THE PATH TO JAZZ IMPROVISATION

A compilation of previously published magazine
articles by Emile and Laura De Cosmo

Special thanks to:
Dave Gibson, Dr. Oscar Muscariello, Louis De Cosmo and Kevin Hagen for music graphics;
Everyone at Hal Leonard Corporation

This books is dedicated to:
Crisanne Simeone, Louis De Cosmo and Jeanette De Cosmo

ISBN 978-0-634-04826-5

7777 W. BLUEMOUND RD. P.O. BOX 13819 MILWAUKEE, WI 53213

Visit Hal Leonard Online at www.halleonard.com

FOREWORD

by David J. Gibson, Editor, Jazz Player

Emile De Cosmo is one of the most creative writers of our time. I first learned how Emile De Cosmo's mind works when I published one of his early articles on jazz improvisation in *Jazz Player* magazine. His columns quickly turned into masterpieces of thought and energy. Each time I read a new column from Emile I felt like I was discovering a missing link in the art of jazz improvisation. I told him many times that I considered his writing to be on the level of a genius and that he should publish an authoritative book on the art of jazz improvisation. We would laugh because we both knew it probably wouldn't happen, but I kept telling him anyway.

Emile De Cosmo's new book, *The Path to Jazz Improvisation*, is like no other book ever published on jazz improvisation. I can truthfully say this because I have read every chapter. It is a continuation of his dedicated writings for *Jazz Player* magazine, yet you have it all in one definitive book. Using his sequential writing style, everything is spelled out clearly. It's funny, nowhere does he say you must do this, or you must do that, to become a good improvisor of jazz. Instead Emile chooses to stimulate one's imagination by simply presenting essays on an almost unlimited palate of options.

Besides all the information on jazz fundamentals in Emile's new book (traditional rules, guidelines and suggestions), there are three additional great strengths that set *The Path to Jazz Improvisation* apart from all other publications on jazz improvisation. First is Emile's great talent for making complex things simple and easy to understand in a step-by-step sequential presentation. There are many musical examples to support his essays, and additional playing exercises that will put Emile De Cosmo's ideas into that part of your brain where you store all your jazz improvisation thoughts. He also includes interesting lists of related jazz repertoire (tunes), which in their own compositional makeup, utilize his topic of the moment, and I find this to be particularly useful.

The second great strength that Emile possesses is his deep understanding of history. When I read his chapter on the Byzantine Scale I almost fell off my chair. I had never thought about jazz in those terms. I suddenly realized that jazz improvisation has roots, which go back much further than the jazz masters of the 1920s, 30s, 40s and beyond.

The third strength is Emile's ability as an organizer of words. This is where the true genius is most gifted and Emile has this gift. The chapters in this book are written in a style that will have you reading them more than once. There is nothing boring here. There is style, knowledge, and presentation of a unique kind.

All jazz musicians strive to obtain a unique style and sound. Yet I think the highest level of achievement any musician, or writer can obtain, is to become an artist at his or her craft. Artists are not made, they are born with this great gift. Emile De Cosmo's book, *The Path to Jazz Improvisation*, is an artistic achievement in our time. It is quite simply a masterpiece of writing that could easily be called the bible of jazz.

In spite of what Dave Gibson writes, I have to give an imense amount of credit to my wife Laura who has inspired me over and over, again and again.

–Emile De Cosmo

TABLE OF CONTENTS

ABOUT THE AUTHORS

Emile De Cosmo has been active as a teacher, musician, and jazz educator for over 30 years. Playing woodwind instruments, he has freelanced in the New York area with many noted musicians on television and radio commercial soundtracks, club dates, concerts, and shows.

Formerly an adjunct professor of jazz improvisation at Jersey City State College (now New Jersey City University), an applied music instructor at Jersey City State College and Fairleigh Dickinson University, and concert/marching/jazz band director at Fort Lee High School. He has also been a feature writer for Jazz Player magazine and an artist in residence/teacher/mentor for the Jersey City school district.

He is author and publisher of the Polytonal Rhythm Series, a 19-book collection that has been endorsed by Paquito D'Rivera, Jamey Abersold, Denis De Blasio, Slide Hampton, John Faddis, Clem De Rosa, Clark Terry, Bill Watrous, Friday the 13th film composer Harry Manfredini, Pat La Barbara, symphony conductor Gerard Schwarz, and many other leading professionals. He is co-author for the Woodshedding Source Book, with Laura De Cosmo, published by Hal Leonard.

His performance and recording credits include Sarah Vaughn, Dizzy Gillespie, Dinah Washington, Joe Farrell, Vic Damone, Milt Hinton, Slide Hampton, Bucky Pizzarelli, Gregory Hines, Pepper Adams, Terry Gibbs, Sonny Stitt, Four Tops and many more.

He is currently teaching privately, playing and writing in Florida where he lives with his wife, Laura De Cosmo.

Laura De Cosmo is a teacher and musician who has worked in the New Jersey and New York metropolitan area playing flute, saxophone, clarinet and singing. She has experience playing in big band, small group, and orchestra. She has taught high school chorus and jazz band in the Jersey City school district. She has been assistant to Emile De Cosmo in various jazz clinics and workshops; a feature writer for Jazz Player magazine; a staff writer for Northeast Neighborhood News; assisted in the writing of text for 19 books, from the Polytonal Rhythm series; and co-authored the Woodshedding Source Book, with Emile De Cosmo, published by Hal Leonard.

Currently, she is teaching music in St. Petersburg and Seminole Florida where she continues to play professionally and write with her husband, Emile De Cosmo.

For more information, visit their website at:
http://www.home_earthlink.net/bigears23
email: edecosmo@yahoo.com

CHAPTER 1

PATH TO IMPROVISATION: A JAZZ PHILOSOPHY

Jazz performers and educators continue to search for shortcuts to improvisation. Unfortunately, there are no shortcuts. When an author writes a book and a publisher decides to publish it, they both want the book to sell. If jazz improvisation is the subject, the publisher packages the book as if it will make improvisation immediately possible. Aside from the well-conceived books on the market, many are incomplete and are merely misleading how-to books promising the impossible, but unable to deliver. Reading between the lines quickly reveals that hours and hours of work are required to produce a jazz improvisor.

A student interested in learning how to improvise should hear a few great jazz players, either live or on recordings, and then start practicing and learning. This means reading and playing many jazz heads or melodies and, if possible, many transcribed solos of jazz greats.

In the early days of the big bands, the term woodshedding was introduced by jazz musicians to indicate long practice sessions in a private place where the musician could practice alone and undisturbed. Frank Tirro, in his book, *Jazz, A History* states, "Woodshedding refers to practicing or rehearsing in private, in order to gain technical mastery of one's instrument before going into a jam session." Woodshedding to many jazz players also means practicing as a group, practicing a new song in private, or practicing to get a part down. Many great jazz players have taken a period of time off from public performance and recording to practice alone to rethink improvisational techniques and create new material. Woodshedding is a self-imposed exile, which any creative musician must endure to reach his or her true potential.

Practicing alone, as all successful jazz musicians know, is also an important component in the acquisition of music reading ability, technical facility, tone production, range and endurance, sight-reading ability, and theoretical knowledge, which all lead to improvisational skills. For too many students, practicing alone is reduced to practicing lessons assigned by a teacher in preparation for the next lesson. Rarely is the student actually taught how to go about studying the material. Instead, the student is expected to devise ways of practicing and learn the assigned lesson.

Learning how to practice requires many years of experience, and students should be guided by the experienced teacher.

THE MUSICAL LANGUAGE AND ITS DIALECTS

The old adage that music is a language is somewhat simplistic. Music is a language, but one which is complex and composed of twenty-four dialects. Within a language, a dialect, among other dialects, is a variant form of the standard language. The variations occur as alterations of pronunciation, colloquial vocabulary, idiomatic expression, spelling, syntax, and grammar. In the United States, the principal regional dialects are those of New England, the Eastern Seaboard, New York Metropolitan area, Southern, Deep Southern, Southwestern, Northwestern, Midwestern, and Pacific Coastal. Each of these dialects is distinguishable from the others by most native speakers of English as departures from "standard English." The important matter is that speakers of the same language be able to understand one another in spite of dialectic differences.

In music, as in spoken language, it is important that a musician be fluent in all the "dialectal keys" of music. The musical dialects consist of twelve diatonic major keys or tonal centers, and twelve relative diatonic minor keys or tonal centers.

In all music, there is one basic harmonic urge: the tendency of a tone or chord to move or fall cadentially to a tone, chord, scale, or mode whose root is a fifth below. This compulsion, or natural gravitation, is responsible for establishing the term "cycle of fifths."

The cycle of fifths has elsewhere been employed to identify key signatures, but the more important function of the cycle of fifths is to explain chord relationships and show the natural movement or progression of chords. Composers apply the cycle in constructing chord sequences. The cycle of fifths is the key to understanding the most common cadential progression in music: that of the Dominant V chord moving to the tonic major I chord or tonic minor I chord.

Within the musical universe of the cycle of fifths, there occurs another twenty-four cycles, which are dialects of music moving diatonically in descending fifths. The twenty-four cycles are called "diatonic cycles," which means that they stay in one key or tonal center, either major or minor. The cycle of fifths, encompassing all of the diatonic cycles, constitutes the twenty-four dialects of the musical language.

Students are dismayed to realize how much background and experience, including the mastery of the twelve major and minor dialectical keys, are essential to becoming a proficient jazz improvisor. At first, they express disbelief, and then become resistive. Let the facts be made clear here and now that acquisition of fluency in the musical language of the twenty-four dialectical keys does require study and cannot be avoided. There are no shortcuts.

All diatonic seventh chords and their corresponding modes must be mastered in all dialectical keys as a prerequisite to improvising. Improvisational study must be pursued by learning basic music theory, gaining technical skills, and studying the jazz language through its literature, which necessitates proficient music reading ability. The history of jazz is not in the brand of instruments, mouthpieces, reeds, strings, picks, or amplifiers great performers used, but should rather be sought in the music they played, which includes both composed melodies and improvisations.

SIGHT-READING PROFICIENCY

In order to take advantage of the jazz language available, the student of jazz must become a proficient reader and sight-reader of music. Most students who wish to play jazz do not realize that being a good reader is an essential skill. Much has been said about the importance of rapid sight-reading, but little about the importance of accurate depth reading (melodic and harmonic comprehension) of musical notation. A student whose depth reading of written music is deficient cannot be expected to sight-read with comprehension and conceptualization.

In reading music, a player's ability is determined both by the speed and accuracy of his reactions to the visual stimuli of musical notation. Sight-reading can hardly be said to occur when the student requires an inordinate amount of time to decipher a simple rhythmic pattern. Notation in varying rhythmic patterns must be experienced so often that they can be recalled quickly and easily. The student is sight-reading proficiently when recognizing a pattern and notation, and executing it correctly, almost instantaneously, the first time the music is read.

After the study of musical reading techniques, which improves depth reading, students can improve sight-reading ability by sight-reading new material often. The music should be played at a tempo at which the student can apply his sight-reading ability without making too many mistakes. When practicing sight-reading, the student should pass over errors. If too many errors are committed, the tempo should be reduced. The student will find the level of playing the piece or exercise at a functional tempo, while still making the notations being read sound musical. Usually, when reading, a student will find trouble spots and work on them. The student should first look at the new material, find the most difficult parts, and then play the music at a tempo at which the difficult areas are playable. The way to learn how to read music better is by reading new music often.

THE READING PROCESS EXPLAINED

When reading text, the eyes do not move letter by letter, or word by word, but rather by groups of words. The better the reader, the larger the groups of words encompassed in a single eye movement. The same principle applies to music reading. A student is taught at first to react to each note, but eventually learns to group notes together and perform them as a single unit by drawing on previous experience with musical phrases.

Other factors which help in the sight-reading of materials are: perception of intervals, scale patterns, chordal patterns, direction of melodic movements up or down, rhythms, and accidentals. Music theory studies relate directly to the ability to sight-read.

At a high level, sight-reading and depth reading can be said to be the same, but sight-reading is reading for note production when confronted with a brand new piece of music; depth reading is reading with comprehension and conceptualization of the composer's intent. A reader can finish a paragraph of text in a short time, but he may not understand what is read, or be able to completely interpret the intent of the notation. In music, a student might profess reading ability because of ability to understand some of the concepts, i.e., know the names of the notes, note values, recognize different rhythms, and know what a major and minor scale is. But, if confronted with a piece of unfamiliar music, the student sometimes cannot play it because notation does not totally convey the musical intent. Mere note reproduction is not necessarily music in the higher sense, but is, to borrow terms, "artless and non-poetic."

Of course, the more the student knows about theory, the better a sight-reader the student can become.

In order to group large amounts of notes together, a student must be able to recognize chords and scales. A student who cannot recognize a succession of notes as an Ab scale, for example, will have a more difficult time playing the succession than a student who can.

Knowledge of music theory is helpful to the jazz improvisor, who must be able to read chord symbols and know what keys the chords represent. The improvisor must be able to do this at sight, having no time to sit and figure it out. A jazz player who plays "by ear" must rely solely on the ear to carry him though a piece. The jazz player who knows theory, however, can look at the chord symbols, recognizing the keys and the corresponding modes signaled, and use the notes of those dialectical keys or modes to improvise. The knowledgeable improvisor can go much farther than the "ear player," and can also play with more confidence and deliver a more interesting solo.

PRIVATE PRACTICE VERSUS LISTENING

Practice is more important than listening. Too often, excessive time is spent listening and insufficient time is spent practicing. Listening to sound recordings is important to student conceptualization, but listening alone is not enough. Just as the melody comes first and the improvisation comes afterward, so do the learning of the jazz repertoire and the improvisation come after the student is familiar with the literature and able to utilize jazz phraseology in improvising. Jazz tunes and improvisations are, in fact, the language of jazz. A student can learn more about improvisation if he has the technique to play and analyzes many jazz tunes.

Many methods suggest that the student write out melodies and thoughts, but a student would consume a lifetime attempting to recreate all the jazz that is readily available in the literature. Writing melodies is worthwhile, but only after the student has been exposed to one hundred or more jazz tunes; otherwise, it is like asking a student to write a speech, knowing only a few words of a language. It is better to take from the literature a language already available than to isolatedly contrive a "new" language. All of the past and present professional jazz players, whether they realize it or not, have the command of the existing language of their own period and previous periods of jazz, while continuing to keep abreast of changing trends. Modern jazz language has evolved through a synthesis of all the jazz literature, jazz melodies or tunes, and jazz improvisations of the past century. Just as great innovators of science, theater, art, architecture, poetry, mathematics, languages, music, and sports explore the past and take advantage of their predecessors' experiences and knowledge, so must the jazz player do the same without detracting from the creative process. In fact, knowledge of the past one hundred years of jazz history and its literature makes a jazz artist more creative, through the influences of many sources.

Imitating recorded jazz by ear alone would require an inestimable amount of time because the student's ear and instrument are not synchronized and able to immediately reproduce what is heard on the recording. The jazz music of the past is more advantageously reproduced from written jazz melodies and transcriptions. There is no shortcut, but proficient reading ability is the most efficient way of exploring jazz literature in transcription as preparation for actual jazz improvisation.

THE PROCESS OF INSTRUMENTAL TRANSFERAL

Children learn to use their voices from infancy. Those preparing to become musicians begin to learn to produce sounds from man-made musical instruments later. Almost any music student can hum a note struck on a piano keyboard by matching it because the voice does not have to be concerned with a key. When students are asked to reproduce that same note on their instrument, it takes about three, four, or more tries to match the note because the ear and instrument are not synchronized as the ear and the voice. The student must identify which one of the twelve notes of music has been played before he can reproduce it on his instrument. Likewise, a student may be able to identify the quality or type of chord, scale, or melodic fragment that he hears, but when asked to play it on his instrument, will have a problem identifying which one of the twelve it is. The ability to remember and hum, whistle, or sing a vast number of tunes is not uncommon, but ask students to duplicate the hum or whistle, or to play a song on their instruments, and the same problem is experienced. To become a professional musician, a student must acquire as much facility for reproducing melodic lines on his musical instrument as he is able to reproduce with his voice. Furthermore, an improvising musician must be able to reproduce melodies originating in his imagination.

In order to achieve instrumental facility and a smooth flow of melodic lines, either as reproductions from memory or origination from the imagination, and in order to hear sounds and then play them on a musical instrument, all major and minor scales or dialects and their respective chord progressions should be memorized.

THE DEVELOPMENT OF THE MUSICAL EAR

The normal ear is a receiving instrument that begins hearing sounds at birth. The ear receives music, speech, singing, and environmental sounds. The newborn's first sending instrument is the voice, which begins functioning when the first slap on the baby's bottom stimulates or causes its first cry. Using its voice, the child begins to develop its first sending instrument. One must realize that the normal ear receives naturally, and the voice, by limitation of sounds learned from parents, begins to function as a natural instrument by sending what the ear hears. The brain learns to decipher what the ear is hearing so that the voice can begin transmitting what it has heard and assimilated.

As the child grows, his hearing is constantly being bombarded with the music of television, radio, and recordings. The child continues his musical education with musical activities in the early grades, including singing, dancing, and playing rhythm instruments. His hearing and voice are tied together, enabling the child to learn and sing the lyrics and melodies of numerous songs. Usually at the fourth grade level, the child will have an instrument placed in his hands by the music teacher. Precisely at this moment in time, the child is reborn again. In place of the natural sending instrument, his voice, he now has a new voice, or sending instrument, in his hands through which he must learn to speak musical sounds.

Assuming that the child is ten years old, his natural receiving instrument (his hearing) and his natural sending instrument (his voice) have been synchronized since birth, receiving and sending at will, and are ten years more musically advanced than his new sending instrument or new voice. His hearing and the new musical sending instrument, now held in his hands, are now unsynchronized.

Now begins the long process of catching up to the musically educated hearing. The ears have heard enough music! The student now has to begin practicing in order to try to play the sounds that he hears in the present and the sounds that have been heard in the past, and are now in his memory waiting to be expressed. A student can be frustrated in the attempt to produce these sounds and does not understand why they will not come out of his instrument.

The majority of beginning "ear players" try to play what is in the mind's ear by "fishing around," trying to find the notes to melodies that have been heard before and are familiar. If the student works on learning to read better, the ability to lift the melodies immediately from the written page and the skill to play melodies "by ear" will come sooner. The ability of playing by ear must also be learned, but it is more productive to improve one's reading of music first.

Students who read fairly well can learn to play by ear sooner, but sometimes, good readers have a tendency to shy away from playing by ear. However, many students who read music well memorize the music being played and are actually playing by ear, but may not realize it. Consequently, ear players should work on reading as they attempt to play by ear, and good readers should begin playing by ear as they go forward with reading studies. Beginning lessons, which must include reading musical notation, can seem trite and boring compared to the years of musical sounds a student has heard and collected in the mind's ear. The student will spend the rest of his musical life trying to catch up to his mind's ear because, as he is learning his instrument, his ear is continuously receiving and learning more musical sounds. The mind's ear and the musical instrument will probably never be completely synchronized, but after many years of arduous practice, the gap will be lessened considerably. Practicing chords, scales, modes, fragments, melodies, and jazz literature in all twelve keys develops the facility to send out what the ear hears, thus developing the musical instrument as an extension of the musician's body, and connecting it more directly with the mind. Consequently, the ear does not need developing, but the mind does, in order to understand and perceive what the ear is hearing. The student must, therefore, begin to develop the technical ability to produce on the instrument what is heard in the mind's ear.

To sum up, a student must be prepared for each improvisational demand, as it arises under actual performance conditions, being able to express himself in all twenty-four dialectical keys melodically, harmonically, and rhythmically. The recommendation is made to study jazz theory or method books and jazz literature, which is available through the use of jazz fake books and jazz solo transcriptions to expose the student to the panorama of melodies and masterful improvisations of the past and present. This formula is no shortcut, but apprises the student of how much effort is required in becoming a good improvisor and is the shortest realistic route to a direct path, which leads to better sight-reading, interpretive reading, and jazz improvisational ability.

As jazz melodies and improvisations are practiced and learned, they will become part of the student's language and memory. The mind's ear will develop through understanding, recalling, and playing what the ear has heard. Most importantly, improvisations will flow musically and melodically rather than mechanically.

Improvisation is the spontaneous production of music, calling upon all available resources: musical knowledge, instrumental or vocal technique, emotions, and concentration. How a musician blends these vari-

ous components determines the stylistic artistry and originality of his improvisation. During a solo, an improvisor may incorporate general melodic patterns and specific bits of jazz tunes he has committed to memory. Whatever his product, however, it is clear that improvisation is a complex, many-faceted process. Experience has shown that a performer's improvisational ability is in direct proportion to the number of jazz melodies memorized; therefore, it is important to learn the jazz literature, through both reading and hearing.

Learning jazz ideas in twelve dialectical keys is as important as learning the jazz literature itself. Because of the difficulty involved, these directions are frequently ignored; however, the advisability of learning to play scales, chords, and melodic ideas in every dialectical key is that jazz tunes can and usually will contain many dialectical modulations and tonal centers. Most students do not realize that an improvisor who does not have command of all dialectical keys, both major and minor, finds it difficult to improvise and communicate musical thoughts. Currently, students must assimilate these skills within a relatively short period of time, in order to begin performing on the same level as modern jazz players, and it is the purpose of this chapter to present a broad, eclectic, original approach to the learning and teaching of jazz improvisation—an approach which can be utilized by inexperienced and experienced musicians alike. Jazz improvisation does not derive from inspiration alone, but requires all of the previously mentioned directions, which will develop an individual's style, and make the difference between ordinary instrumentalists and an outstanding performer.

CHAPTER 2

THE CYCLE OF FIFTHS:
THE GRAVITATIONAL PULL IN MUSIC

Now that you have (hopefully) read my previous chapter on "The Path to Improvisation," I would now like to address one of the most important subjects a jazz improvisor (and any other musician) must comprehend. This is music's primary progression, most commonly known as "The Cycle of Fifths." This subject is for the majority of musicians who have heard the term but need to gain a complete understanding of this progression. It is the first and most important chord progression that a musician must hear, play, and put into practice.

THE GRAVITATIONAL PULL OF "THE CYCLE"

Because of the gravity, or natural progression in music, any chromatic tone is compelled to progress or fall to a tone or note an interval of a fifth below. This compulsion or natural musical gravitation is responsible for establishing the term "cycle of fifths." For example, the fundamental note C wants to resolve down a fifth to the fundamental note F, while a chord (major or minor) built on the root C wants to resolve down a fifth to a chord whose root is F. As gravity is to the earth, so the cycle of fifths is to music. The cycle may be graphically described as a continuous spiral of descending fifths falling endlessly. Each tone or chord is the fifth of the next, in the cycle.

The cycle of fifths has elsewhere been employed to identify key signatures, but the more important func-tion of the cycle of fifths is to explain chord relation-ships and show the natural movement or progression of chords. Composers apply the cycle in constructing chord sequences. The cycle of fifths is the key to under-standing the most common cadential progression in music, that of the dominant (V7) chord moving to the tonic major (I) chord or tonic minor (i) chord.

THE DOMINANT SEVENTH CHORD

The fact that the strongest pull in music is from a dominant chord to its tonic chord cannot be over emphasized because this relationship is the doorway to understanding the harmonic movement, or delay, of resolution to the tonic for all progressions in all music from classical, popular, jazz, rock, and folk. A delay of resolution to the tonic creates the interesting forward motion of music. When resolution to the tonic is effect-ed the motion comes to rest, and the piece is heard as having reached an ending.

DOMINANT (V7) TO TONIC (I7) CHORDS IN EVERY KEY

The C dominant chord (C7) gravitates to its tonic:
The F chord

The F dominant chord (F7) gravitates to its tonic:
The B♭ chord

The B♭ dominant chord (B♭7) gravitates to its tonic:
The E♭ chord

The E♭ dominant chord (E♭7) gravitates to its tonic: The A♭ chord

The A♭ dominant chord (A♭7) gravitates to its tonic: The D♭ chord

The D♭ dominant chord (D♭7) gravitates to its tonic: The G♭ chord

The G♭7 chord spelled enharmonically becomes an F♯7 chord

The F♯ dominant chord (F♯7) gravitates to its tonic: The B chord

The B dominant chord (B7) gravitates to its tonic: The E chord

The E dominant chord (E7) gravitates to its tonic: The A chord

The A dominant chord (A7) gravitates to its tonic: The D chord

The D dominant chord (D7) gravitates to its tonic: The G chord

The G dominant chord (G7) gravitates to its tonic: The C chord

When we accept the fact that roots of chords are attracted to roots of chords a fifth lower, then we can better analyze how other chord progressions in music are produced. Using the magnetism of the Cycle of Fifths we can create chord progressions of all diatonic keys, major and minor. For example in the key of C major (CMaj7 to FMaj7 to Bm7♭5 to Em7 to Am7 to Dm7 to G7 to CMaj7) and in the key of C minor (Cm(Maj7) to Fm7 to Bdim7 to E♭Maj7+5 to A♭Maj7 to Dm7♭5 to G7 to Cm(Maj7).

CONFUSION OF "THE CYCLE OF FIFTHS" NOMENCLATURE

Other terms are frequently applied as misnomers for the cycle of fifths by many educators, musicians, and students. For example, it is often called the circle of fourths, the cycle of fourths, and the spiral of fourths. In fact, on a recent trip that my wife and I took to Ellwood City, Pa., to visit relatives, I happened to read an article in the local newspaper (dated April 19, 1995) about a

musical group called "The Circle of Fourths." The group's guitarist Joe Lynch stated, "The band's name was derived from music theory; the circle of fourths is based on a progression of harmonies." This perpetual confusion of terms results from thinking in intervals instead of harmonic function. Let the fact be made clear here and now, that when an interval of a fourth is inverted it does become an interval of a fifth, and when an interval of a fifth is inverted it does become an interval of a fourth, but the harmonic function V to I remains the same, thus the correct term "the cycle of fifths."

No matter in which direction the V7 moves, whether down a fifth to its tonic (I) or up a fourth to its tonic (I) it is still the V7 chord moving to the tonic (I) chord. Any fifth degree of any scale always retains its gravitational V to I relationship to its tonic and will always fall or move to its tonic tone or chord when coming to a conclusion. The interval changes in accordance with the direction of flow, but the harmonic relationship is still V to I.

In addition, Many alternate terms are used by music theorists for the cycle of fifths. The cause of frequent communications breakdown in musical discourses is revealed by the partial but copious list of alternate terms for the cycle of fifths which follows:

OTHER TERMS FOR "THE CYCLE OF FIFTH" USED BY USED BY MUSIC THEORISTS

1. Root movement

2. Root progressions

3. Harmonic progressions

4. Cycle of fifths (the correct term)

5. Circle of fifths

6. Spiral of fifths

7. Fifth falls

8. Dominant cycle

9. Circle of chords

10. Laboratory Progressions

11. Functional harmony

12. Authentic cadence

13. Enchained dominant harmonies

14. First class chords

15. Regular Resolution

THE OVERTONE SERIES: SOURCE FOR THE CYCLE OF FIFTHS

The phenomena manifested by the gravity of music are many and interrelated. Principally important is the understanding that when an instrument produces a musical tone as the consequence of vibration in parts of a column of air or a string, the tones produced, heard as a single pitch, are actually physical combinations of a fundamental tone in conjunction with upper partials or overtones. The fundamental, the most prominent tone heard by the human ear, is produced by the longest and, therefore, most slowly vibrating portion of the column of air or string. As the column of air or string is shortened by valves or fingers, the pitch rises. The upper partials or overtones are secondarily audible in comparison with the fundamental tone. The parts naturally assume relative positions represented by the overtone series. Although heard as single tones, each individual pitch consists of a fundamental tone and a series of six principal overtones referred to as either harmonics or partials. The overtones are higher in pitch than the fundamental tone. The overtones of a given pitch have been reported to extend to sixteen, twenty-two, and beyond. The fundamental and its overtones produce an altered dominant seventh chord containing tensions extending to diminished or flatted fifth, augmented fifth, ninth, augmented eleventh, and thirteenth.

The fundamental and its subsequent overtones or partials create a magnetic or gravitational force, that puts the fundamental in motion causing it to resolve or fall to another fundamental a fifth below, and begin the cadential flow of the cycle of fifths.

The overtone series from the fundamental tone C (C, E, G, B♭, C, D, E, F♯, G, A, B♭, B, C) can be seen as the origin of the theoretical information as follows:

C triad = C, E, G

C seventh chord = C, E, G, B♭

C ninth chord = C, E, G, B♭, D

C thirteenth + augmented eleventh chord = C, E, G, B♭, D, F♯, A

G minor sixth chord = G, B♭, D, E

E half diminished or E minor seventh flat five = E, G, B♭, D

A tetrachord from the C whole tone scale = C, D, E, F♯

G melodic minor scale ascending = G, A, Bb, C, D, E, F♯, G

C overtone scale = C, D, E, F♯, G, A, Bb, C

D major tetrachord = D, E, F♯, G

D seventh chord = D, F♯, A, C

D mixolydian mode = D, E, F♯, G, A, B, C, D

D ninth chord = D, F♯, A, C, E

D thirteenth chord = D, F♯, A, C, E, G, B

E minor tetrachord = E, F♯, G, A

F♯ half diminished seventh chord = F♯, A, C, E

G pentatonic blues scale = G, A, B♭, B, D, E, G

One third of the chromatic scale from A = A, B♭, B, C

Two tritones = C to F♯ and E to B♭

Each new fundamental tone produces a new set of theoretical information.

THE TRITONE

The tritone, an interval of an augmented fourth, was called the "devil's interval" or it was called the diabolus in music during the Middle Ages and avoided melodically; but, when used harmonically, it is the most powerful force of harmonic action within the musical universe. When heard harmonically the augmented fourth creates a tremendous need for resolution and is more properly to be regarded as the "angel of resolution." The tritone provides the most distinctive characteristic of the dominant seventh chord creating individual tension and unrest, increasing the tonal magnetism, causing a greater need for resolution.

Although the leap of a tritone melodically was generally avoided in traditional music, the momentum produced by the strong harmonic motion of the cycle of fifths was considered powerful enough to justify its use between IV and vii in the bass in major or minor keys. The chord progression stays in the same tonal center when going from IV7 to vii7 in all tonal centers or keys.

A demand for resolution of overtones as chords or clusters to a fifth below sets up new overtones which also demand resolution.

LEARNING MUSICAL THEORIES

During the growth period when a child starts learning and using his native language, constant use of the language refines the way of speaking words, sentences and paragraphs. Even during normal daily conversation it takes a great amount of study of the language to use even the smallest of words grammatically correct. It is said that when learning a new word the best way for the word to become part of your vocabulary is to use the new word many times in conversation and writing. So it is with music! When learning new musical theories, a student has to commit that theory to memory, learn it in every key or dialect, and then begin to use those theories in performing or writing. For example, if a student learns what a cycle progression is, for performance or writing he has to commit that progression to memory and learn the spelling of all the dominant seventh chords in the cycle of fifths. For performance he has to be able to execute this progression chordally, modally and melodically. After using the cycle of fifths progression many times, sometimes years, the jazz improvisor or writer is able to handle the progression fluently.

The importance of the cycle of fifths can be illustrated by analyzing the song "Skippy," composed by jazz great Thelonious Monk using the "I Got Rhythm" AABA form but substituting and using sixty-two dominant seventh chords as a progression. The dominant seventh chords move harmonically through the cycle of fifths and chromatically. The song "Skippy" contains only one tonic chord appearing in the final measure as the final chord of the piece.

In the past and even today jazz educators instruct students to reproduce everything they play chromatically on their instruments, which is usually ignored because of its difficulty. Practicing this way was suggested because most of the educators were either pianists, instrumentalists who possessed piano skills, composers, or theorists. As the piano is a visual instrument, practicing chromatically is accomplished more easily. The cycle of fifths was understood thoroughly by those who were able to play the piano because most of the musical literature made use of the cycle of fifths in part or completely. Chromatic progressions are an outgrowth of the cycle of fifths and therefore should be learned after one has immersed oneself in the cycle of fifths and the diatonic cycle of fifths and all its dialects.

In all major keys the dominant seventh chord built on the fifth degree of the major scale is a V7 chord. Upon seeing a dominant seventh chord a student, when improvising, must immediately recognize the key from which it is derived (V7 = Key or dialect of the moment is five steps lower than the root of the V7 chord). For example C7 = V7 of key of the moment = F major.

The following is a list of the twelve V7, or dominant seventh chords, and their respective tonal centers:

When a C7 occurs improvise in the key of the F major tonal center.

When a F7 occurs improvise in the key of the B♭ major tonal center.

When a B♭7 occurs improvise in the key of the E♭ major tonal center.

When an E♭7 occurs improvise in the key of the A♭ major tonal center.

When an A♭7 occurs improvise in the key of the D♭ major tonal center.

When a D♭7 occurs improvise in the key of the G♭ major tonal center.

When a F#7 occurs improvise in the key of the B major tonal center.

When a B7 occurs improvise in the key of the E major tonal center.

When an E7 occurs improvise in the key of the A major tonal center.

When an A7 occurs improvise in the key of the D major tonal center.

When a D7 occurs improvise in the key of the G major tonal center.

When a G7 occurs improvise in the key of the C major tonal center.

If a dominant seventh chord occurs as a V7 chord in a minor key, the student should then improvise in the key of the minor tonal center. For example, if a C7 appears as a V7 chord of the key of F minor and the C7 chord precedes an F minor chord, the student should then improvise in the key of F minor.

When a student practices the cycle of fifths in each of the twelve tonal centers, they will be able to hear and react more easily to dominant seventh chord changes and express more of what he imagines producing quicker ear/instrument response, whether reading music or improvising.

Although it is important to learn the cycle of fifths in all keys or dialects; it is imperative for today's novice composer or improviser to become familiar with the jazz literature that makes use of the cycle of fifths. If the student learns, analyses, and memorizes these melodies, improvising on cycle changes and tunes that use cycle changes will become easier.

The following is a list of standard, popular, and jazz tunes containing cycle of fifths changes. Cycle of fifth changes are usually found in the bridge or B section of many AABA tunes, and many tunes begin with cycle changes.

"After You've Gone" – Creamer/Layton

"All Blues" – Miles Davis

"All of Me" – S.Simons/G.Marks

"Anthropology" – C. Parker/D. Gillespie

"Blue Room" – Rodgers/Hart

"Blue Monk" – Thelonious Monk

"Broadway" – Wood/McCrae/Bird

"Celebrity" – Charlie Parker

"Chasin' the Bird" – Charlie Parker

"Country Roads" – Steve Swallow

"Crazy Rhythm" – Caesar/Kahn

"Dansero" – Hayman/Daniels/Parker

"Dewey Square" – Charlie Parker

"Dig" – Miles Davis

"Don't Get Around Much Anymore" – Duke Ellington

"Doxy" – Sonny Rollins

"Exactly Like You" – J. McHugh

"Four Brothers" – Jimmy Guiffre

"Freddy Freeloader" – Miles Davis

"Get Me To The Church on Time" – Lerner/Loewe

"Honeysuckle Rose" – Fats Waller

"I Can't Believe That You're in Love with Me" – McHugh/Gaskill

"I've Got it Bad and That Ain't Good" – Duke Ellington

"I've Got Rhythm" – George Gershwin

"I've Got a Right to Sing the Blues" – Arlen/Koehler

"In a Mellow Tone" – Duke Ellington

"Jordu" – Duke Jordon

"Killer Joe" – Benny Golson

"Kim" – Charlie Parker

"Lazy River" – Hoagy Carmichael

"Leap Frog" – Charlie Parker

"Lil' Darlin'" – Neil Hefti

"Loads of Love" – Richard Rodgers

"Lulu's Back in Town" – H. Warren

"Misterioso" – Thelonious Monk

"Moody's Got Rhythm" – James Moody

"Moose the Mooche" – Charlie Parker

"Perdido" – J. Tizol

"Scrapple From the Apple" – Charlie Parker

"Sermonette" – Cannonball Adderley

"Sister Sadie" – Horace Silver

"Skippy" – Thelonious Monk

"Spanish Flea" – Julius Wechter

"Spinning Wheel" – D.C. Thomas

"Straight Life" – Freddie Hubbard

"Sweet Georgia Brown" – Bernie/Pinkard

"The Preacher" – Horace Silver

"Watermelon Man" – Herbie Hancock

"Well You Needn't" – Thelonious Monk

It would take an insurmountable number of pages of songs to list all the ones which contain the "cycle" movement in them. The cycle progression has been used by the greatest, and least, of composers. Consequently, we would have to list all composed music since the tempered scale came into use. The tempered scale was first suggested by Chinese prince Tsai-yu in 1596 (over 400 years ago)!

As can be seen by the length of the above partial list of jazz literature that contains cycle of fifth changes, a jazz player acquires an abundance of jazz language and style while learning melodies. These tunes, as melodic information stored in the mind's ear, then become part of the total melodic recall to be played in bits or at length when improvising. All great jazz players have hundreds and maybe thousands of jazz tunes at their fingertips that can be used to put together as a puzzle in thousands of different ways over endless chord changes. This process occurs automatically as the improvisor reacts to many new tunes and many new sets of chord changes. The novice player should begin to memorize as many different jazz tunes as possible to expand improv-

isational fluency and acquire jazz vocabulary and language which should be a continuing process. After memorizing some of the jazz literature above, the student should then transpose portions and eventually complete tunes into as many different keys as possible (in the cycle of fifths order) to expand the student's jazz vocabulary even further.

Many high school and even college students have a problem learning the V7 to I relationship and how strongly it relates to other chord sequences when studying classical harmony. Memorizing the cycle of fifths and practicing it would greatly improve the understanding of this chain of dominants and its relationship to the progression or movement of chords used in music. For students of jazz improvisation, music theory, or composition learning the cycle of fifths is a must!

CYCLE OF FIFTHS: TREBLE CLEF

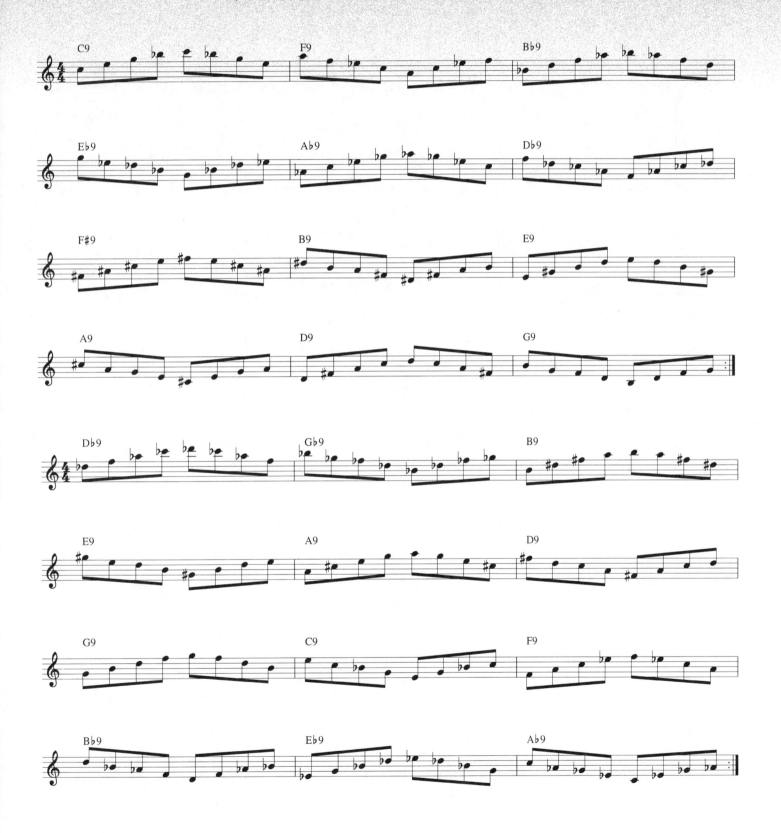

CYCLE OF FIFTHS: BASS CLEF

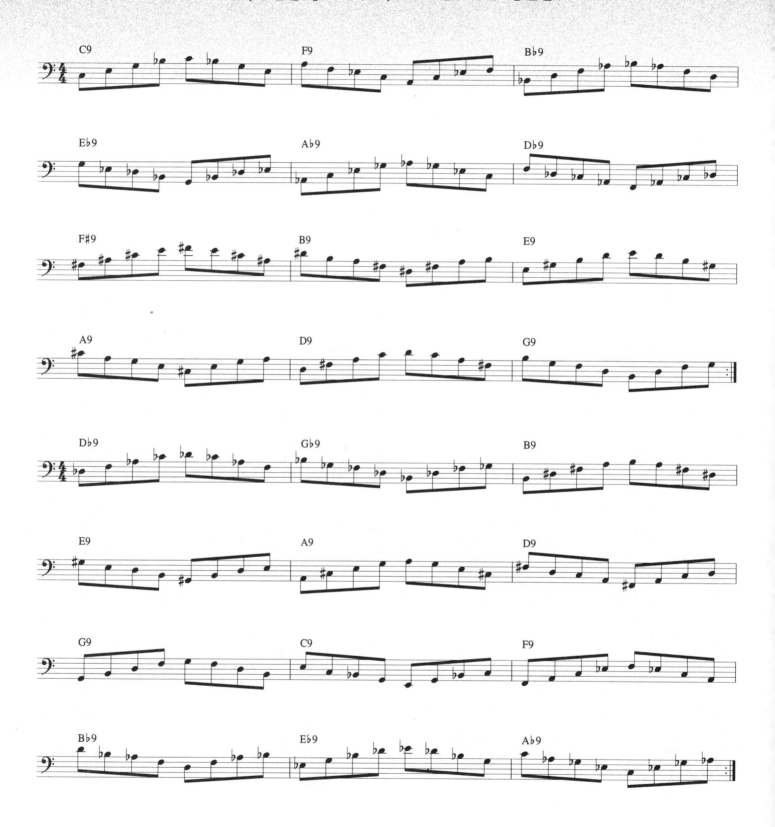

CHAPTER 3

THE DIATONIC CYCLE

You should now understand the gravitational pull of the cycle and its importance to composers, arrangers, and improvisors. However, in order to understand how progressions move within songs, we will discuss the gravitational pull of the diatonic cycle and its implications.

The old adage that music is a language is somewhat simplistic. Music is a language, but one which is complexity composed of twenty-four dialects. Within a language a dialect, among other dialects, is a variant form of the standard language.

Each of these dialects is distinguishable from the others by most native speakers of English, as departures from standard English. The important matter is that speakers of the same language be able to understand one another, in spite of dialectic differences.

As in a language, in music it is important that a musician be fluent in all the dialectal keys of music. The musical dialects consist of twelve diatonic major keys or tonal centers and twelve relative diatonic minor keys or tonal centers. When a musician improvises he or she must immediately recognize a chord symbol as a dialect or tonal center and be able to "speak" (play) fluently in that dialect or tonal center.

In all music, there is one basic harmonic urge: the tendency of a tone, chord, scale, or mode to move or fall cadentially to a tone, chord, scale, or mode whose root is a fifth below. (C, F, B♭, E♭, A♭, D♭, G♭ (F♯), B, E, A, D, G).

Within the cycle of fifths there occurs another twenty-four cycles which are dialects of music moving in the same direction in fifths. The twenty-four cycles are called "diatonic cycles," which means that each cycle stays in one key or dialectal tonal center, either major or minor. The cycle of fifths, encompassing all of the diatonic cycles, constitutes the musical language.

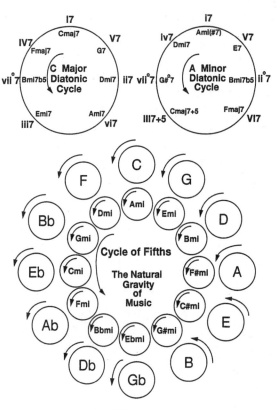

Cycle of Fifths and twenty-four diatonic cycles

PROGRESSION OF THE DIATONIC CYCLE

Normally in the cycle of fifths the next note after F would be B♭. However, in order to keep within the tonal center of C major the F moves in cycle to a B natural, which is a tritone away from F. In this way it short circuits the normal cycle of fifths and moves across the cycle to the B natural, thus remaining in the key or tonal center of C. This is true to all keys major or minor.

Although the melodic leap of a tritone was generally avoided in traditional music, the momentum produced by the strong harmonic motion of the cycle of fifths was considered powerful enough to justify its use between the fourth and seventh degrees of the scale being used.

THE ROOT MOVEMENT OF THE TWELVE DIATONIC CYCLES IN ALL MAJOR KEYS

Key of C major: C, F, B, E, A, D, G

Key of F major: F, B♭, E, A, D, G, C

Key of B♭ major: B♭, E♭, A, D, G, C, F

Key of E♭ major: E♭, A♭, D, G, C, F, B♭

Key of A♭ major: A♭, D♭, G, C, F, B♭, E♭

Key of D♭ major: D♭, G♭, C, F, B♭, E♭, A♭

Key of F♯ major: F♯, B, E♯, A♯, D♯, G♯, C♯

Key of B major: B, E, A♯, D♯, G♯, C♯, F♯

Key of E major: E, A, D♯, G♯, C♯, F♯, B

Key of A major: A, D, G♯, C♯, F♯, B, E

Key of D major: D, G, C♯, F♯, B, E, A

Key of G major: G, C, F♯, B, E, A, D

THE ROOT MOVEMENT OF THE TWELVE DIATONIC CYCLES IN ALL MINOR KEYS

Key of C minor: C, F, B, E♭, A♭, D, G

Key of F minor: F, B♭, E, A♭, D♭, G, C

Key of B♭ minor: B♭, E♭, A, D♭, G♭, C, F

Key of E♭ minor: E♭, A♭, D, G♭, C♭, F, B♭

Key of G♯ minor: G♯, C♯, F𝄪, B, E, A♯, D♯

Key of C♯ minor: C♯, F♯, B♯, E, A, D♯, G♯

Key of F♯ minor: F♯, B, E♯, A, D, G♯, C♯

Key of B minor: B, E, A♯, D, G, C♯, F♯

Key of E minor: E, A, D♯, G, C, F♯, B

Key of A minor: A, D, G♯, C, F, B, E

Key of D minor: D, G, C♯, F, B♭, E, A

Key of G minor: G, C, F♯, B♭, E♭, A, D

The melodic study written in bass and treble clef in this article uses the flow of the diatonic cycle. The study helps the jazz player and student learn all diatonic modes and diatonic seventh chords of each major and minor key as it progresses through the diatonic cycle. This is accomplished by playing this study through all keys—changing the key signature, not transposing the melody. (Refer to Chapter 12, "How Chords Change A-Chording to POOK".)

While improvising over chord changes, a jazz player must make the melodic improvisation fit the harmonic progression, as the chords drop in and out of the melody being played. Practicing this melodic study in all major and minor keys establishes the process that must take place when improvising. Most educators realize that mastery of playing in all keys or tonal centers is essential to enabling students to begin functioning as performers and improvisors.

Playing through the major and minor tonal centers is accomplished easily by practicing keys in a specific order that I call "The Polytonal Order of Keys." Abbreviated it is called "P.O.O.K."

The Diatonic Cycle exercise helps the student surmount the advanced key signatures by employing the Polytonal Order of Keys which introduces the sharps and flats, one-at-a-time, in a specific order.

1. C major
2. A minor (add G♯)
3. G major
4. E minor (add D♯)
5. F major
6. D minor (add C♯)
7. D major
8. B minor (add A♯)
9. B♭ major
10. G minor (add F♯)
11. A major
12. F♯ minor (add E♯)
13. E♭ major
14. C minor (add B♮)
15. E major
16. C♯ minor (add B♯)
17. A♭ major
18. F minor (add E♮)
19. B major
20. G♯ minor (add F𝄪)
21. D♭ major
22. B♭ minor (add A♮)
23. F♯ major
24. D♯ minor (add C𝄪)
25. G♭ major
26. E♭ minor (add D♮)

As demonstrated, the student should follow the P.O.O.K. order when playing through this study. After the first major key is applied, the student should immediately go to its relative harmonic minor key. (The same key signature is used for the relative harmonic minor except the seventh degree is raised by one half-step.) The study should be played through all twenty-six keys following the numbered order. Refer to page 25 – Polytonal Order Of Keys

INFLUENCE OF THE DIATONIC CYCLE

The diatonic cycle forms the strongest progression of diatonic harmony. The diatonic seventh chords and their corresponding modes present the most basic melodic and harmonic elements needed to begin functioning and developing as a jazz improvisor or composer. A student must be able to know and immediately recognize the relationship existing between a diatonic chord and its related mode or scale, in order to produce melodies from either a vertical (chord information) or horizontal (mode or scale information) approach.

The diatonic cycle progression in all major keys consists of the I7 chord moving to the IV7 chord, the IV7 chord moving to the vii half-dim7 chord, the vii half-dim7 chord moving to the iii7 chord, the iii7 chord moving to the vi7 chord, the vi7 chord moving to the ii7 chord, the ii7 chord moving to the V7 chord, and the V7 chord returning back to the I7 chord creating a descending spiral of fifths.

The diatonic cycle progression in all minor keys consists of the i7 chord moving to the iv7 chord, the iv7 chord moving to the vii dim7 chord, the vii dim7 chord moving to the III7 chord, the III7 chord moving to the VI7 chord, the VI7 chord moving to the ii half-dim7 chord, the ii half-dim7 chord moving to the V7 chord and the V7 chord returning back to the i7 chord creating a descending spiral of fifths.

It should be understood that the diatonic chords and modes in all major keys are always of the same species or qualities. It should also be understood that the diatonic chords and modes in all minor keys are of the same species or qualities.

EMPLOYMENT OF THE DIATONIC CYCLE

Whether in a major or minor key, all styles of music, including jazz and pop tunes employ this diatonic flow of chord changes. Both composers and improvisors add variety and interest to their music by moving from one tonal center to another, thereby creating many different chord progressions. When moving to other tonal centers the flow of the diatonic cycle may be retained within each tonal center. Playing this study will accomplish the following:

1. The memorization of the natural sound or gravity of the diatonic cycle for each tonal center

2. Ability to react to and reproduce sounds heard by the ear

3. The playing of scales, modes, and chords, in their natural progression

4. Quicker ear/instrument responses whether reading or improvising

5. The learning of all keys or tonal centers, both major and minor, with equal proficiency

DIALECTAL TONAL CENTERS OR KEYS SIGNALED

The key signature is only a partial indication of the dialectal tonal centers or keys contained in a given piece of music. Novice improvisors and many semi-professional performers improvise in the key of the signature and then rely upon the ear to hear non-diatonic chords and tonal changes and sometimes are not even aware that a tonal center change has occur. Chords other than diatonic chords from the key being played signal changes of tonal centers or dialects to use when improvising.

A popular song, a standard, or any musical composition frequently does not remain in the tonal center indicated by the key signature, but may change several times throughout a given piece of music.

The most common use of tonal center changes can be found in the B section or bridge of many AABA tunes.

The overall design of a song using the musical form of AABA is 32 measures in length and consists of four 8-measure sections.

1. The A-section (main idea) contains 8 measures which is repeated.

2. The B-section or bridge (contrasting with the A-section) contains 8 measures, often constructed of two 4-measure phrases; the last phrase usually prepares for the return of the A-section.

3. Repetition of the A-section

The standard, "I Got Rhythm," a song composed in the AABA musical form, passes through several tonal centers during the bridge section using "cycle of fifths" chord changes.

Many musicians are aware that the chorus and the release or bridge of a song are often composed in differ-

ent tonal centers, even though there are no key signature indications of change provided. Too many improvisors, however, are not aware that tonal centers change within the traditional AABA structural components of a song.

Any seventh chord that is different from the diatonic chords of the key usually indicates a change of tonal centers within the song's progression and requires a shift to the tonal center of that key.

Functional chords that signal tonal center changes approximately seventy-five percent of the time that are not related to the tonal center of the key signature being used are: a major seventh chord, a minor seventh chord, and a dominant seventh chord foreign to the key of the tune being improvised.

Chord types from non-related keys that signal tonal center changes are: the tonic chord, IMaj7, the supertonic chord, iim7, the dominant seventh, V7 the most common signals to be recognized as tonal center changes. In the minor keys the ii chord is a iim7♭5.

The next common chord in the chain of functional chords is the subdominant chord, IV7. In the minor key the iv7 is a minor chord.

The submediant chord, vi7, is the next most common chord followed by the mediant chord, iii7, and the leading tone chord, vii7♭5. These three chords are usually found as a part of a longer progression in changing tonal centers.

After practicing this diatonic cycle study with all its dialectal tonal centers, the student should then commit all tonal centers with their corresponding chords and modes to memory. When different chord changes appear in the music, new tonal centers will be easily recognized, and improvising will become easier.

When a piece is written entirely within one tonal center indicated by the key signature, improvisation is easier, but when internal tonal center changes occur, improvisational demands become more complex.

The tonal center approach to improvisational study encourages fluency in the whole spectrum of the language and dialects of music from which an individual's style can properly be developed.

Following is a list of standard, popular jazz tunes that contain the Diatonic Cycle completely or in part. Although it is important to learn the diatonic cycle in all keys or dialects; it is imperative for today's novice composer or improvisor to become familiar with the jazz literature that makes use of the diatonic cycle. The more tunes that a student learns, analyses, and memorizes the easier it will be to improvise on diatonic chord changes.

Standard, Pop, Jazz Tunes That Use the Diatonic Cycle of Fifths Chord Progressions Completely or Partially in Various Tonal Centers.

"All of Me," S.Simons/G.Marks

"Along Came Betty," Benny Golson

"All the Things You Are," Oscar Hammerstein II/Jerome Kern

"Anthropology," C. Parker/D. Gillespie

"Autumn Leaves," Johnny Mercer/Joseph Kosma

"Baubles, Bangles and Beads," Forest/Wright

"Blue Moon," Richard Rodgers/ Lorenz Hart

"Bluesette," Jean "Toots" Tielemans/Norman Gimbel

"Boplicity," Miles Davis/Gil Evans

"But Not for Me," Ira Gershwin/George Gershwin

"Chasin' the Bird," Charlie Parker

"Cherokee," Ray Noble

"Confirmation," Charlie Parker

"Countdown," John Coltrane

"Cute," Neil Hefti

"Daahoud," Clifford Brown

"Del Sasser," Sam Jones

"Dewey Square," Charlie Parker

"Donna Lee," Miles Davis

"Fly Me to the Moon (aka, "In Other Words")," Bart Howard

"Four Brothers," Jimmy Guiffre

"Four," Miles Davis

"Get Happy," Ted Koehler/Harold Arlen

"Giant Steps," John Coltrane

"Good Bait," Tad Dameron

"Groovin' High," Dizzy Gillespie

"How High the Moon," Morgan/Lewis

"I Got Rhythm," George Gershwin/Ira Gershwin

"I Love You," Cole Porter

"I Remember Clifford," Benny Golson

"I'll Remember April," Raye/DePaul

"In a Mellow Tone," Duke Ellington

"Jordu," Duke Jordon

"Joy Spring," Clifford Brown

"Just in Time," Betty Comden/Adolph Green/Jule Styne

"Kim," Charlie Parker

"Ko-Ko," Charlie Parker

"Lady Bird," Tad Dameron

"Little Willie Leaps," Miles Davis

"Loads of Love," Richard Rodgers

"Lover Man," Davis/Ramirez

"Lover," Richard Rodgers

"Meditation," A.C.Jobim

"Misty," Erroll Garner

"On Green Dolphin Street," Bronislav Kaper

"Ornithology," Charlie Parker

"Out of Nowhere," Green

"Parisian Thoroughfare," Bud Powell

"Round Midnight," Thelonious Monk

"Saint Thomas," Sonny Rollins

"Satin Doll," Duke Ellington

"Scrapple from the Apple," Charlie Parker

"Sister Sadie," Horace Silver

"Skylark," Carmichael/Mercer

"Soon," George Gershwin

"Sophisticated Lady," Duke Ellington

"Stella By Starlight," Victor Young

"Stranger in Paradise," Robert Wright/George Forest

"Sweet Georgia Brown," Bernie/Pinkard

"The Shadow of Your Smile," Paul Francis Webster/ Johnny Mandel

"The Song is You," Kern/Hammerstein

"Tune Up," Eddie Vinson and Mile Davis

"Watch What Happens," Michel LeGrand and Ceora, Lee Morgan

"Yardbird Suite," Charlie Parker

As can be seen by the length of this list of jazz literature which contains the diatonic cycle progression, a jazz player acquires an abundance of jazz language and style while learning melodies. These tunes, as melodic information stored in the mind's ear, then become part of the total melodic recall to be played in bits or at length when improvising.

All great jazz players have hundreds and maybe thousands of jazz tunes at their fingertips that can be used to put together as a puzzle in thousands of different ways over endless chord changes. This process occurs automatically as the improvisor reacts to many new tunes and many new sets of chord changes.

The novice player should begin to memorize as many different jazz tunes as possible to expand improvisational fluency and acquire jazz vocabulary and language which should be a continuing process. After memorizing some of the jazz literature listed above, the student should then practice the tunes in as many different keys as possible to expand the student's jazz language even further.

Practicing the diatonic cycle study along with jazz literature develops the facility to send out what the ear hears, thus developing the musical instrument as an extension of the musician's body and connecting it more directly with the mind. Consequently, the ear does not need developing, but the mind does, in order to understand and perceive what the ear is hearing. Now the student must begin to develop the technical ability to produce on the instrument what is heard in the mind's ear.

Enjoy the diatonic cycle and keep on "Pooking."

POLYTONAL ORDER OF KEYS

THE TONAL CENTERS follow a definite order based upon EMILE DE COSMO'S POLYTONAL ORDER OF KEYS. It's purpose is to help the student learn how to play in any key. It is essential that this order of keys be followed. The student will discover that upon approaching the tonal center of D Major he has laready been prepared for the tones F♯ and C♯. The same holds true with all subsequent tonal centers. Apply these signatures to the following exercises.

Will help you learn to play in all keys.
Gives you the experience of playing through the keys which facilitates sight reading.

THE DIATONIC CYCLE – TREBLE CLEF INSTRUMENTS

Diatonic Modes

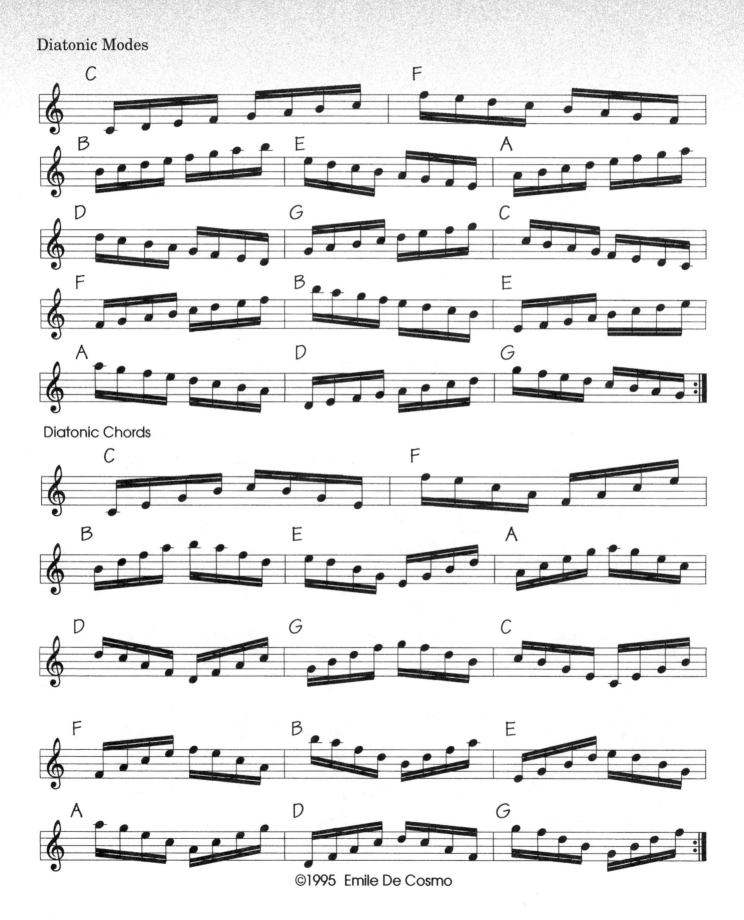

Diatonic Chords

©1995 Emile De Cosmo

THE DIATONIC CYCLE — BASS CLEF INSTRUMENTS

Diatonic Modes

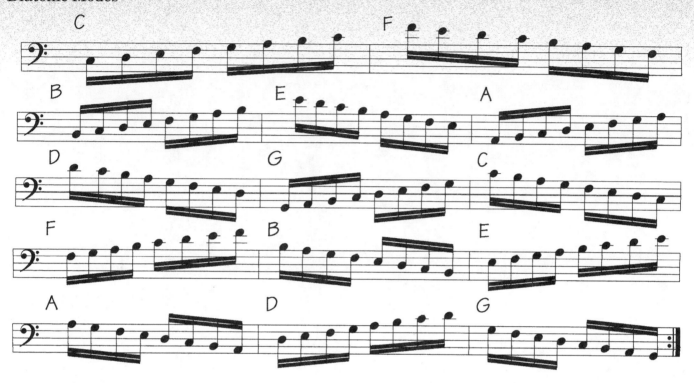

Diatonic Chords

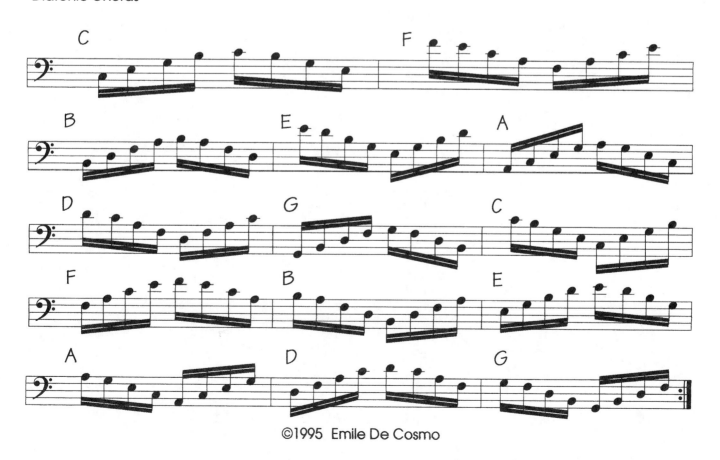

©1995 Emile De Cosmo

CHAPTER 4

LEARNING THEORY USING THE OVERTONE SERIES

In this chapter, I will explain what is known as the overtone, or the harmonic, series. By analyzing the overtone series, one can learn the source of all the musical theory which it produces: intervals of minor seconds, major seconds, minor thirds, major thirds, fourths, augmented fourths, fifths, augmented fifths, flatted fifths, sixths, minor sevenths, major sevenths, octaves, ninths, tenths, augmented elevenths, and thirteenths.

Importance of the overtone series cannot be underestimated. The history and growth of the music through the centuries directly relates to the overtone series.

The musical example in this chapter illustrates the overtones in every key moving through the cycle of fifths. This exercise should be played with some changes made in octaves to accommodate the range of any particular instrument.

OVERTONAL INFLUENCE

Although heard as single tones, each individual pitch consists of a fundamental tone and a series of six principal overtones referred to as either harmonics or partials. Example:

The dominant 7th chord (C7) in the tonic key of F, which contains one flat, is built on the note C, the fifth of the F scale, and contains the notes: C (the root), E (the third), G (the fifth), and Bb (the seventh), corresponding to the first six overtones produced by the fundamental C. The overtones are higher in pitch than the fundamental tone.

The overtones of a given pitch have been reported to extend to sixteen, twenty-two, and beyond. The fundamental and its overtones produce an altered dominant seventh chord containing tensions extending to diminished or flatted fifth, augmented fifth, ninth, augmented eleventh, and thirteenth.

The fundamental and its subsequent overtones or partials create a magnetic or gravitational force that puts the fundamental in motion, causing it to resolve or fall to another fundamental fifth below, and begin the cadential flow of the cycle of fifths.

The upper partials or overtones are secondarily audible, in comparison with the fundamental tone. The parts naturally assume relative positions represented by the overtone series.

The sequence of notes produced when any tone or chord is played are audible in accordance with a universal principle of nature, as fundamental to music as gravity is to motion. Fifths (V) fall to tonics (I), just as physical objects fall to the earth. For example, if C is played, the ear actually hears not only the C, but the series of overtones: C, E, G, Bb, D, E, F#, G, A, Bb, B, C. The first six overtones produce a dominant 7th chord. The remaining overtones, from the seventh to the fifteenth partial, are actually sounding a highly altered dominant seventh chord.

ORDER OF OVERTONES

Inclusion of overtones beyond the first six intensify the gravitational pull toward resolution, especially as the diminished fifth, augmented fifth, the ninth, and the augmented eleventh occur. Notice, that due to the tempered tuning, the diminished fifth and augmented eleventh are synonymous.

The sixth overtone, when added to the first five, produces a dominant seventh chord, which contains a tritone (the augmented fourth, lowered fifth, or augmented eleventh).

The overtone series from the fundamental tone C (C, E, G, Bb, C, D, E, F#, G, A, Bb, B, C) contains a tremendous amount of musical theory. The harmonic relationships that encompass the series is as follows (refer to musical examples):

C triad = C, E, G

E Minor triad = E, G, B

G Minor triad = G, Bb, D

F# dimished triad = F#, A, C

A minor triad = A, C, E

Bb Augmented triad = Bb, D, F#

C seventh chord = C, E, G, Bb

C major 7th chord = C, E, G, B

G major 7th chord = G, B, D, F#

A minor 7th chord = A, C, E, G

C ninth chord = C, E, G, Bb, D

C major ninth chord = C, E, G, B, D

E minor ninth chord = E, G, B, D, F#

C thirteenth + augmented eleventh chord = C, E, G, Bb, D, F#, A

E half diminished or E minor seventh flat five = E, G, Bb, D

The lower tetrachord of the C whole-tone scale = C, D, E, F#

G melodic minor scale ascending = G, A, Bb, C, D, E, F#

G minor sixth chord = G, Bb, D, E

D major tetrachord = D, E, F#, G

D seventh chord = D, F#, A, C

D Mixolydian mode = D, E, F#, G, A, B, C

D ninth chord = D, F#, A, C, E

D thirteenth chord = D, F#, A, C, E, G, B

E minor tetrachord = E, F#, G, A

F# half diminished seventh chord = F#, A, C, E

G major pentatonic scale = G, A, B, D, E

G pentatonic blues scale = G, A, Bb, B, D, E

One third of the chromatic scale from A = A, Bb, B, C

Two tritones = C to F# and E to Bb

Consequently, when every other of the eleven chromatic tones is struck as fundamentals, a new set of theoretical information appears.

THE TRITONE DEFINED

The tritone, an interval of an augmented fourth, called the devil's interval ("diabolus in musica") during the Middle Ages, was avoided melodically, but when used harmonically, it is the most powerful force of harmonic action within the musical universe. When heard harmonically, the augmented fourth (tritone) creates a tremendous need for resolution and is more properly to be regarded as the "angel of resolution."

The two tritones from the overtone series provide the most distinctive characteristics of the overtones, creating individual tension and unrest, increasing the tonal magnetism, causing a greater need for resolution to a tonic chord whose root is a fifth below the root of the dominant seventh chord. One of these tritones is naturally found between the fourth and seventh degrees of any major scale.

The dominant seventh chord (V7) of any key contains both of these scale degrees, which create forward motion pressing for resolution to the tonic (I) chord, making the dominant seventh to tonic the most prevalent chord progression.

THE CHAIN OF DOMINANTS

The overtone series serves as the magnetic vehicle of all cadential movement. The fundamental bass moves in descending fifths (C, F, Bb, Eb, Ab, Db, Gb/F#, B, E, A, D, G). Because of the Overtonal influence discussed earlier, the overtone series is in reality a cycle of altered dominant sevenths moving in an endless harmonic spiral of descending fifths. The fundamental and its overtones establish the force of gravity of the musical universe, the strongest and most natural harmonic progression in music.

Because of the fifth relationship, which exists between each chord in the chain of dominants, the term "cycle of fifths" is employed and established; each note is the fifth of the note it precedes.

The C fundamental and its overtones gravitate down to an F.

The F fundamental and its overtones gravitate down to a Bb.

The Bb fundamental and its overtones gravitate down to an Eb.

The Eb fundamental and its overtones gravitate down to an Ab.

The Ab fundamental and its overtones gravitate down to a Db.

The Db fundamental and its overtones gravitate down to a Gb.

The Gb fundamental and its overtones gravitate down to a Cb (B).

The B fundamental and its overtones gravitate down to an E.

The E fundamental and its overtones gravitate down to an A.

The A fundamental and its overtones gravitate down to a D.

The D fundamental and its overtones gravitate down to a G.

The G fundamental and its overtones gravitate down to a C.

The gravitational force produced by the fundamental and its overtones causes the forward motion of chord progressions in all styles and improvised music.

Many high school and even college students have a problem learning this dominating relationship when studying jazz or classical harmony. Memorizing the overtone series and practicing it would greatly improve the understanding of this chain of dominants and its relationship to the progression or movement of chords used in music.

For students of jazz improvisation, music theory, or composition learning the cycle of fifths and its relationship to the overtone series is a must.

OVERTONE STUDY — ALL TREBLE CLEF INSTRUMENTS

by Emile De Cosmo

OVERTONE STUDY – ALL BASS CLEF INSTRUMENTS

by Emile De Cosmo

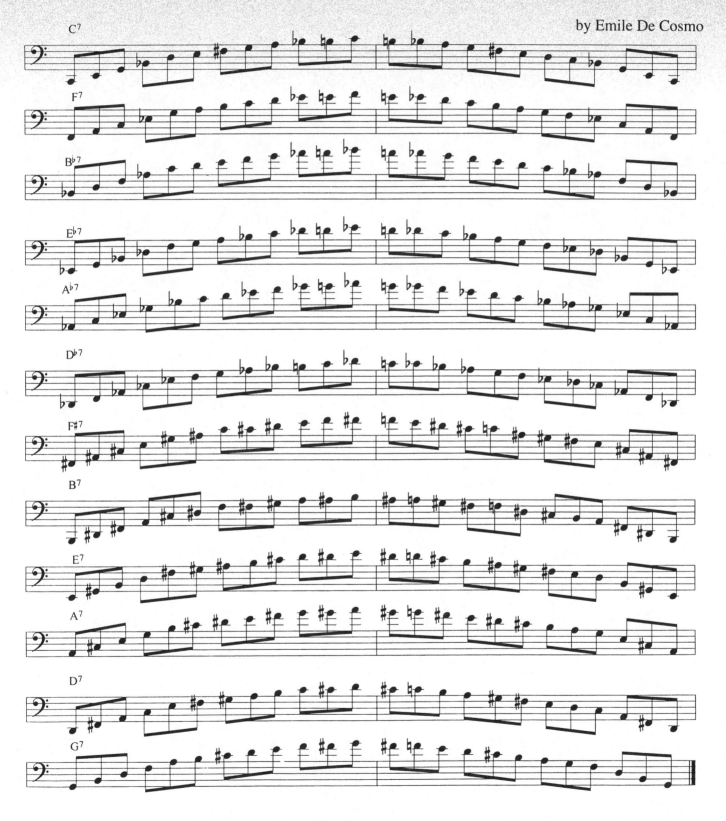

CHAPTER 5

THE PENTATONIC SCALE
THE SCALE OF CENTURIES PAST AND PRESENT

The melodic strains of the five-tone pentatonic scale span the history of music from 3000 B.C. to the present. It was developed by the Chinese in the order of the overtone series (nature's chord) taking five ascending notes from the cycle of fifths and rearranging them in scale form. The notes taken from the cycle were C, G, D, A, and E. When rearranged in scale form they become a C major pentatonic scale with the final note being C: C, D, E, G, A, C.

If you compare it with our western major scale you will notice that F, the fourth degree, and B, the seventh degree, are not present. The pentatonic scale can serve as a solid basis for both melody and harmony. This scale has been used extensively and universally and has endured for centuries due to its unique shape and sound.

In the 1974 edition of *The Harvard Dictionary of Music* Willi Apel states, "Many melodies of the great composers begin with a chordal motion and continue with scalar motion, thus showing a progression from a 'static' beginning to a 'dynamic' continuation."

The C pentatonic scale contains three chord tones C, E, G (chordal motion) and five scale tones C, D, E, G, and A (scalar motion) which when combined in any order satisfies the definition of melody. The pentatonic scale continues in its popularity and is still a major part of composed and improvised melodic music to this day.

EXPLANATION OF THE MAJOR PENTATONIC SCALE MODES OR INVERSIONS

In the key of C the notes of the scale are C, D, E, G, A which produce the first mode of the pentatonic scale numbered 1, 2, 3, 5, 6 and uses the harmony of a C Major chord. Other modes or inversions are produced by taking the same five notes and rearranging them in groups.

The second mode or inversion is D, E, G, A, C numbered 2, 3, 5, 6, 1 which uses the harmony of a D minor chord.

The third mode or inversion is E, G, A, C, D numbered 3, 5, 6, 1, 2 which uses the harmony of an E minor chord.

The fourth mode or inversion is G, A, C, D, E numbered 5, 6, 1, 2, 3 which uses the harmony of a G Major chord.

The fifth mode or inversion is A, C, D, E, G numbered 6, 1, 2, 3, 5 which uses the harmony of an A minor chord.

All of these modes or inversions may also be used or written in reverse order using it's appropriate harmonic chord. In addition to modes and inversions, the pentatonic scale may also be broken into four-note fragments used as partials of melodies.

Scale fragments are groups of four notes that can be taken from any of the hundreds of existing scales. They can be partials of scales or partials of chords ascending

The pentatonic scale is the FIRST and most IMPORTANT scale that an improvising musician or composer must learn in order to have endless melodic curves under his fingers and in his mind's ear.

When a studying musician practices the pentatonic scale and all its inversions in all keys, he or she will be exposed to and experience all possible melodic patterns. Accomplishing this, results in a tremendous amount of melodic shapes being at his/her command.

or descending. Fragments can be started from roots, thirds, fifths, sevenths, ninths, elevenths, and thirteenths of any species or type chord.

The pentatonic scale results in having ten shapes of four note fragments. The uniqueness of the pentatonic scale causes it to stand alone as consonant, melodic, shapes and sounds that have been sounding for thousands of years, and still going!

MAJOR PENTATONIC SCALE FRAGMENTS

Various jazz educators have chosen different terms as labels for scale fragments. I learned the term "scale fragments" when I read a book titled *Jazz Improvisation*, published in 1959 by Watson-Guptill Inc. It was written by pianist, theorist, and jazz critic John Mehegan.

Famous jazz educator David Baker uses the term "Digital Patterns."

Jerry Coker, another well known jazz educator, has recently written an excellent book titled *Elements of the Jazz Language for the Developing Improviser*, published in 1991 by Studio 224. In chapter two of Coker's book he introduces digital and scalar patterns credited to David Baker but terms them 4-note cells.

"Four note groupings" is the term used by Scott Reeves in a book published by Prentice-Hall 1989 titled *Creative Jazz Improvisation*.

In chapter eighteen Reeves deals with improvising "outside" the tonal center and returning to the key center. He states, "Often jazz musicians will improvise with groups of four eighth notes instead of complete scales. In previous chapters we have used the 1-2-3-5 grouping to outline major and dominant chords and the 1-2-b3-5 grouping to outline minor chords. In contemporary improvisation, however, four-note groupings are often used to go outside the key center."

The main reason that these four-note groups are often used for outside playing is because they are complete melodic fragments that are good sounding when playing over stagnant or moving harmony. Though I am accustomed to using the term scale fragments I prefer to label them as "melodic scale fragments." When these fragments are played over any chord they can keep moving or can become final.

MAJOR PENTATONIC HARMONIES

Four basic harmonies available for the C major pentatonic scale are: C triad, C sixth chord, Cmaj7, and a C7 chord. There are three fourth chords that can also be used: (D, G, C), (E, A, D), and (A, D, G). When these fourth chords are inverted they are spelled (C, G, D), (D, A, E), and (G, D, A) and become fifth chords.

Following is a detailed list of the first mode of the twelve major pentatonic scales. The scales ascend and descend using the identical notes, and can use a Major 6 chord or the two respective seventh chords.

C major pentatonic scale: C, D, E, G, A, C uses the CMaj7 or uses the C7 chord.

F major pentatonic scale: F, G, A, C, D, F uses the FMaj7 or uses the F7 chord.

Bb major pentatonic scale: Bb, C, D, F, G, Bb uses the BbMaj7 or uses the Bb7 chord.

Eb major pentatonic scale: Eb, F, G, Bb, C, Eb uses the EbMaj7 or uses the Eb7 chord.

Ab major pentatonic scale: Ab, Bb, C, Eb, F, Ab uses the AbMaj7 or uses the Ab7 chord.

Db major pentatonic scale: Db, Eb, F, Ab, Bb, Db uses the DbMaj7 or uses the Db7 chord.

F# major pentatonic scale: F#, G#, A#, C#, D#, F# uses the F#Maj7 chord or uses the F#7 chord.

B major pentatonic scale: B, C#, D#, F#, G#, B uses the BMaj7 chord or uses the B7 chord.

E major pentatonic scale: E, F#, G#, B, C#, E uses the EMaj7 chord or uses the E7 chord.

A major pentatonic scale: A, B, C#, E, F#, A uses the AMaj7 chord or uses the A7 chord.

D major pentatonic scale: D, E, F#, A, B, D uses the DMaj7 chord or uses the D7 chord.

G major pentatonic scale: G, A, B, D, E, G uses the GMaj7 chord or uses the G7 chord.

As stated earlier, the major pentatonic scale sounds best when played over the harmony of a major triad or major sixth chord and over a major seventh or dominant seventh chord built on the root of the scale.

The pentatonic scale and all of its modes, inversions, fragments and their respective melodic retrogrades have a complete melodic consonant sound. Because of this each of these partials can be considered a short melody that is usable in any compositional or improvisational situation—over any harmony at the discretion of the individual.

In fact, many composers have used fragments or inversions of this scale to begin a melodic line. In 1926 George and Ira Gershwin composed "Someone To Watch Over Me," a song that begins with the first five notes or first fragment of the Eb pentatonic scale, plus the first two notes repeated again an octave higher making seven notes. This scale is used for the melody throughout the entire song rhythmically and sequentially.

In 1935, nine years later, Duke Ellington used the same seven notes of the pentatonic scale to begin the melody of "In A Sentimental Mood."

"Always," another pentatonic song, written by Irving Berlin for a Broadway show in 1923 named *Music Box Revue* starts on the fourth mode or inversion of an

F pentatonic ascending scale written over an F Major chord. Another Irving Berlin yearly favorite, also pentatonic, is "Easter Parade" (1933).

Leroy Anderson, a highly educated musician, has written many well known pentatonic oriented songs. Some of the famous ones are: "The Blue Bells of Scotland," "Fiddle Faddle," "Sleigh Ride," "Blue Tango," "China Doll," "The Syncopated Clock," "Forgotten Dreams," "A Trumpeters Lullaby," "Chicken Reel," "The Bugler's Holiday," "The Typewriter," and many more.

The TV theme from the Archie Bunker show, *All In The Family*, is completely notated with the use of the F pentatonic scale. This song Those Were The Days, by Lee Adams and Charles Strouse was written in 1971 is still being heard on all the re-runs of the show.

Two recent Disney movies contain songs that are pentatonically composed. The two tunes from the score of *The Lion King* (1994), music by Elton John with lyrics by Tim Rice are "Circle of Life" and "I Just Can't Wait to Be King."

Pocahontas (1995) is the second movie with music written by Alan Menken with the lyrics by Stephen Schwartz. Due to the fact that the movie is about the American Indians, the music of course is ninety percent pentatonic.

John Coltrane, one of the greatest saxophonists that has ever lived used four note scale fragments while improvising on "Giant Steps" and "Count Down." Both songs were written by Coltrane and recorded on his *Giant Steps* album on December 2, 1959, released by Atlantic Records. Coltrane continued his exploration of pentatonic scales during this period.

Other post bop jazz players such as Freddie Hubbard, McCoy Tyner, Chick Corea, Joe Farrell, and Woody Shaw began to explore perfect 4ths, the characteristic interval or "gap" in the pentatonic scale. Because this scale was conceived with the ascending fifths of the cycle of fifths which when inverted become fourths, jazz players of that period began using penta-tonic scales and patterns and its fourths and fifths as a means of improvisation in which to express their music.

The pentatonic scale is the FIRST and most IMPORTANT scale that an improvising musician or composer must learn in order to have endless melodic curves under his fingers and in his mind's ear.

When a studying musician practices the pentaton-ic scale and all its inversions in all keys, he or she will be exposed to and experience all possible melodic pat-terns. Accomplishing this results in a tremendous amount of melodic shapes being at his/her command.

In this chapter I have included an etude of the pen-tatonic scale written in both treble and bass clefs to be played and memorized.

My next chapter will explain the minor pentaton-ic scale and the confusion that exists among many edu-cators who teach the theory and use of this scale.

THE MAJOR PENTATONIC SCALE – TREBLE CLEF INSTRUMENTS

by Emile De Cosmo

THE MAJOR PENTATONIC SCALE —
BASS CLEF INSTRUMENTS

by Emile De Cosmo

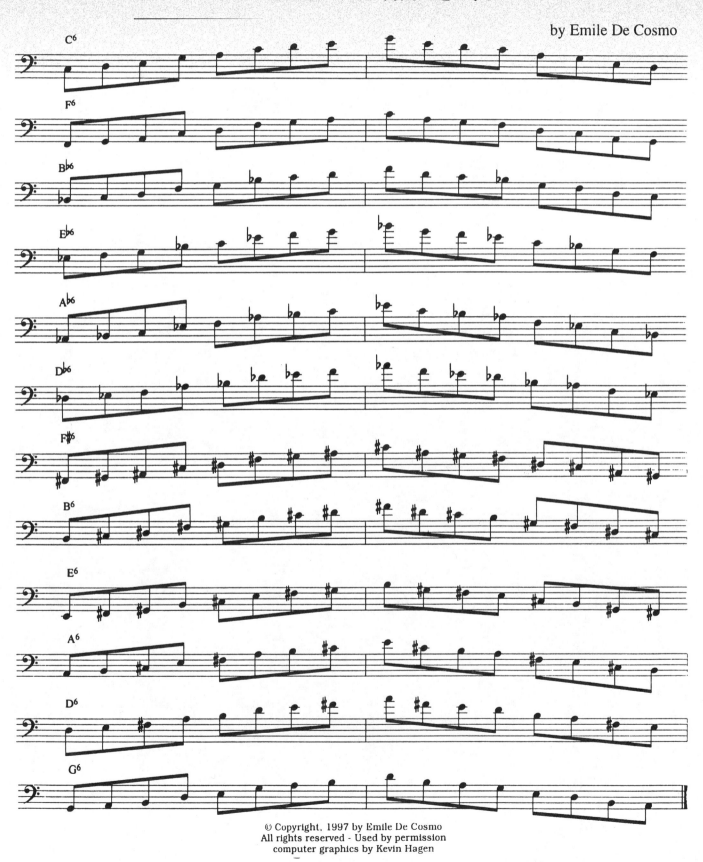

CHAPTER 6

THE AUTHENTIC MINOR PENTATONIC SCALE

The minor pentatonic scale has been taught incorrectly by many classical and jazz music educators. *The Harvard Dictionary of Music*, by Willi Apel, (c) 1974 states (under key relationships), "All keys are related, but in different degrees. The most important such relationships are as follows: (a) parallel keys, major and minor key with the same tonic (C major and C minor); (b) relative keys, major and minor key with the same signature (C major and A minor)..." A majority of jazz educators suggest or use incorrect versions of the minor pentatonic scale. I will try to show the confusion that exists.

Ramon Ricker, internationally known professor of music has written a popular book titled, *Pentatonic Scales for Jazz Improvisation*. In this book, comprised of six transcribed solos, two pages of altered pentatonics, and thirty-seven pages of major pentatonic scale exercises, there is no mention of a minor pentatonic scale.

Two renowned jazz educators/performers Gary Campbell and Mark Levine have each written an improvisation book. In Campbell's book titled *Expansions* he devotes five pages to the proper minor pentatonic scale. The notes of the scale are: C, D, E♭, G, A which are taken from the C melodic minor scale. In Levine's book titled *The Jazz Piano Book* he devotes a whole chapter of twelve pages to pentatonic scales. On the first page of this section there is a song by Johnny

Mandel and Dave Frishberg titled "You Are There." This ballad contains fragments of both major and minor pentatonic scales in the melody. Levine states, "pentatonic scales occur naturally in C major and C melodic minor." On page 134 he shows a Japanese "In-Sen" scale that is an inversion of an ascending D melodic minor scale. However, on page 135 he is in conflict with himself when he shows an example of the incorrect minor pentatonic scale. Shown is a C minor pentatonic scale spelled from the root: C, E♭, F, G, B♭, C which is actually the fourth inversion of an E♭ major pentatonic scale.

AND SO THE CONFUSION GOES ON

As stated earlier the minor pentatonic scale is made up of the first, second, third, fifth, and sixth steps of the ascending melodic minor scale with the fourth and seventh steps omitted. Any student who is familiar with basic music theory, and the music educators who teach music theory, should learn and know that it is an accepted practice that when changing a chord, scale or a melody from major to minor it is necessary to lower the third of that chord, scale, or melody a half step.

Examples: C major chord = C E G, C minor chord = C E♭ G, C Major scale = C D E F G A B C, C minor scale = C D E♭ F G A B C, C Major pentatonic = C D E G A C, C minor pentatonic = C D E♭ G A C.

Bruce Mishkit, a talented saxophone/flute player, active as a writer/producer in the San Francisco bay area, co/produced a book titled *Sax/Flute Lessons with the Greats*. In his lessons he confirms a few basic concepts one of which is the pentatonic scales, "The most common pentatonic scales are major and minor. The formula for the major pentatonic is 1-2-3-5-6. That is the formula you would use to construct a major pentatonic from a major scale. The minor pentatonic, however, is not as clear-cut. I think of a minor pentatonic as 1-2-♭3-5-6. It seems logical to me that if you flat the third of a major pentatonic scale, the result would be a 'true', minor pentatonic." As you can see Mishkit states the correct concept and goes on to say, "Why give the same scale two different names"?

It seems that because the pentatonic scale is so often associated with Oriental music many composers of all types and styles and authors of texts on music never mention pentatonic scales (both major and minor) as the best source for good melodic writing. It may also be due to the fact that the most successful composers of catchy or popular compositions do not want to let their secret be known that pentatonic-conceived melodies with all its many fragments are the way to go. This is why I have concluded that the incorrect C minor pentatonic scale in vogue (C E♭ F G B♭ C) is in reality the third inversion or mode of an E♭ major pentatonic scale using the sixth degree as the root of the scale. Although this modal pentatonic scale sounds good it cannot or should not take precedence over the first choice: the root or basic inside sound of the parallel minor pentatonic scale. Consequently, the closest key relationship to a C major pentatonic scale is its parallel C minor pentatonic scale, and this is arrived at by lowering the third of the major pentatonic scale by a half step.

In chapter twelve of Jerry Coker's book *Elements of the Jazz Language for the Developing Improviser* he introduces the twelfth of the eighteen jazz elements he writes about in the book. This chapter is titled the "Cry Me a River Lick," and he begins by defining the element in the title. The "Cry Me a River Lick" is a specific melodic fragment, (my term) named after the tune from which it comes. The lick is the opening melodic statement of the tune, "Cry Me a River." The line from the song is a descending melody starting from A, the second note of the G minor pentatonic scale: A, G, D, B♭, A, G (a four note 2-1-5-3 fragment). He goes on to say, "There are two reasons why the 'Cry Me a River' lick merits its own segment, they are: 1. the frequency of its use (and by all players); and 2. its extraordinary versatility, capable of accommodating five different chord types without being altered!"

The minor pentatonic scale that Arthur Hamilton used as a basis to compose the song *Cry Me A River* is the C minor pentatonic four note fragment used over the harmony of a C minor chord. Coker's two reasons are really four reasons; namely 1. frequency of use, 2. versatility, 3. five chord types, 4. use over stagnant harmony.

These four reasons are in agreement with the reasons I had given in my last chapter on the major pentatonic scale. This is the rationale I used for the longevity and endurance of the tonic major and tonic minor pentatonic scales through the history of melody and music!

The great saxophonist John Coltrane uses the E minor pentatonic scale on his improvisations on Roger and Hammerstein's song "My Favorite Things." Some other famous musicians/educators in agreement with the minor pentatonic concept are pianist/conductor/composer Leonard Bernstein, pianist John Mehegan, percussionists Phil Kraus, Bob Tilles, Doug Allan, saxophonist Gary Campbell and guitarist Sal Salvador.

MODES AND INVERSIONS OF THE MINOR PENTATONIC SCALE

The minor pentatonic scale is made up of the first, second, third, fifth, and sixth steps of the ascending melodic minor scale with the fourth and seventh steps omitted. When these five steps are rearranged in groups they are called modes or inversions. In the key of C melodic minor ascending the notes are C, D, E♭, G, A. This produces the first mode of the minor pentatonic scale numbered 1, 2, ♭3, 5, 6 which uses the harmony of a C minor chord.

The second mode or inversion is D, E♭, G, A, C numbered 2, ♭3, 5, 6, 1, which uses the harmony of a D minor chord.

The third mode or inversion is E♭, G, A, C, D numbered ♭3, 5, 6, 1, 2, which uses the harmony of an E♭ major chord.

The fourth mode or inversion is G, A, C, D, E♭ numbered 5, 6, 1, 2, ♭3, which uses the harmony of a G minor chord.

The fifth mode or inversion is A, C, D, E♭, G numbered 6, 1, 2, ♭3, 5, which uses the harmony of an A diminished triad.

All of these modes or inversions may also be used or written in reverse order using its appropriate harmonic chord.

MINOR PENTATONIC SCALE FRAGMENTS

Pentatonic scale fragments are four-note partials of any mode or inversion of a major or minor pentatonic scale. To reiterate the notes of a C minor pentatonic scale are C, D, E♭, G, A, numbered as 1, 2, ♭3, 5, 6.

The first four note minor fragment is C, D, E♭, G or numbered by scale degrees 1, 2, ♭3, 5.

By taking four notes of the first inversion D, E♭, G, A and numbering them by scale degrees we arrive at the second minor fragment numbered 1, 2, 4, 5.

By taking four notes of second inversion E♭, G, A, C and numbering them by scale degrees we arrive at the third minor fragment numbered 1, ♭3, 4, 6.

By taking four notes of third inversion G, A, C, D and numbering them by scale degrees we arrive at the fourth minor fragment numbered 1, 2, 4, 5.

By taking four notes of fourth inversion A, C, D, E♭ and numbering them by scale degrees we arrive at the fifth minor fragment numbered 1, ♭3, 4, 5.

The pentatonic scale and all of its modes, inversions, fragments, and their respective retrogrades have a complete melodic consonant sound.

MINOR PENTATONIC HARMONIES

Basic harmonies available for the C minor pentatonic are, C minor triad, C minor sixth chord and the C minor seventh chord. There are also three fourth chords that can be used: D-G-C, E♭-A-D, A-D-G. When these three fourth chords are inverted they are spelled C-G-D, D-A-E♭, G-D-A and are called fifth chords.

A dominant seventh chord whose root lies a fifth below the root of a minor pentatonic scale may be used for its harmony. A C minor pentatonic scale can be played over an F7th chord.

A flatted fifth substitute of this same dominant seventh chord may be also used. A C minor pentatonic scale can be played over a B7 chord. This particular scale is also called the altered scale when it is written starting on the note B, the root of the B7 chord.

The minor pentatonic scale is another of the numerous scales which may be used to compose or improvise melodies over minor triads and minor seventh chords. In this chapter I have included an etude of the minor pentatonic scale written in both treble and bass clefs to be played and memorized. The study can also be played in down across fashion. (Chapter 13)

As stated earlier, the minor Pentatonic Scale sounds most inside when played over the harmony of a minor triad or minor sixth chord and over a minor seventh chord built on the root of the scale.

MINOR PENTATONIC SCALE: TREBLE CLEF

Graphics by Kevin Hagen

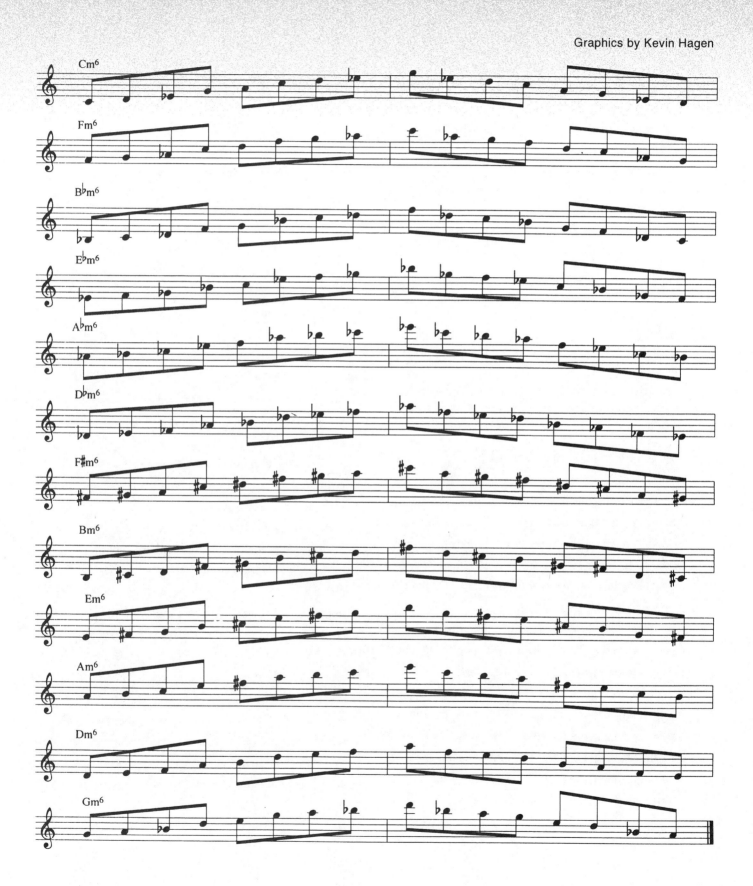

MINOR PENTATONIC SCALE: BASS CLEF

Graphics by Kevin Hagen

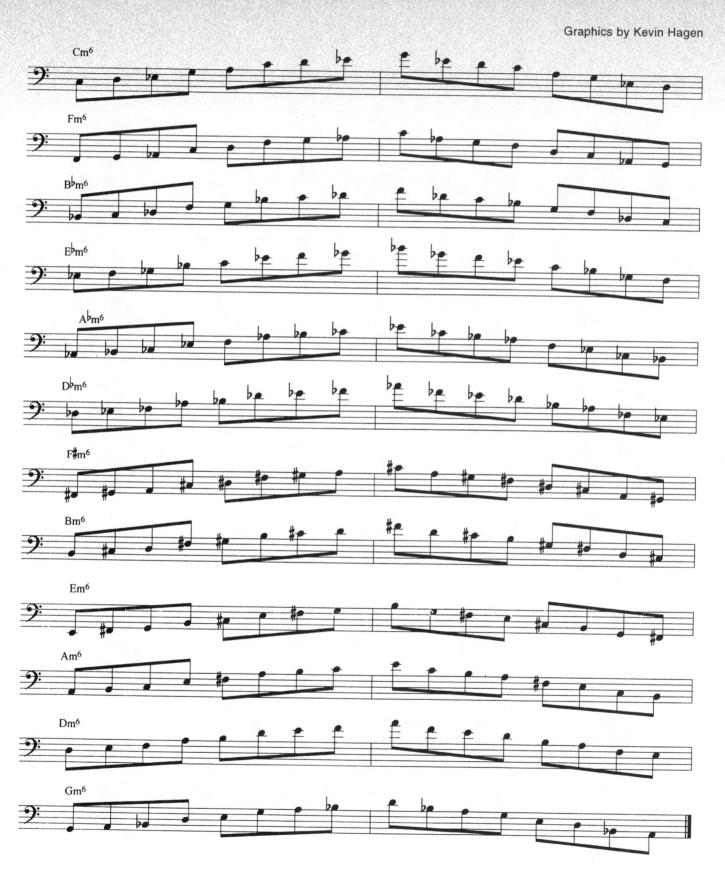

CHAPTER 7

THE ii7/V7 PROGRESSION

In all music, the most basic and natural progression is the V7, or in other words the dominant seventh chord's need to resolve a fifth below, i.e., to a I chord in a major key or to a i chord in a minor key. For example:

• G7 to C Maj = V7 to I in a major key

• G7 to C min = V7 to i in a minor key

The diatonic cycle of fifths reveals that a minor seventh chord (ii7 chord) a fifth higher than the dominant seventh chord (V7 chord) always preceded the dominant V7 chord. This movement from ii7 to V7 results in the term "The ii7/V7 Progression."

The ii7/V7 and I7 have basically three different harmonic functions in the context of the ii7/V7/I7 progression. In all major keys or tonal centers the ii7 chord contains a minor triad with a minor seventh added. The ii7 progresses down a fifth to the V7 chord by way of the diatonic cycle of fifths.

The V7 chord contains a major triad with a minor seventh added. The V7 dominates the key and progresses down a fifth to the I7 chord thus returning to the tonic or chord of the tonal center or key. The I7 chord contains a major triad with the major seventh added. The I7 chord, which establishes the tonal center, does not need to progress, but when it does progress, it can go anywhere. During some progressions in various jazz tunes pursuing the diatonic flow the I7 progresses very smoothly down a fifth to the IV7 chord (Example: ii7/V7/I7/IV7 progression).

In all minor keys or tonal centers the ii7♭5 chord contains a diminished triad with a minor seventh added. The ii7♭5 progresses down a fifth to the V7♭9 chord by way of the diatonic cycle of fifths.

The V7♭9 chord contains a major triad with a minor seventh and lowered ninth added. The V7♭9 dominates the key and progresses down a fifth to the I-7 chord thus returning to the tonic chord of the tonal center or key. The I-7 chord contains a minor triad with the major seventh added. The I-7 chord which establishes the tonal center, does not need to progress, but when it does progress, it can go anywhere. Sometimes during some progressions pursuing the diatonic flow in various jazz tunes the I-7 progresses very smoothly down a fifth to the iv7 chord (Example: ii7/V7/I-7/iv7 progression.

In major keys the ii-7 chord resolves five steps lower to the V7 chord by the natural gravitation of the diatonic cycle of fifths. Next to the V7 to I, the ii7/V7 progression is the most important one found in jazz and classical harmony. When a ii7/V7 chord progression appears other than the diatonic ii7/V7 of the original key, the tonal center that it is derived from must be quickly recognized as a modulation regardless of the key signature in which the music is written, and regardless of whether it moves to the I chord or not. For example:

If a jazz composition is written in the key of D major, the diatonic ii7/V7 progression would be Emi7 to

note: (−) = minor chord   eg. I−7

47

A7. If a Cmi7 to F7 suddenly appears, the key of the moment will be B♭ major (Cmi7 to F7 = ii7/V7 in the key of I or B♭ major).

In this same composition in D major if a Cmi7♭5 to F7♭9 appears, the key of the moment will be Bb minor (Cmi7♭5 to F7♭9 = ii7♭5/V7♭9 in the key of i or B♭ minor).

Mastering the ii7/V7 progression in both major and minor keys is an important step in developing good flowing jazz lines using the chord progressions at hand which may contain many ii7/V7 in many different keys.

A ii7 to V7 is usually found at the end of a progression, but can also be found in the middle of a progression and not necessarily in the original key. The ii7 to V7 to I7 is a longer progression employed in many compositions to modulate to different keys or suggest different keys, thus, making the composition more interesting. The ii7/V7/I7 is usually found at the end of a progression. Next to the V to I progression the ii7 to V7 to I7 progression is the most important group of chords.

All jazz improvisers have to learn how to respond melodically to ii7/V7 chord changes as they appear in different jazz compositions or arrangements. The better one can react to these changes, by playing in the tonal centers they imply, the better the improvisation will sound. Practically every musical composition consists of some or many combinations of the ii7/V7 progression. When the combination of the minor seventh and dominant seventh appear, the key that they are derived from must be quickly recognized. The improvisor can compose many melodies in the corresponding key using basic chords and scales of the ii7/V7. The player also has at his disposal all of the diatonic chords and scales in that key to use at his discretion.

RECOGNIZING DIFFERENT TONAL CENTERS OR DIALECTS

The old adage that music is a language is somewhat simplistic. Music is a language, but one which is complexly composed of twenty-four dialects representing the twelve major tonal centers or keys and the twelve minor tonal centers or keys. Within a language a dialect, among other dialects, is a variant form of the standard language. The variations occur as alterations of pronunciation, colloquial vocabulary, idiomatic expression, spelling, syntax, and grammar. In the United States of America the principal regional dialects are those of New England, The Eastern Seaboard, New York Metropolitan, Southern, Deep Southern, South Western, North Western, Midwestern, and Pacific Coastal.

Each of these dialects is distinguishable from the others by most native speakers of English, as departures from standard English. The important matter is that speakers of the same language be able to understand one another, in spite of dialectic differences.

As in a language, in music it is important that a musician be fluent in all the dialectal keys of music. The musical dialects consist of twelve diatonic major keys or tonal centers and twelve relative diatonic minor keys or tonal centers. When a ii7/V7 chord progression appears in a jazz composition the student must immediately recognize it as a dialectic tonal center or key.

In any jazz composition the ii7/V7 progression does not have to move anywhere else, but when it does appear, and for whatever length of time it appears, the dialectic key or tonal center has, for the moment, changed in that composition. Even if a singular ii7 or V7 or I7 appears in a jazz piece, the key that these individual chords come from is used as the key or dialect of the moment. For example:

If a jazz composition is written in D major and a Gmi7 chord appears, the key or dialect of the moment is F major, because recognizably the Gmi7 chord is a ii7 chord in the key of F major and requires playing in the key of F major instead of D major.

If in the same composition in D major a B♭7 chord appears, the key of the moment is E♭ major, because the B♭7 chord is recognized as a V7 chord in E♭ major and requires playing in the key or dialect of E♭ major instead of D major.

If the next single chord in the same composition is D♭ maj7 the key or dialect of the moment is D♭ major, because recognizably the D♭ maj7 chord is a I7 chord in the key of D♭ major and requires playing in the key of D♭ major.

The previous analysis reveals the following qualities of the ii7 V7/I7 diatonic chords of the major key. In all major keys the minor seventh chord built on the second degree of the major scale is a ii7 chord:

ii7 = Key of the moment is a whole step lower than the root of the ii7 chord. Ex. Bmi7 = ii7 of key of the moment = A major.

The following is a list of the twelve ii7 chords and their respective tonal centers or dialects:

- When a Bmi7 occurs: Improvise in the key or dialect of the A major tonal center.

- When an Emi7 occurs: Improvise in the key or dialect of the D major tonal center.

- When an Ami7 occurs: Improvise in the key or dialect of the G major tonal center.

- When a Dmi7 occurs: Improvise in the key or dialect of the C major tonal center.

- When a Gmi7 occurs: Improvise in the key or dialect of the F major tonal center.

- When a Cmi7 occurs: Improvise in the key or dialect of the B♭ major tonal center.

- When a Fmi7 occurs: Improvise in the key or dialect of the E♭ major tonal center.

- When a B♭mi7 occurs: Improvise in the key or dialect of the A♭ major tonal center.

- When an E♭mi7 occurs: Improvise in the key or dialect of the D♭ major tonal center.

- When an A♭mi7 occurs: Improvise in the key or dialect of the G♭ major tonal center.

- When a C♯mi7 occurs: Improvise in the key or dialect of the B major tonal center.

- When a F♯mi7 occurs: Improvise in the key or dialect of the E major tonal center.

In all major keys the dominant seventh chord built on the fifth degree of the major scale is a V7 chord:

V7 = key or dialect of the moment is five steps lower than the root of the V7 chord (Example E7 = V7 of key of the moment = A major).

The following is a list of the twelve V7 chords and their respective tonal centers or dialects:

- When an E7 occurs: Improvise in the key or dialect of the A major tonal center.

- When an A7 occurs: Improvise in the key or dialect of the D major tonal center.

- When a D7 occurs: Improvise in the key or dialect of the G major tonal center.

- When a G7 occurs: Improvise in the key or dialect of the C major tonal center.

- When a C7 occurs: Improvise in the key or dialect of the F major tonal center.

- When a F7 occurs: Improvise in the key or dialect of the B♭ major tonal center.

- When a B♭7 occurs: Improvise in the key or dialect of the E♭ major tonal center.

- When an E♭7 occurs: Improvise in the key or dialect of the A♭ major tonal center.

- When an A♭7 occurs: Improvise in the key or dialect of the D♭ major tonal center.

- When a D♭7 occurs: Improvise in the key or dialect of the G♭ major tonal center.

- When a F♯7 occurs: Improvise in the key or dialect of the B major tonal center.

- When a B7 occurs: Improvise in the key or dialect of the E major tonal center.

In all major keys the major seventh chord built on the first degree of the major scale is a I7 chord (Example: Amaj7 = I7 of key of the moment = A major).

The following is a list of twelve I7 chords and their respective tonal centers or dialects:

- When a Amaj7 occurs: Improvise in the key or dialect of the A major tonal center.

- When a Dmaj7 occurs: Improvise in the key or dialect of the D major tonal center.

- When a Gmaj7 occurs: Improvise in the key or dialect of the G major tonal center.

- When a Cmaj7 occurs: Improvise in the key or dialect of the C major tonal center.

- When a Fmaj7 occurs: Improvise in the key or dialect of the F major tonal center.

- When a B♭maj7 occurs: Improvise in the key or dialect of the B♭ major tonal center.

- When a E♭maj7 occurs: Improvise in the key or dialect of the E♭ major tonal center.

- When a A♭maj7 occurs: Improvise in the key or dialect of the A♭ major tonal center.

- When a D♭maj7 occurs: Improvise in the key or dialect of the D♭ major tonal center.

- When a G♭maj7 occurs: Improvise in the key or dialect of G♭ major tonal center.

- When a Bmaj7 occurs: Improvise in the key or dialect of the B major tonal center.

- When a Emaj7 occurs: Improvise in the key or dialect of the E major tonal center.

In any jazz composition written in a minor key the ii-7♭5 or half-dim7 (V7♭9) progression does not have to move anywhere else, but when it does appear and for whatever length of time it appears the key or tonal center has changed in that composition for the moment. Even if a singular ii-7♭5 or V7♭9 or I-7 appears in a jazz piece the key that these individual ii-7♭5, V7♭9 , I-7 chords come from is used as the key or dialect of the moment. For example:

If a jazz composition is written in D minor and a Gmi7♭5 or minor half-diminished chord appears, the key or dialect of the moment is F minor because we recognize the Gmi7♭5 chord as a ii-7♭5 chord in the key of F minor and we play in the key of F minor instead of D minor.

If in the same composition in D minor a B♭7♭9 chord appears, the key of the moment is E♭ minor because the B♭7♭9 chord is recognized as a V7♭9 chord in E♭ minor and we play in the key or dialect of E♭ minor instead of D minor.

If the next single chord in the same composition is Db minor the key or dialect of the moment is Db minor because we recognize the Db minor chord as a I-7 chord in the key of Db minor and we play in the key of Db minor.

We can deduce from the above analysis the following qualities of the ii-7♭5/V7♭9/I-7 diatonic chords in the minor key. In all minor keys the minor seventh flat five chord built on the second degree of the minor scale is a ii-7♭5 chord.

- ii-7♭5 = Key of the moment is a whole step lower than the root of the ii7♭5 chord. Ex. Bmi7♭5 = ii7♭5 of key of the moment = A minor.

The following is a list of the twelve ii-7b5 chords and their respective tonal centers or dialects:

- When a Bmi7♭5 occurs: Improvise in the key or dialect of the A minor tonal center.
- When a Emi7♭5 occurs: Improvise in the key or dialect of the D minor tonal center.
- When a Ami7♭5 occurs: Improvise in the key or dialect of the G minor tonal center.
- When a Dmi7♭5 occurs: Improvise in the key or dialect of the C minor tonal center.
- When a Gmi7♭5 occurs: Improvise in the key or dialect of the F minor tonal center.
- When a Cmi7♭5 occurs: Improvise in the key or dialect of the B♭ minor tonal center.
- When a Fmi7♭5 occurs: Improvise in the key or dialect of the E♭ minor tonal center.
- When a B♭mi7♭5 occurs: Improvise in the key or dialect of the A♭ minor tonal center.
- When a E♭mi7♭5 occurs: Improvise in the key or dialect of the D♭ minor tonal center.
- When a A♭mi7♭5 occurs: Improvise in the key or dialect of the G♭ minor tonal center.

- When a C#mi7♭5 occurs: Improvise in the key or dialect of the B minor tonal center.
- When a F#mi7♭5 occurs: Improvise in the key or dialect of the E minor tonal center.

In all minor keys the dominant seventh chord built on the fifth degree of the major scale is a V7♭9 chord.

V7♭9 = Key or dialect of the moment is five steps lower than the root of the V7♭9 chord (Example: E7♭9 = V7♭9 of key of the moment = A minor).

The following is a list of the twelve V7♭9 chords and their respective tonal centers or dialects.

- When an E7♭9 occurs: Improvise in the key or dialect of the A minor tonal center.
- When an A7♭9 occurs: Improvise in the key or dialect of the D minor tonal center.
- When a D7♭9 occurs: Improvise in the key or dialect of the G minor tonal center.
- When a G7♭9 occurs: Improvise in the key or dialect of the C minor tonal center.
- When a C7♭9 occurs: Improvise in the key or dialect of the F minor tonal center.
- When a F7♭9 occurs: Improvise in the key or dialect of the B♭ minor tonal center.
- When a B♭7♭9 occurs: Improvise in the key or dialect of the E♭ minor tonal center.
- When an E♭7♭9 occurs: Improvise in the key or dialect of the A♭ minor tonal center.
- When an A♭7♭9 occurs: Improvise in the key or dialect of the D♭ minor tonal center.
- When a D♭7♭9 occurs: Improvise in the key or dialect of the G♭ minor tonal center.
- When a F#7♭9 occurs: Improvise in the key or dialect of the B minor tonal center.
- When a B7♭9 occurs: Improvise in the key or dialect of the E minor tonal center.

In all minor keys the minor chord built on the first degree of the minor scale is a I-7 chord (Example: Ami = I-7 of key of the moment = A minor).

The following is a list of twelve I-7 chords of the minor keys and their respective tonal centers or dialects:

- When an Ami occurs: Improvise in the key or dialect of the A minor tonal center.
- When a Dmi occurs: Improvise in the key or dialect of the D minor tonal center.
- When a Gmi occurs: Improvise in the key or dialect of the G minor tonal center.
- When a Cmi occurs: Improvise in the key or dialect of the C minor tonal center.
- When a Fmi occurs: Improvise in the key or dialect of the F minor tonal center.
- When a B♭mi occurs: Improvise in the key or dialect of the B♭ minor tonal center.
- When an E♭mi occurs: Improvise in the key or dialect of the E♭ minor tonal center.
- When an A♭mi occurs: Improvise in the key or dialect of the A♭ minor tonal center.
- When a D♭mi occurs: Improvise in the key or dialect of the D♭ minor tonal center.
- When a G♭mi occurs: Improvise in the key or dialect of the G♭ minor tonal center.
- When a Bmi occurs: Improvise in the key or dialect of the B minor tonal center.
- When an Emi occurs: Improvise in the key or dialect of the E minor tonal center.

The following is a list of standard popular jazz tunes that contain the ii7/V7 progression completely or in part. Although it is important to learn the ii7/V7 progression in all keys or dialects, it is imperative for today's novice composer or improviser to become familiar with the jazz literature that makes use of the ii7/V7 progression. If the student learns, analyses, and memorizes these melodies, improvising on tunes which contain the ii7/V7 progression will become easier.

THE PATH TO JAZZ IMPROVISATION

A LIST OF TUNES THAT SHOULD BE MEMORIZED USING THE ii-7/V7 PROGRESSION

"All The Things You Are," Oscar Hammerstein/ Jerome Kern

"Along Came Betty," Benny Golson

"Autumn Leaves," Johnny Mercer

"Baubles, Bangles and Beads," Forest/Wright

"Beyond All Limits," Woody Shaw

"Boplicity," Miles Davis/Gil Evans

"Cherokee," Ray Noble

"Con Alma," Dizzy Gillespie

"Confirmation," Charlie Parker

"Countdown," John Coltrane

"Crosscurrent," Lenny Tristano

"Daahoud," Clifford Brown

"Del Sasser," Sam Jones

"Dewey Square," Charlie Parker

"Donna Lee," Miles Davis

"Embraceable You," George and Ira Gershwin

"Four," Miles Davis

"Giant Steps," John Coltrane

"Groovin' High," Dizzy Gillespie

"Half Nelson," Miles Davis/N.Boyd

"How High the Moon," Morgan/Lewis

"I Love You," Cole Porter

"I Remember Clifford," Benny Golson

"I Can't Get Started," V. Duke/I. Gershwin

"I Let a Song Go Out of My Heart," Duke Ellington

"I'll Remember April," Raye/DePaul

"Joy Spring," Clifford Brown

"Ko-Ko," Charlie Parker

"Lady Bird," Tad Dameron

"Little Willie Leaps," Miles Davis

"Lover Man," Davis/Ramirez

"Lover," Richard Rodgers

"Meditation," A.C.Jobim

"Milestones," Miles Davis

"Misty," Erroll Garner

"Moon River," Henry Mancini

"My Old Flame," Johnson/Coslow

"On Green Dolphin Street," Bronislav Kaper

"Ornithology," Charlie Parker

"Out of Nowhere," Green

"Round Midnight," Thelonious Monk

"Saint Thomas," Sonny Rollins

"Satin Doll," Duke Ellington

"Secret Love," Webster/Fain

"Skylark," Carmichael/Mercer

"Soon," George Gershwin

"Sophisticated Lady," Duke Ellington

"Stablemates," Benny Golson

"Stella By Starlight," Victor Young

"The Days of Wine and Roses," Henry Mancini

"The Song is You," Kern/Hammerstein

"There Will Never Be Another You," Warren

"Tune Up," Eddie Vinson and Mile Davis

"Watch What Happens," Michel LeGrand

"Ceora," Lee Morgan

"Yardbird Suite," Charlie Parker

As can be seen by the length of the above partial list of jazz literature which contain the ii7/V7 progression, a jazz player acquires an abundance of jazz language and style while learning melodies. These tunes, as melodic information stored in the mind's ear, then become part of the total melodic recall to be played in bits or at length when improvising. All great jazz players have hundreds and maybe thousands of jazz tunes at their fingertips that can be used to put together as a puzzle in thousands of different ways over endless chord changes. This process occurs automatically as the improviser reacts to many new tunes and many new sets of chord changes. The novice player should begin to memorize as many different jazz tunes as possible to expand improvisational fluency and acquire jazz vocabulary and language which should be a continuing process. After memorizing some of the jazz literature listed above, the student should then practice the tunes in as many different keys as possible to expand the student's jazz language even further.

Development of ability to execute the ii7/V7 progression anywhere on an instrument and learning to hear chordal changes by recognizing the sounds of the twelve dialects or tonal centers of the minor seventh chords and the dominant seventh chords will result in enhanced hearing, reading ability, and improvisational fluency. The tonal center approach to improvisational study encourages fluency in the whole spectrum of the language of music from which a unique style can be developed.

The ii7/V7 progression exercise included with this article takes the player through all twelve keys by the use of the cycle of fifths. The exercise is written in both treble and bass clef versions. Woodshedding (practicing) the exercise will put the sound of each individual tonal center at the student's fingertips where it belongs for practical application, will program the student's ears and mind with the basic sound of the ii7/V7 changes, and will identify the notes that sound right over the ii7/V7 in all major keys or dialects.

Chord symbols have been provided to familiarize the student with the proper chord names and the corresponding keys for the arpeggios being practiced.

This information in this article is taken from a book by Emile De Cosmo titled *The ii7/V7 Progression*, which may be ordered from Jamey Aebersold, 1211 Aebersold Drive, New Albany, Indiana 47151-1244 USA. The ii7/V7 Progression book is endorsed by leading educators and instrumentalists including Jamey Aebersold, Pat LaBarbera, Denis DiBlasio, Bucky Pizzarelli, Arnie Lawrence, Clark Terry, Bill Watrous, Clem DeRosa, John Faddis and Slide Hampton, Vincent Bell, Trade Martin, Jack Grassel, Eddie Bert, Joe Cinderella, Harold Lieberman, Leon Russianoff, Harry Manfredini, and conductor Gerard Schwarz.

THE II−7/V7 PROGRESSION: TREBLE CLEF

THE II-7/V7 PROGRESSION: BASS CLEF

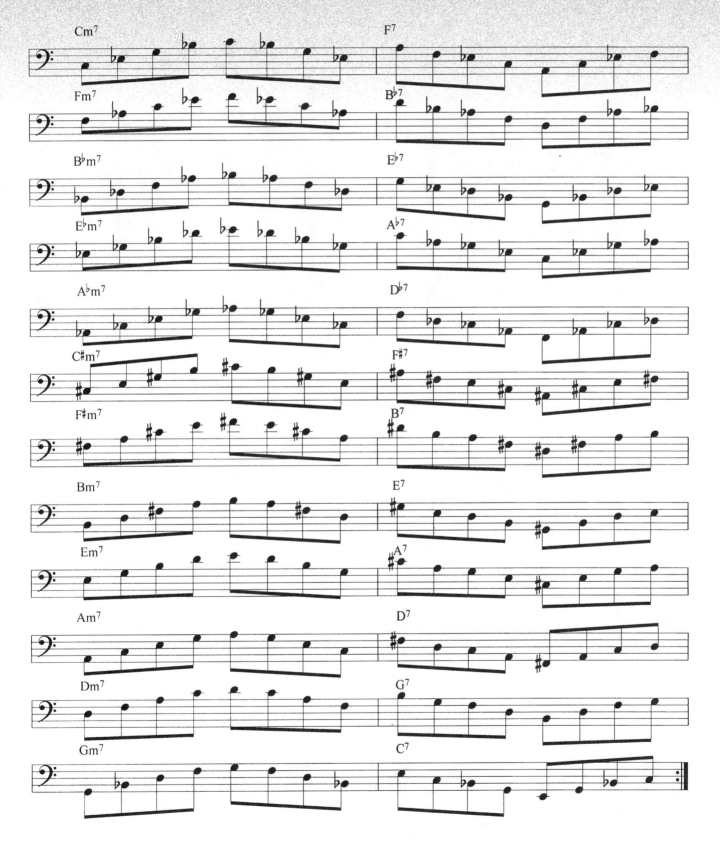

Music graphics by Louis De Cosmo

CHAPTER 8

THE HARMONIC MINOR SCALE

The melodic sound of the harmonic minor scale surrounds us and is heard many times through the various media: radio, television, tapes, CDs, films, played by orchestras, concert, marching, jazz, rock, and country bands. In his book, *Harmony Structure and Style*, published by McGraw-Hill Book Co., Inc., 1962, Leonard G. Ratner states: "To Western ears, the major scale is one of the most familiar and convincing musical statements that can be made. This pattern, which we know so well and which we take so much for granted, has values and relationships within it that have tremendous significance for the harmonic procedures of centuries of Western music. Although the minor mode, by virtue of its borrowed leading tone, has virtually the same structural strength as the major mode, its particular appeal lies in its rich palette of colors. The influence of the major scale has made the harmonic minor mode a virtual partner in the key-centered harmonic system of Western music."

Melodies heard today come from varying the succession of musical pitches known as the scale. Each musical pitch that comprises a scale is termed a degree of that scale. The most common scales used when composing music are the major scale, and the three minor scales: the harmonic minor, the melodic minor, and the natural minor. These three minor scales may be used melodically when composing or improvising and pro-

vide an abundance of material for melodic ideas within a given harmonic background.

In this article the harmonic minor, and it's seven minor modes, will be discussed. Each mode shall be named using the term "harmonic" for each harmonic minor mode followed by the names given to the church or medieval modes.

THE SEVEN HARMONIC MINOR MODES

First mode harmonic (ionian), second mode harmonic (dorian), third mode harmonic (phrygian), fourth mode harmonic (lydian), fifth mode harmonic (mixolydian), sixth mode harmonic (aeolian), and the seventh mode harmonic (locrian).

Each minor key will contain a harmonic minor scale built on the first degree of the scale. Every minor key will also contain seven diatonic modes, one built on each scale degree.

When composing or improvising, it is necessary to become familiar with the seven diatonic minor modes and the corresponding diatonic chords that appear in every minor key or minor modal center.

The term "mode" is used interchangeably to mean scale; referring to modal steps as opposed to scale steps; referring to the different scale steps as first mode, second mode, third mode, fourth mode, fifth mode, sixth mode, and seventh mode. A minor mode is determined by its position in the minor key. Each minor mode presents the half steps, whole steps and step and a half, in different positions and creates the difference in character of the seven minor modes and of music utilizing them. Each minor mode presents a great source of material when constructing melodies and the specific characteristics of each mode are necessary to conceive well written or improvised minor modal melodies. The new names suggested and created for the harmonic modes using the term harmonic are added to the names used for the Church modes in Medieval times.

In the key of C harmonic minor:

The **First Mode** is named harmonic ionian and contains the notes:

C, D, E♭, F, G, A♭, B, C.

The diatonic seventh chord used harmonically is the Cmi (maj7).

The **Second Mode** is named harmonic dorian and contains the notes:

D, E♭, F, G, A♭, B, C, D.

The diatonic seventh chord used harmonically is the Dmi7♭5.

The **Third Mode** is named harmonic phrygian and contains the notes:

E♭, F, G, A♭, B, C, D, E♭.

The diatonic seventh chord used harmonically is the E♭maj7+5.

The **Fourth Mode** is named harmonic lydian and contains the notes:

F, G, A♭, B, C, D, E♭, F.

The diatonic seventh chord used harmonically is the Fmi7.

The **Fifth Mode** is named harmonic mixolydian and contains the notes:

G, A♭, B, C, D, E♭, F, G.

The diatonic seventh chord used harmonically is the G7 or G dominant seventh.

The **Sixth Mode** is named harmonic aeolian and contains the notes:

A♭, B, C, D, E♭, F, G, A♭.

The diatonic seventh chord used harmonically is A♭maj7.

The **Seventh Mode** is named harmonic locrian and contains the notes:

B, C, D, E♭, F, G, A♭, B.

The diatonic seventh chord used harmonically is the Bdim7.

By making use of the way the active tones of the harmonic minor scale degrees move and relating the direction each one of these tones resolve to each modal degree of the key, the proper resolution for each modal tone is realized.

ACTIVE AND INACTIVE TONES OF ALL HARMONIC MINOR MODES

In the key of C harmonic minor:

The **Harmonic Ionian Mode** contains these active and inactive tones:

G, the fifth, an active tone, resolves down a fifth or up a fourth to the root C: (5 to 1)(V to I).

B, the seventh, an active tone, resolves up a half step to the root C: (7 to 8) (VII to VIII).

D, the second, an active tone, resolves down a whole step to the root C: (2 to 1)(II to I).

F, the fourth, an active tone, resolves down a whole step to the third E♭: (4 to 3)(IV to III).

A♭, the sixth, an active tone, resolves down a half step to the fifth G: (6 to 5)(VI to V).

The remaining tones C, E♭, and G produce a tonic chord and create a feeling of resolution, repose, or rest when the active tones resolve to them, or in the case of the note G, can move or remain stationary.

The **Harmonic Dorian Mode** contains these active and inactive tones:

A♭, the fifth, an active tone, resolves down a diminished fifth to the root D: (5 to 1)(V to I).

C, the seventh, an active tone, resolves up a whole step to the root D:

(7 to 8) (VII to VIII).

G, the fourth, an active tone, resolves down a whole step to the third F: (4 to 3)(IV to III).

B, the sixth, an active tone, resolves down a step and a half to the fifth A♭: (6 to 5)(VI to V).

E♭, the second, an active tone, resolves down a half step to the root D: (2 to 1)(II to I).

The remaining tones D, F, and A♭ produce a modal tonic chord that tends to create a feeling of modal resolution, repose, or rest when the active tones resolve to them, or in the case of the note Ab, can move or remain stationary.

The **Harmonic Phrygian Mode** contains these active and inactive tones:

B, the fifth, an active tone, resolves down an augmented fifth to the root E♭: (5 to 1)(V to I).

D, the seventh, an active tone, resolves up a half step to the root E♭: (7 to 8)(VII to VIII).

A♭, the fourth, an active tone, resolves down a half step to the third G: (4 to 3)(IV to III).

C, the sixth, an active tone, resolves down a half step to the fifth B: (6 to 5)(VI to V).

F, the second, an active tone, resolves down a whole step to the root E♭: (2 to 1)(II to I).

The remaining tones E♭, G, and B produce a modal tonic chord that tends to create a feeling of modal resolution, repose, or rest when the active tones resolve to them or, in the case of the note B, can move or remain stationary.

The **Harmonic Lydian Mode** contains these active and inactive tones:

C, the fifth, an active tone, resolves down a fifth or up a fourth to the root F: (5 to 1)(V to I).

E♭, the seventh, an active tone, resolves up a whole step to the root F: (7 to 8) (VII to VIII).

B, the fourth, an active tone, resolves down a step and a half to the third A♭: (4 to 3)(IV to III).

D, the sixth, an active tone, resolves down a whole step to the fifth C: (6 to 5)(VI to V).

G, the second, an active tone, resolves down a whole step to the root F: (2 to 1)(II to I).

The remaining tones F, A♭, and C produce a modal tonic chord that tends to create a feeling of modal resolution, repose, or rest when the active tones resolve to them or in the case of the note C, can move or remain stationary.

The **Harmonic Mixolydian Mode** contains these active and inactive tones:

D, the fifth, an active tone, resolves down a fifth or up a fourth to the root G: (5 to 1)(V to I).

F, the seventh, an active tone, resolves up a whole step to the root G: (7 to 8) (VII to VIII).

C, the fourth, an active tone, resolves down a half step to the third B: (4 to 3)(IV to III).

E♭, the sixth, an active tone, resolves down a half step to the fifth D: (6 to 5)(VI to V).

A♭, the second, an active tone, resolves down a half step to the root G: (2 to 1)(II to I).

The remaining tones G, B, and D produce a modal tonic chord that tends to create a feeling of modal resolution, repose, or rest when the active tones resolve to them or, in the case of the note D, can move or remain stationary.

The **Harmonic Aeolian Mode** contains these active and inactive tones:

Eb, the fifth, an active tone, resolves down a fifth or up a fourth to the root Ab: (5 to 1)(V to I).

G, the seventh, an active tone, resolves up a half step to the root Ab: (7 to 8)(VII to VIII).

D, the fourth, an active tone, resolves down a whole step to the third C: (4 to 3)(IV to III).

F, the sixth, an active tone, resolves down a whole step to the fifth Eb: (6 to 5)(VI to V).

B, the second, an active tone, resolves down a step and a half to the root Ab: (2 to 1) (II to I).

The remaining tones Ab, C, and Eb produce a modal tonic chord that creates a feeling of modal resolution, repose or rest when the active tones resolve to them or, in the case of the note Eb, can move or remain stationary.

The **Harmonic Locrian Mode** contains these active and inactive tones:

F, the fifth, an active tone, resolves down a diminished fifth to the root B: (5 to 1)(V to I).

Ab, the seventh, an active tone, resolves up a step and a half to the root B: (7 to 8) (VII to VIII).

Eb, the fourth, an active tone, resolves down a half step to the third D: (4 to 3)(IV to III).

G, the sixth, an active tone, resolves down a whole step to the fifth F: (6 to 5)(VI to V).

C, the second, an active tone, resolves down a half step to the root B: (2 to 1)(II to I).

The remaining tones B, D, and F produce a modal tonic chord that tends to create a feeling of modal resolution, repose, or rest when the active tones resolve to them or, in the case of the note F, can move or remain stationary.

The harmonic minor scale sounds best when played over the harmony of the diatonic minor chord used as the Imi (maj7) chord of the key. The color tones of the harmonic minor scale are the second, third, sixth and seventh degrees. Melodically, it is better, when improvising, to use the tonic note of the mode at the ending rather than beginning with it. The fifth degree is one of the best notes to precede the tonic when starting a solo because it sets up the sound of the harmonic minor scale as heard by the listener.

DETAILS OF THE HARMONIC MINOR SCALE

The harmonic minor scale is comprised of two similarly constructed four-note groups of notes called tetrachords using one as a lower tetrachord beginning on the tonic minor note followed by an upper tetrachord a whole step away from the lower tetrachord. The harmonic minor scale ordinarily consists of scale degrees of two sizes, half steps and whole steps, and occur as: whole step, half step, whole step, whole step, half step, a step and a half, and a half step.

The harmonic minor scale consists of eight consecutive notes written on the staff ascending or descending, ending on the tonic note. In the key of C minor the scale ascending is C, D, Eb, F, G, Ab, B, C and in descending order C, B, Ab, G, F, Eb, D, C. Most tetrachords include one half step and two whole steps or occasionally a step and one half, as is the case in the harmonic minor scale. These various size steps may occur in one of three positions: at the bottom, in the middle, or at the top of the tetrachord. When constructing the harmonic minor scale, half steps occur between the second and third scale degrees and also between the fifth and sixth and the seventh and eighth scale degrees. The step and a half occurs between the sixth and seventh degrees, and all other degrees of the scale are separated by whole steps. Minor scale degrees are usually numbered using Arabic or Roman numerals and letters to correspond to a specific key.

The Minor Scale Degrees for
All Harmonic Minor Scales:

1 2 3 4 5 6 7 1

I II III IV V VI VII I

Scale degrees in the key of C minor:

C D E♭ F G A♭ B C

Scale degrees in the key of F minor:

F G A♭ B♭ C D♭ E F

Scale degrees in the key of B♭ minor:

B♭ C D♭ E♭ F G♭ A B♭

Scale degrees in the key of E♭ minor:

E♭ F G♭ A♭ B♭ C♭ D E♭

Scale degrees in the key of A♭ minor:

A♭ B♭ C♭ D♭ E♭ F♭ G A♭

Scale degrees in the key of D♭ minor:

D♭ E♭ F♭ G♭ A♭ B♭♭ C D♭

Scale degrees in the key of F♯ minor:

F♯ G♯ A B C♯ D E♯ F♯

Scale degrees in the key of B minor:

B C♯ D E F♯ G A♯ B

Scale degrees in the key of E minor:

E F♯ G A B C D♯ E

Scale degrees in the key of A minor:

A B C D E F G♯ A

Scale degrees in the key of D minor:

D E F G A B♭ C♯ D

Scale degrees in the key of G minor:

G A B♭ C D E♭ F♯ G

Each harmonic minor scale contains certain active scale degrees that have a tendency to move or resolve to another scale tone or degree. By combining active tones with inactive tones many pleasant melodies can be composed using this tendency to resolve.

The active tones of the harmonic minor scale in the key of C minor are: G, the fifth scale degree, B, the seventh scale degree, D, the second scale degree, F, the fourth scale degree, and A♭, the sixth scale degree. These notes spell out a dominant seventh flat ninth chord: G, B, D, F, A♭.

The inactive tones of the harmonic minor scale that give the tonal color of the key of C minor are: C, the first scale degree, E♭, the third scale degree and G, the fifth scale degree, which can be either active or inactive depending on its use.

RESOLUTIONS OF ACTIVE TONES

In the key of C minor:

G, the fifth, an active tone, resolves to the root C: (5 to 1)(V to I). B, the seventh, an active tone, resolves up a half step to the root C:(7 to 8) (VII to VIII).

D, the second, an active tone, resolves down a whole step to the root C: (2 to 1)(II to I).

F, the fourth, an active tone, resolves down a whole step to the third E♭: (4 to 3)(IV to III).

A♭, the sixth, an active tone, resolves down a half step to the fifth G: (6 to 5)(VI to V).

The remaining tones C, E♭ and G produce a tonic chord and create a feeling of resolution, repose or rest when the active tones resolve to them, or in the case of the note G, can move or remain stationary.

As stated earlier, the harmonic minor scale sounds best when played over the harmony of a diatonic minor chord used as the Im (Maj7) chord of the key.

Following is a list of standard, popular jazz tunes that contain the harmonic minor scale completely or in part along with various other minor scales. Although it is important to learn the harmonic minor scale in all keys or dialects; it is imperative for today's novice composer or improvisor to become familiar with the jazz literature that makes use of all minor scales. If the student learns, analyses, and memorizes these melodies, improvising on tunes that are in minor keys will become easier.

LIST OF STANDARD JAZZ TUNES TO BE LEARNED THAT USE THE SOUND OF VARIOUS MINOR SCALES MELODICALLY

"Airegin," Sonny Rollins

"African Flower," Duke Ellington

"Angel Eyes," Matt Dennis

"Blue Bossa," Kenny Dorham

"Bikini," Dexter Gordon

"Blue Serge," Duke Ellington

"The Core," Freddy Hubbard

"Django," John Lewis

"East St. Louis Toodle-oo," Duke Ellington

"Four on Six," Wes Montgomery

"Hot House," Charlie Parker

"In a Sentimental Mood," Duke Ellington

"It Don't Mean a Thing," Duke Ellington

"Jordu," Duke Jordon

"Jump Mon," Thelonious Monk

"Lament," J.J. Johnson

"La Rue," Clifford Brown

"Lullaby of Birdland," George Shearing

"Minority," Gigi Gryce

"Mo Jo," Joe Henderson

"Moonchild," Kenny Jarrett

"My Funny Valentine," Richard Rodgers/Lorenz Hart

"Nica's Dream," Horace Silver

"Night in Tunisia," Dizzy Gillespie

"Off Minor," Thelonious Monk

"Pithycanthropus Erectus," Charles Mingus

"'Round Midnight," Thelonious Monk

"Shutterbug," J.J. Johnson

"Sky Dive," Freddie Hubbard

"Solar," Miles Davis

"Soul Eyes," John Coltrane

"Somebody Loves Me," MacDonald/Gershwin/DeSylva

"Sugar," Stanley Turrentine

"Summertime," George Gershwin

"Valse Hot," Sonny Rollins

"Wild Flower," Wayne Shorter

"Woody 'N You," Dizzy Gillespie

"Yesterdays," Jerome Kern

"Zoot Case," Zoot Sims

As can be seen by the length of the above partial list of jazz literature which contain the harmonic minor scale in many melodic shapes, a jazz player acquires an abundance of jazz language and style while learning melodies. These tunes, as melodic information stored in the mind's ear, then become part of the total melodic recall to be played in bits or at length when improvising. All great jazz players have hundreds and maybe thousands of jazz tunes at their fingertips that can be used to put together as a puzzle in thousands of different ways over endless chord changes. This process occurs automatically as the improvisor reacts to many new tunes and many new sets of chord changes. The novice player should begin to memorize as many different jazz tunes as possible to expand improvisational fluency and acquire jazz vocabulary and language which should be a continuing process. After memorizing some of the jazz literature listed above, the student should then practice the tunes in as many different keys as possible to expand the student's jazz language even further.

The *Pook 7/9 Harmonic Minor Scale* exercises included with this article are written in both treble and bass clef versions. The study moves through the cycle of fifths progression. Playing this exercise will increase the ability to hear and play the sound of the harmonic minor scale anywhere on your instrument.

The information in this chapter was taken from *The Harmonic Minor Scale* by Emile De Cosmo. It is endorsed by leading educators and instrumentalists including: Jamey Aebersold, Paquito D'Rivera, Denis De Blasio, Pat La Barbera Bucky Pizzarelli, Clark Terry, Snooky Young, Arnie Lawrence, Bill Watrous, Clem DeRosa, John Faddis, Slide Hampton, Vincent Bell, Trade Martin, Jack Grassel, Eddie Bert, Joe Cinderella, Friday the 13th film composer Harry Manfredini, Seattle Symphony orchestra conductor Gerard Schwarz, Dizzy Gillespie, Ray Copeland, and Leon Russianoff.

BOOK 7/9 HARMONIC MINOR SCALE: TREBLE CLEF

BOOK 7/9 HARMONIC MINOR SCALE: BASS CLEF

CHAPTER 9

THE MELODIC MINOR SCALE

The melodic minor scale is the source of the seven diatonic minor modes. The melodic sound of the melodic minor scale is used in the composing of many melodies in jazz, classical, various popular and Broadway musical songs. These various melodies are familiar to us as they are heard many times through the various media: radio, television, records, tapes, CDs, films—played by orchestras, concert, marching, jazz, rock, and country bands.

In his book, *Harmony Structure and Style*, published by McGraw-Hill Book Co., Inc., 1962, Leonard G. Ratner states: "Although the minor mode, by virtue of its borrowed leading tone, has virtually the same structural strength as the major mode, its particular appeal lies in its rich palette of colors. As its two variable tones, the sixth and seventh degrees, are incorporated into various harmonies, they can create striking nuances, intermingling major and minor in a rich chiaroscuro."

Melodies heard today come from varying the succession of musical pitches known as the scale. Each musical pitch that comprises a scale is termed a degree of that scale.

The most common scales used when composing music are the major scale, and the three minor scales: the harmonic minor, the melodic minor, and the natural minor. These three minor scales may be used melod-

ically when composing or improvising, and provides an abundance of material for melodic ideas within a given harmonic background.

Derived from one of these scales, the melodic minor are the seven minor modes that shall be named using the term "melodic" for the melodic minor modes followed by the names used for the church or medieval modes.

THE SEVEN MELODIC MINOR MODES

First mode melodic ionian, second mode melodic dorian, third mode melodic phrygian, fourth mode melodic lydian, fifth mode melodic mixolydian, sixth mode melodic aeolian and the seventh mode melodic locrian.

Each minor key may contain either a harmonic minor or a melodic minor scale built on the first degree of the scale. Every minor key will also contain seven diatonic modes, one built on each scale degree.

When composing or improvising, it is necessary to become familiar with the seven diatonic minor modes and the corresponding diatonic chords that appear in every minor key or minor modal center.

The term mode is used interchangeably to mean scale; referring to modal steps as opposed to scale steps; referring to the different scale steps as first mode, second mode, third mode, fourth mode, fifth mode, sixth mode and seventh mode. A mode is determined by its position in the minor key. Each minor mode presents the half steps and whole steps in different positions and creates the difference in character of the seven minor modes and of music utilizing them. Each minor mode presents a great source of material when constructing melodies and the specific characteristics of each mode are necessary to conceive well-written or improvised minor modal melodies.

THE MELODIC MINOR MODES

The new names suggested and created for the melodic modes using the term "melodic" are added to the names used for the church modes in Medieval times.

In the key of C melodic minor:

The **first mode** is named melodic ionian and contains the notes:

C, D, Eb, F, G, A, B, C.

The diatonic seventh chord used harmonically is the Cmi(maj7).

The **second mode** is named melodic dorian and contains the notes:

D, Eb, F, G, A, B, C, D.

The diatonic seventh chord used harmonically is the Dmi7.

The **third mode** is named melodic phrygian and contains the notes:

Eb, F, G, A, B, C, D, Eb.

The diatonic seventh chord used harmonically is the Ebmaj7+5.

The **fourth mode** is named melodic lydian and contains the notes:

F, G, A, B, C, D, Eb, F.

The diatonic seventh chord used harmonically is the F7.

The **fifth mode** is named melodic mixolydian and contains the notes:

G, A, B, C, D, Eb, F, G.

The diatonic seventh chord used harmonically is the G7.

The **sixth mode** is named melodic aeolian and contains the notes:

A, B, C, D, Eb, F, G, A.

The diatonic seventh chord used harmonically is Ami7b5.

The **seventh mode** is named harmonic locrian and contains the notes:

B, C, D, Eb, F, G, A, B.

The diatonic seventh chord used harmonically is the Bmi7b5.

By making use of the way the active tones of the melodic minor scale degrees move and relating the direction each one of these tones resolve to each modal degree of the key, the proper resolution for each modal tone is realized.

ACTIVE AND INACTIVE TONES OF ALL MELODIC MINOR MODES

In the key of C melodic minor:

The **Melodic Ionian Mode** contains these active and inactive tones:

- G, the fifth, an active tone, resolves down a fifth or up a fourth to the root C: (5 to 1)(V to I).

- B, the seventh, an active tone, resolves up a half step to the root C: (7 to 8) (VII to VIII).

- D, the second, an active tone, resolves down a whole step to the root C: (2 to 1)(II to I).

- F, the fourth, an active tone, resolves down a whole step to the third Eb: (4 to 3)(IV to III).

- A, the sixth, an active tone, resolves down a whole step to the fifth G: (6 to 5)(VI to V).

The remaining tones C, E♭, and G produce a tonic chord and create a feeling of resolution, repose or rest when the active tones resolve to them, or in the case of the note G, can move or remain stationary.

The **Melodic Dorian Mode** contains these active and inactive tones:

- A, the fifth, an active tone, resolves down a fifth or up a fourth to the root D: (5 to 1)(V to I).
- C, the seventh, an active tone, resolves up a whole step to the root D: (7 to 8) (VII to VIII).
- G, the fourth, an active tone, resolves down a whole step to the third F: (4 to 3)(IV to III).
- B, the sixth, an active tone, resolves down a whole step to the fifth A: (6 to 5)(VI to V).
- E♭, the second, an active tone, resolves down a half step to the root
- D: (2 to 1)(II to I).

The remaining tones D, F, and A produce a modal tonic chord that tends to create a feeling of modal resolution, repose, or rest when the active tones resolve to them or, in the case of the note A, can move or remain stationary.

The **Melodic Phrygian Mode** contains these active and inactive tones:

- B, the fifth, an active tone, resolves down an augmented fifth to the root E♭: (5 to 1)(V to I).
- D, the seventh, an active tone, resolves up a half step to the root E♭: (7 to 8)(VII to VIII).
- A, the fourth, an active tone, resolves down a whole step to the third G: (4 to 3)(IV to III).
- C, the sixth, an active tone, resolves down a half step to the fifth B: (6 to 5)(VI to V).
- F, the second, an active tone, resolves down a whole step to the root E♭: (2 to 1)(II to I).

The remaining tones E♭, G, and B produce a modal tonic chord that tends to create a feeling of modal resolution, repose, or rest when the active tones resolve to

them or, in the case of the note B, can move or remain stationary.

The **Melodic Lydian Mode** contains these active and inactive tones:

- C, the fifth, an active tone, resolves down a fifth or up a fourth to the root F: (5 to 1)(V to I).
- E♭, the seventh, an active tone, resolves up a whole step to the root F: (7 to 8) (VII to VIII).
- B, the fourth, an active tone, resolves down a whole step to the third A: (4 to 3)(IV to III).
- D, the sixth, an active tone, resolves down a whole step to the fifth C: (6 to 5)(VI to V).
- G, the second, an active tone, resolves down a whole step to the root F: (2 to 1)(II to I).

The remaining tones F, A♭, and C produce a modal tonic chord that tends to create a feeling of modal resolution, repose, or rest when the tones resolve to them or, in the case of the note C, can move or remain stationary.

The **Melodic Mixolydian Mode** contains these active and inactive tones:

- D, the fifth, an active tone, resolves down a fifth or up a fourth to the root G: (5 to 1)(V to I).
- F, the seventh, an active tone, resolves up a whole step to the root G: (7 to 8) (VII to VIII).
- C, the fourth, an active tone, resolves down a half step to the third B: (4 to 3)(IV to III).
- E♭, the sixth, an active tone, resolves down a half step to the fifth D: (6 to 5)(VI to V).
- A, the second, an active tone, resolves down a whole step to the root G: (2 to 1)(II to I).

The remaining tones G, B, and D produce a modal tonic chord that tends to create a feeling of modal resolution, repose, or rest when the active tones resolve to them or, in the case of the note D, can move or remain stationary.

The **Melodic Aeolian Mode** contains these active and inactive tones:

- E♭, the fifth, an active tone, resolves down a augmented fifth to the root A: (5 to 1)(V to I).

- G, the seventh, an active tone, resolves up a whole step to the root A: (7 to 8)(VII to VIII).

- D, the fourth, an active tone, resolves down a whole step to the third C: (4 to 3)(IV to III).

- F, the sixth, an active tone, resolves down a whole step to the fifth E♭: (6 to 5)(VI to V).

- B, the second, an active tone, resolves down a whole step to the root A: (2 to 1) (II to I).

The remaining tones A, C, and E♭ produce a modal tonic chord that tends to creates a feeling of modal resolution, repose, or rest when the active tones resolve to them or, in the case of the note E♭, can move or remain stationary.

The **Melodic Locrian Mode** contains these active and inactive tones:

- F, the fifth, an active tone, resolves a diminished fifth to the root B: (5 to 1)(V to I).

- A, the seventh, an active tone, resolves up a whole step to the root B: (7 to 8) (VII to VIII).

- E♭, the fourth, an active tone, resolves down a half step to the third D: (4 to 3)(IV to III).

- G, the sixth, an active tone, resolves down a whole step to the fifth F: (6 to 5)(VI to V).

- C, the second, an active tone, resolves down a half step to the root B: (2 to 1)(II to I).

The remaining tones B, D, and F produce a modal tonic chord that tends to create a feeling of modal resolution, repose, or rest when the active tones resolve to them or, in the case of the note F, can move or remain stationary.

MELODIC MINOR SCALE

The melodic minor scale sounds best when played over the harmony of the diatonic minor chord used as the Imi(maj7) chord of the key. The color tones of the melodic minor scale are the second, third, sixth and seventh degrees. Melodically, it is better, when improvising, to use the tonic note of the mode at the ending rather than beginning with it. The fifth degree is one of the best notes to precede the tonic when starting a solo because it sets up the sound of the melodic minor scale as heard by the listener.

DETAILS OF THE MELODIC MINOR SCALE

The melodic minor scale is comprised of two similarly constructed four-note groups of notes called tetrachords using one as a lower tetrachord beginning on the tonic minor note followed by an upper tetrachord a whole step away from the lower tetrachord. The melodic minor scale ordinarily consist of scale degrees of two sizes, half steps and whole steps, and occur as: whole step, half step, whole step, whole step, whole step, whole step, and half step.

The melodic minor scale consists of eight consecutive notes written on the staff ascending using one succession of notes and then descending, using a different succession of notes, and then ending on the tonic note. Since the melodic minor scale descending is spelled or constructed in the same manner as the natural minor scale or aeolian mode, only the ascending form will be detailed. In the key of C minor the scale ascending is C, D, E♭, F, G, A, B, C and in descending order C, B♭, A♭, G, F, E♭, D, C. As can be seen the melodic minor scale ascends like a major scale with a flatted third scale degree and descends like natural minor or aeolian mode. Most tetrachords include one half step and two whole steps. The half steps may occur in one of three positions: at the bottom, in the middle, or at the top of the tetrachord. When constructing the melodic minor scale, half steps occur between the second and third scale degrees and also between the seventh and eighth scale degrees. All other degrees of the scale are separated by whole steps. Minor scale degrees are usually numbered using Arabic or Roman numerals and letters to correspond to a specific key.

THE MINOR SCALE ASCENDING DEGREES FOR ALL MELODIC MINOR SCALES:

1 2 3 4 5 6 7 1

I II III IV V VI VII I

Scale degrees in the key of C minor:

C D E♭ F G A B C

Scale degrees in the key of F minor:

F G A♭ B♭ C D E F

Scale degrees in the key of B♭ minor:

B♭ C D♭ E♭ F G A B♭

Scale degrees in the key of E♭ minor:

E♭ F G♭ A♭ B♭ C D E♭

Scale degrees in the key of A♭ minor:

A♭ B♭ C♭ D♭ E♭ F G A♭

Scale degrees in the key of D♭ minor:

D♭ E♭ F♭ G♭ A♭ B♭ C D♭

Scale degrees in the key of F♯ minor:

F♯ G♯ A B C♯ D♯ E♯ F♯

Scale degrees in the key of B minor:

B C♯ D E F♯ G♯ A♯ B

Scale degrees in the key of E minor:

E F♯ G A B C♯ D♯ E

Scale degrees in the key of A minor:

A B C D E F♯ G♯ A

Scale degrees in the key of D minor:

D E F G A B C♯ D

Scale degrees in the key of G minor:

G A B♭ C D E F♯ G

Each melodic minor scale contains certain active scale degrees that have a tendency to move or resolve to another scale tone or degree. By combining active tones with inactive tones many pleasant melodies can be composed using this tendency to resolve.

The active tones of the melodic minor scale in the key of C minor are: G the fifth scale degree, B the seventh scale degree, D the second scale degree, F the fourth scale degree, and A the sixth scale degree. These notes spell out a dominant ninth chord: G, B, D, F, A.

The inactive tones of the melodic minor scale that give the tonal color of the key of C minor are: C, the first scale degree, E♭, the third scale degree and G, the fifth scale degree which can be either active or inactive depending on its use.

RESOLUTIONS OF ACTIVE TONES

In the key of C minor:

- G, the fifth, an active tone, resolves to the root C: (5 to 1)(V to I).

- B, the seventh, an active tone, resolves up a half step to the root C:(7 to 8) (VII to VIII).

- D, the second, an active tone, resolves down a whole step to the root C: (2 to 1)(II to I).

- F, the fourth, an active tone, resolves down a whole step to the third E♭: (4 to 3)(IV to III).

- A, the sixth, an active tone, resolves down a whole step to the fifth G: (6 to 5)(VI to V).

The remaining tones C, E♭, and G produce a tonic chord and create a feeling of resolution, repose, or rest when the active tones resolve to them or, in the case of the note G, can move or remain stationary.

As stated earlier, the melodic minor scale sounds best when played over the harmony of a diatonic minor chord used as the Im(Maj7) chord of the key.

THE NATURAL MINOR SCALES IN DESCENDING DEGREES FOR ALL MELODIC SCALES:

1 7 6 5 4 3 2 1

I VII VI V IV III II I

Scale degrees in the key of C minor:

C B♭ A♭ G F E♭ D C

Scale degrees in the key of F minor:

F E♭ D♭ C B♭ A♭ G F

Scale degrees in the key of B♭ minor:

B♭ A♭ G♭ F E♭ D♭ C B♭

Scale degrees in the key of E♭ minor:

E♭ D♭ C♭ B♭ A♭ G♭ F E♭

Scale degrees in the key of A♭ minor:

A♭ G♭ F♭ E♭ D♭ C♭ B♭ A♭

Scale degrees in the key of D♭ minor:

D♭ C♭ B♭♭ A♭ G♭ F♭ E♭ D♭

Scale degrees in the key of F♯ minor:

F♯ E D C♯ B A G♯ F♯

Scale degrees in the key of B minor:

B A G F♯ E D C♯ B

Scale degrees in the key of E minor:

E D C B A G F♯ E

Scale degrees in the key of A minor:

A G F E D C B A

Scale degrees in the key of D minor:

D C B♭ A G F E D

Scale degrees in the key of G minor:

G F E♭ D C B♭ A G

Each descending melodic minor scale contains certain active scale degrees that have a tendency to move or resolve to another scale tone or degree. By combining active tones with inactive tones many pleasant melodies can be composed using this tendency to resolve.

The active tones of the descending melodic minor scale in the key of C minor are: G, the fifth scale degree, B♭, the seventh scale degree, D the second scale degree, F the fourth scale degree, and A♭ the sixth scale degree. These notes spell out a G minor 7th ♭9 chord: G, B♭, D, F, A♭.

The inactive tones of the melodic minor scale that give the tonal color of the key of C minor are: C the first scale degree, E♭ the third scale degree, and G the fifth scale degree, which can be either active or inactive depending on its use.

RESOLUTIONS OF ACTIVE TONES IN THE KEY OF C MINOR:

- G, the fifth, an active tone, resolves to the root C: (5 to 1)(V to I).

- B♭, the seventh, an active tone, resolves up a half step to the root C:(7 to 8) (VII to VIII).

- D, the second, an active tone, resolves down a whole step to the root C: (2 to 1)(II to I).

- F, the fourth, an active tone, resolves down a whole step to the third E♭: (4 to 3)(IV to III).

- A♭, the sixth, an active tone, resolves down a half step to the fifth G: (6 to 5)(VI to V).

The remaining tones C, E♭, and G produce a tonic chord and create a feeling of resolution, repose, or rest when the active tones resolve to them or in the case of the note G, can move or remain stationary.

THE DESCENDING MELODIC MINOR SCALE

The descending melodic minor scale sounds best when played over the harmony of a diatonic minor seventh chord used as the I minor 7th chord in the key.

Following is a list of standard and popular jazz tunes that contain the melodic minor scale completely or in part. Although it is important to learn the melodic minor scale in all keys or dialects; it is imperative for today's novice composer or improvisor to become familiar with the jazz literature that makes use of the melodic minor scale. If the student learns, analyzes and memorizes the melodies, improvising on tunes that contain the melodic minor scale will become easier.

Standard Jazz Tunes to Be Learned That Use the Sound of the Melodic Minor Scale Melodically

"Airegin," Sonny Rollins

"Bikini," Dexter Gordon

"Blue Serge," Duke Ellington

"East St. Louis Toodle-oo," Duke Ellington

"In a Sentimental Mood," Duke Ellington

"Lament," J.J.Johnson

"Love Me or Leave Me," Gus Kahn/Walter Donaldson

"Lullaby of Birdland," G. Shearing/B.Y. Forster

"My Funny Valentine," Richard Rodgers/Lorenz Hart

"Nica's Dream," Horace Silver

"Shutterbug," J.J.Johnson

"Sky Dive," Freddie Hubbard

"Solar," Miles Davis

"Somebody Loves Me," MacDonald/Gershwin/DeSylva

"Summertime," George Gershwin

"Yesterdays," Jerome Kern

Songs Using Hybrid Minor Scales With Various Minor Harmony

"And I Love Her," Lennon, McCartney

"Anniversary Song," Dubin, Franklin

"Big Red," Earnie Wilkins

"The Bird," Charlie Parker

"Bird Gets the Worm," Charlie Parker

"Black Magic Woman," P. Green

"Blue and Green," Miles Davis

"Caravan," Duke Ellington

"Dear Old Stockholm," Varmeland

"Diverse," Charlie Parker

"Dopolous," Yusef Lateef

"Fall," Wayne Shorter

"Four Up and Four Down," Sam Noto

"Full House," Wes Montgomery

"Getting It Together," Bobby Timmons

"Jug Eyes," Gene Ammons

"Moanin'," Bobby Timmons

"Oye Negres," Noro Morales

"Scan," Gene Ammons

"Segment," Charlie Parker

"Serenade to a Cuckoo," Roland Kirk

"Take Five," Paul Desmond

"Treux Bleu," Gene Ammons

As can be seen by the length of the above partial lists of jazz literature which contain the melodic minor scale in many melodic shapes and various hybrid minor scales, a jazz player acquires an abundance of jazz language and style while learning melodies. These tunes, as melodic information stored in the mind's ear, then become part of the total melodic recall to be played in bits or at length when improvising. All great jazz players have hundreds and maybe thousands of jazz tunes at their fingertips that can be used to put together as a puzzle in thousands of different ways over endless chord changes. This process occurs automatically as the improvisor reacts to many new tunes and many new sets of chord changes. The novice player should begin to memorize as many different jazz tunes as possible to expand improvisational fluency and acquire jazz vocabulary and language, which should be a continuing process. After memorizing some of the jazz literature listed above, the student should then practice the tunes in as many different keys as possible to expand the student's jazz language even further.

The Pook 7/9 Melodic Minor Scale exercise included in this chapter is written in both treble and bass clef versions. The study moves through the cycle of fifths progression. Playing this exercise will increase the ability to hear and play the sound of the melodic minor scale anywhere on your instrument.

The information in this chapter was taken from *The Melodic Minor Scale* by Emile De Cosmo has been endorsed by leading educators and instrumentalists including Jamey Abersold, Paquito D'Rivera, Denis Di Blasio, Pat La Barbera Bucky Pizzarelli, Clark Terry, Snooky Young, Arnie Lawrence, Bill Watrous, Clem DeRosa, John Faddis, Slide Hampton, Vincent Bell, Trade Martin, Jack Grassel, Eddie Bert, Joe Cinderella, Friday the 13th film composer Harry Manfredini, Seattle Symphony orchestra conductor Gerard Schwarz, Dizzy Gillespie, Ray Copeland, and Leon Russianoff.

POOK 7/9 MELODIC MINOR SCALE: TREBLE CLEF

POOK 7/9 MELODIC MINOR SCALE: BASS CLEF

Music graphics by Louis De Cosmo

CHAPTER 10

P.O.O.K AND DON'T ARGUE

One of the principal requirements the beginning improvisor must fulfill is the ability to play melodic ideas in the jazz language, instead of merely running scales without "saying anything" musically. Most studied players have at their fingertips technical exercises learned from standard method books, including, scales, chords, intervals, and partials of each. When improvising, novice students of jazz tend to play technical exercises as improvisation, instead of using the melodic contours of the jazz language. In order to take advantage of the written jazz language and transcribed solos available, the student of jazz must become a proficient reader and sight-reader of music. Most students need a method to prepare them to read the available jazz language and transcriptions.

POOK AND DON'T ARGUE

The purpose of the present study is to help improve the reading and sight-reading ability of the jazz novice and also to accustom the student to playing jazz melodic shapes, instead of technical exercises, when improvising. I have chosen and composed "POOK and Don't Argue" in the style of trombone jazz greats J.J. Johnson and Kai Winding. This study will expose the player/student to melodic shapes in the jazz idiom to be played in every key, so the shapes will be under his or her fingertips when actually performing.

The "POOK" approach presents a unique way of playing melodic jazz ideas in all keys or tonal centers, both major and minor, with equal proficiency. "POOK and Don't Argue" is written in the modal tonal center of C, employing the diatonic cycle of fifths, which creates the underlying harmonic progression. The melodic jazz lines and shape of this study are conceived and written using a pandiatonic style of composing. Pandiatonic, which means all diatonic, is a term that was first introduced by the Russian/American composer Nicolas Slominsky in 1937. Pandiatonic writing is accomplished by freely using the seven notes of a diatonic scale, either melodically or harmonically.

This melody must be played through all major and minor keys by changing the key signature only—not by transposing the exercise. Chord letter names appear over the melodic curve of this POOK study. Pianists and guitarists should use seventh chords while playing this study. The diatonic quality of each seventh chord (major seventh, dominant seventh, minor seventh, half diminished, diminished, or augmented) automatically changes as each new key signature is applied.

THE POLYTONAL ORDER OF KEYS (POOK)

Practice of this jazz melody in all major and minor keys is facilitated because the student/player does not have to transpose these melodic shapes. The study requires that the player mentally change the key signature each time the exercise is played. Practicing melodies in all major and minor keys over changing chords establishes the process that must take place when improvising. While playing over chord changes, the improvised melody must fit the harmonic progression, as the chords drop in and out of the melodic line being played. Playing through the major and minor tonal centers is accomplished easily in a specific order called "The Polytonal Order of Keys" (POOK).

Most educators, composers, and arrangers expect a student/musician to be able to play in all keys. By employing the POOK approach, the ability becomes easier to acquire. POOKing helps to improve sight-reading ability and tonal memory, and places the key signatures "under your fingers" where keys belong.

Most educators realize that mastery of playing melodic shapes in all keys or tonal centers is essential, so students can begin functioning as performers and improvisors. Playing beyond the keys of E♭ major and A major is difficult, especially their respective relative minor keys, C minor and F♯ minor. The POOK studies help the student surmount the advanced key signatures by employing the Polytonal Order of Keys. The sharps and flats are introduced in a specific order. The POOK order moves from the major key to its relative harmonic minor key and alternates from a sharp key to a flat key by adding one flat or sharp at a time, which prepares the student for each subsequent key:

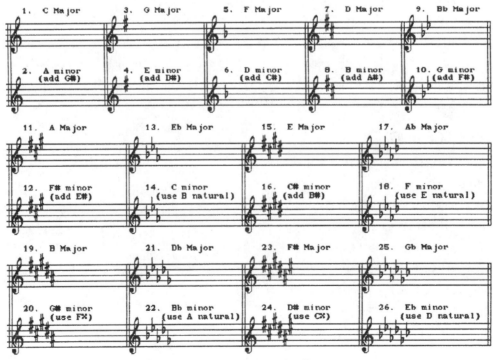

POOK — THE POLYTONAL ORDER OF KEYS

© March 25, 1994 by Emile De Cosmo, *Used by permission*

THE POOK ORDER

1. C major	2. A minor (add G♯)
3. G major	4. E minor (add D♯)
5. F major	6. D minor (add C♯)
7. D major	8. B minor (add A♯)
9. E♭ major	10. G minor (add F♯)
11. A major	12. F♯ minor (use E♯)
13. E♭ major	14. C minor (use B natural)
15. E major	16. C♯ minor (add B♯)
17. A♭ major	18. F minor (use E♮)
19. B major	20. G♯ minor (use F𝄪)
21. D♭ major	22. B♭ minor (use A♮)
23. F♯ major	24. D♯ minor (use C𝄪)
25. G♭ major	26. E♭ minor (use D♮)

As demonstrated in the 26 major/minor key combinations, the student follows the POOK order going immediately to the first relative harmonic minor key after the first major key is learned. After the student has played through the first three major and their respective, relative harmonic minor keys, six fairly easy keys, he or she will have experienced all twelve chromatic tones in the range of this study and should be able to complete the remaining keys without too much difficulty.

As an additional study, the pook melody "POOK And Don't Argue" can be played using the ascending melodic minor scale in all keys. This is accomplished by using the major key signature and flatting the third. Using this process exposes the player to the sounds of the augmented eleventh scale in melodic form.

INFLUENCE OF THE DIATONIC CYCLE OF FIFTHS

The diatonic cycle of fifths forms the strongest progression of diatonic harmony. The diatonic cycle progression in all major keys consists of the following:

I Maj7, IV Maj7, vii half-dim7, iii m7, vi M7, ii M7, V7, I Maj7 creating a descending spiral of fifths.

The diatonic cycle progression in all minor keys consists of:

I minor (Maj7), ivm7, vii dim7, IIIMaj7+5, VIMaj7,

POOK IT

POOK POWER

POOK BEFORE IT POOKS YOU

POOK WITH YOUR PARTNER

DON'T BE A POOR POOKER

HONK IF YOU POOK

GIVE A POOK

HAPPY POOK YEAR

TO POOK OR NOT TO BE

POOK IS FOREVER

PETER PIPER POOKED

DON'T POOK IN YOUR PANTS

COME TO POOK COUNTRY

GIVE POOK A CHANCE

BE THE DUKE OF POOK

DON'T FIGHT POOK

ii half-dim7, V7, I minor (Maj7) also creating a descending spiral of fifths.

Whether in a major or minor key, all styles of music, including jazz and pop tunes employ all or partials of this diatonic flow of chord changes. Both composers and improvisers add variety and interest to their music by moving from one tonal center to another, thereby creating many different chord progressions.

When a student practices these jazz melodic shapes subject to the diatonic cycle of fifths in each tonal center, he or she will be able to produce meaningful melodic lines, react more easily to chord changes, and express more of what he hears in his minds ear. The key signatures may prevail for the entire study or may be changed to other tonal centers at will, from phrase to phrase or section to section, as the player becomes familiar with more keys. Playing melodic shapes in the context of chord progressions produces quicker ear/instrument response, whether reading music or improvising.

I hope you will enjoy this unique approach to improvisation as much as my students and I do. "To POOK or not to Be?" that is the question. Some POOK sayings I've included for good measure.

P.O.O.K, AND DON'T ARGUE — TREBLE CLEF INSTRUMENTS

POOK, AND DON'T ARGUE — BASS CLEF INSTRUMENTS

CHAPTER 11

A BETTER BLUES SCALE

The blues has been in existence since the beginning of improvised music, first as work songs, field hollers, and spirituals. Harmonies used for the blues evolved from the European church hymns and Negro spirituals sung by slaves using the three basic diatonic chords: the tonic or I chord, the subdominant or IV chord, and the dominant seventh or V7 chord which had been in existence since the Renaissance period (1430-1650 A.D.).

Of all the Afro-American forms of jazz literature, the blues form has been the most influential and most performed. The term "blues" has been subject to careless usage and has been greatly misunderstood. For example, the blues has been expressed as a feeling, a slow song, a song of poverty, a sad song of personal misfortunes, and a song using notes "in the cracks" or between the keys of the piano.

Although the blues could be some or all of the aforementioned expressions, in musical terminology, it is considered a form of music consisting of mainly twelve measures, but may have extensions of two, four, six, or possibly even eight measures. The blues and all its variant forms penetrate into all styles of music including pop, rock, country, jazz, and free form.

THE BLUES FORM

The term "blues" means to most jazz players a twelve-measure structured tune. This form usually contains three basic chords arranged in the "basic blues" progression, for reference here, in the concert key of C.

Though basically a I/IV/I/V/IV/I progression, the twelve measures may, at times, contain countless variations of the chord changes used in the blues progression. The blues changes have been altered in many ways through the years by the use of minor seventh chords that preceded the dominant seventh chords. These chords may have been substituted by chords a third above or a third below the basic chord, or by the use of flatted fifth substitutions. There are many variations of the basic progression, and I've shown two samples, top line, and bottom line, in my "variation of the basic blues" example.

THE BASIC BLUES

C7	F7	C7	C7	F7	F7	C7	C7	G7	F7	C7	C7
I	IV	I	I	IV	IV	I	I	V	IV	I	I

VARIATION OF THE BASIC BLUES

C7	F7	Em7♭5	Gm7 C7	F7	Cm7 F7	Gm7	C7	G7	G7	C7	C7
C7	F7	Em7 Dm7	C♯m7 F♯7	F7		F7	C7 B7	B♭7 A7	G7	F7	C7	C7

HISTORY AND DEVELOPMENT OF BLUES SCALES

The blues scale is not a "real" scale because it is not found diatonically; therefore, many different versions of blues scales are suggested by jazz educators. Blues scales are a hybrid of scales in existence and have basically emerged from usage of:

1. The pentatonic scale (a five-tone scale that early jazz players used melodically in compositions and in improvisation), a five note partial of the diatonic scale which includes the first degree, second degree, third degree, fifth degree, and sixth degree. In the key of C, it is composed of C, D, E, G, A, C which produces good sounding melodic notes when played over a C major chord, a C6 chord, a C7 chord, a C9 chord, a Cll chord, and a C13 chord.

2. The diatonic scale, a seven-tone scale which can be used melodically in compositions and in improvisation. In the key of C, the notes are C, D, E, F, G, A, B, C. When playing the blues, the notes to avoid holding on to are F and B. If the F and B are used, they should be played as passing tones and resolved to a chord tone.

3. The chromatic scale, a twelve-tone scale that will produce the most altered or dissonant sounds. A novice improvisor must not over use the chromatic scale, but must learn through experience and analysis when, why, and how to use a chromatic note.

An improvisor must gain a knowledge of these three scales and their usage in order to better under-

stand how the blues notes and then blues scales came into being. We cannot lose sight of the fact that early improvisors were not aware of a blues scale. The evolution of the blues notes was discovered through experimentation by the early blues singers, blues composers, and blues improvisors.

When improvising, the early jazz singers, composers, and improvisors based their melodies and improvisations on chord tones from the principle chords of the key: the I, the IV, and the V7. Other melody notes were derived mainly from the major scale of the key in which the tune was played.

As jazz developed, and knowledge was gained, the added sixth and added ninth came into use, often included in the final chord. The flatted seventh was already being used because it was naturally found in the dominant seventh chord. As the improvisors gained knowledge of the dominant seventh chord, they began changing the qualities of the I chord and the IV chord.

The I chord was changed to the I♭7 chord becoming a dominant of the IV chord, causing a smoother resolution. The flatted seventh was later added to the IV chord, making it a IV♭7 chord. The flatted seventh of the IV♭7 chord is the flatted third or "blue note" of the I chord. The flatted seventh, flatted third, and the major third of the I chord were used during improvisation as the chords changed in the blues progression.

The flatted fifth was used occasionally in early blues as a chromatic passing tone. It came into prominence in the mid-1940s at the beginning of the BeBop era where it was used quite extensively.

JAZZ EDUCATORS' BLUES SCALES

Jamey Aebersold, Adolph Sandole

C, E♭, F, F♯, G, B♭, C

David Baker

C, D, E♭, E, F, F♯, G, A, B♭, C

Emile De Cosmo

C, D♯, E, F, F♯, G, B♭, C

Leonard Feather, Frank Tirro

C, D, E♭, E, F, G, A, B♭, B, C

The Pentatonic Blues Scale
(Emile De Cosmo)

C, D, D♯, E, G, A, C (ascending)

C, B♭, G, G♭, F, E♭, C (descending)

VARIOUS BLUES SCALES IN USE

Many different blues scales have evolved over the past ninety years of blues history, from which an improvisor might draw upon when soloing. Any one of the blues scales presents to the student some good-sounding notes which can be used to improvise over the chord changes of the blues progression. Various blues scales recommended by jazz educators, including some of the examples, are written in the key of C with the chord pattern on top and the jazz artist credited to it listed under each pattern. See the "jazz educators' blues scales" example.

The most common blues scale in use today by jazz students and suggested by many jazz educators, written here in the key of C, is C, E♭, F, F♯, G, B♭, C. The reason most jazz educators use this particular blues scale is because it works well over the entire blues progression and can be used easily by the novice improvisor producing a funky, bluesy sound and eliminating the need to find the right notes to fit the chord changes. This scale sounds more "outside" when played against a I♭7 chord (in its ascending form), but more "inside" when played over the IV♭7 and the V7 chords.

Although this common blues scale contains the root and fifth of the I♭7 chord, it omits the important note E, the third of the I♭7 chord, and does not contain or suggest other important scale tones, such as A, the added sixth, and D, the added ninth (taken from the pentatonic scale).

A BETTER BLUES SCALE

A better choice of notes to be used over the I♭7 chord is, what I call, the pentatonic blues scale. This blues scale makes use of the pentatonic scale adding a raised second (enharmonically it is the flatted third) to accommodate the flatted seventh of the IV♭7 chord sounding "inside" the key. Example: C, D, D♯, E, G, A, C (ascending). In reality the C, E♭, F, F♯, G, B♭, C blues scale used by numerous jazz educators is an inversion of an E♭ major pentatonic scale with a raised second spelled E♭, F, F♯, G, B♭, C, E♭ (that I call the E♭ pentatonic blues scale). It sounds better over the I♭7 chord when used in its descending form: C, B♭, G, G♭, F, E♭, C.

I have chosen a combination of the C pentatonic blues scale (ascending) and the inversion of the E♭ pentatonic blues scale (descending) as a basis for playing over the blues. This gives both a basic "inside" sound and a funky, bluesy "outside" sound when improvising the blues. To reiterate, C, D, D♯, E, G, A, C (ascending) and C, B♭, G, G♭, F, E♭, C (descending)

For a quick reference guide, I've included a treble and bass clef version of my pentatonic blues scale, I call "blues sounds," in every key, to assist you in rapidly developing your skills on this blues progression. This provides a foundation for playing over blues progressions as well as over all dominant seventh chords.

FOUR PROBLEMS WHEN USING THE BLUES SCALE

The first problem is to memorize this scale in all dialects or keys, but, once learned, many beginners rely too heavily on the blues scale and improvise chorus after chorus, running up and down aimlessly. Second, the blues scale becomes a cure-all for any situation because it sounds good over the whole blues progression, becoming a crutch, and hinders a student's development of the blues language.

Third, novice jazz players assume that, upon learning the blues scales, one can "just sort of improvise what you feel" over the chord progression, not realizing that in order to construct a good melodic line making use of the blues scale, a player must have a good knowledge of the literature of blues tunes, rhythms, and rhythmical ideas.

A student of jazz should start to work on a repertoire of blues literature, realizing that early jazz improvisors did not have a blues scale or as much literature to work with. The early jazz improvisors learned step by

BLUES SOUNDS: TREBLE CLEF INSTRUMENTS

BASIC BLUES PROGRESSION IN THE KEY OF C

C7	F7	C7	C7	F7	F7	C7	C7	G7	F7	C7	C7
I♭7	IV♭7	I♭7	I♭7	IV♭7	IV♭7	I♭7	I♭7	V7	I♭7	I♭7	I♭7

The C blues scale should be used over the I♭7 or C7 chord.

The F blues scale should be used over the IV♭7 or F7 chord.

The G blues scale should be used over the V7 or G7 chord.

step which notes fit into the blues progression and, as they became accustomed to more dissonances, their improvised and composed blues melodies became more altered. A student can learn many of the melodic blues phrases that developed throughout jazz history by playing early blues "roots" and proceeding to more modern blues, experiencing and memorizing the blues literature.

Finally, another basic and important factor is that the majority of novice jazz players are not aware of the different forms of the blues.

The improvisor can use the blues scale over the entire blues progression in the key in which the blues is being played. For example, if the blues being played is in the key of C, the C blues scale (in the exercise provided) may be used over the entire progression. To play a more interesting solo and to "zero in" on each chord change, a student should use the notes of the corresponding blues scale for each dominant seventh chord in the blues progression, shown in my "basic blues progression in the key of C" example.

The C blues scale should be used over the I♭7 or C7 chord. The F blues scale should be used over the IV♭7 or F7 chord. The G blues scale should be used over the V7 or G7 chord.

By playing the correct blues scale to correspond to the chord changes, each chorus will be more interesting and, after working and overcoming most of the problems listed, the jazz player can begin developing a solo which is meaningful and enjoyable for himself and his audience.

To derive maximum benefit, students should practice the blues scale in the full range of their respective instruments.

After practicing the blues scale in all keys, the student will be able to hear and react more easily to the blues progression changes and express more of what one imagines, producing quicker ear/instrument response, whether reading or improvising blues.

A jazz player has to draw on all musical experiences learned to improvise creatively. A creative improvisor is only limited by the knowledge of jazz literature which includes theory, chords, scales, modes, and not falling into usual finger patterns or "licks." A creative improvisor is constantly improvising.

Although I have chosen a particular group of notes to represent the blues scale, no one scale can completely represent a particular form of human expression that has come about in the past one hundred years. A blues scale, consisting of six or more notes, cannot encompass the immense range of emotions, tempos, moods, styles, and concepts that this particular form of jazz can convey to an audience. Although it is important to learn blues scales, it is imperative for today's novice jazz student to become familiar and comfortable with learning and memorizing many blues melodies, and in improvising on the many different blues tunes and blues changes that have developed in the past one hundred years.

SAMPLE BLUES LITERATURE FOR LANGUAGE AND IMPROVISATION

This is not a complete list of the thousands of blues songs in existence, but my "sample blues tunes list" will serve as a guide for the student in learning the language of the blues. In order to derive the most benefit from this list of blues songs, and to add a great abundance of blues language a student should transpose and memorize the above melodies in at least three different keys. It would be most beneficial to memorize the above melodies in all twelve keys.

Play-along records, such as Jamey Aebersold's *A New Approach to Jazz Improvisation* book, and recording series *Vol. 42 Blues in All Keys* are available for the student, so various blues melodies and the harmonic background of the blues can be heard and played in all keys.

Practicing blues literature and the blues scale in all keys develops the facility to send out what the ear hears, developing the musical instrument as an extension of the musician's body and connecting it more directly with the mind, thus producing quicker ear/instrument response while improvising over the blues.

SAMPLE BLUE TUNES LIST

Au Privave by Charlie Parker

Back Home Blues by Charlie Parker

Billie's Bounce by Charlie Parker

Blue Monk by Thelonious Monk

Bloomdido by Charlie Parker

Blues by Five by Miles Davis

Blue Seven by Sonny Rollins

Blue Trane by John Coltrane

Blues in the Closet by Oscar Pettiford

Down Tempo by Donald Byrd

Doxy by Sonny Rollins

Duff by Hampton Hawes

Elevation played by Elliot Lawrence

For Stompers Only by Stan Getz

Hamp's Blues by Hampton Hawes

Jumpin' with Symphony Sid by Lester Young

K.C. Blues by Charlie Parker

Mr. P.C. John Coltrane

Morpo by Shorty Rogers

Now's the Time by Charlie Parker

Opus De Funk by Horace Silver

Si Si by Charlie Parker

Twisted Blues by Wes Montgomery

Village Blues by John Coltrane

Wee-Dot by J.J. Johnson

Whose Blues by Lenny Neihaus

Visa by Charlie Parker

BLUES SOUNDS: BASS CLEF INSTRUMENTS

© 1994 by Emile De Cosmo, *Used by permission*
Music graphics by Laura De Cosmo on Music Printer Plus 4.1

CHAPTER 12

HOW CHORDS CHANGE A "CHORDING" TO POOK!

In "POOK AND DON'T ARGUE" I presented a pandiatonic composed jazz POOK melody. This melodic study was written to help the jazz player, and student, learn jazz motifs and to help play jazz language.

A POOK melody is to be played through all the major and minor keys by changing the key signature—not by transposing the melody. By applying new key signatures the melody is changed each time it is played, for a total of twenty-six times. There are also chord letter names placed over the measures to indicate the changing chords that apply during the playing of the study.

After writing my first POOK article I realized the possible need to further explain how the chords change when other key signatures are applied. In order to understand how chord qualities change during POOKing, the player must visualize the chord letter names as seventh chords. All seventh chords are built in thirds upward from the root.

The first thing to memorize is the diatonic letters in each seventh chord as they appear on the staff by their natural letter names (E, G, B, D, F) for the lines of the staff and (F, A, C, E) for the spaces. By listing the chord tones to these seventh chords in ascending scale order we arrive at the following "Seventh Chord" charts later in this column.

The "Polytonal Order Of Keys" (POOK) moves from the major key to its relative harmonic minor key and alternates from a sharp key to a flat key by adding one flat or sharp at a time which prepares the student for each subsequent key.

1. C major   A minor (add G♯)
2. G major   E minor (add D♯)
3. F major   D minor (add C♯)

YODA POOKED!!

I'M THE POOK MAN!

PUT A LITTLE POOK IN YOUR LIFE!

WELCOME TO THE WORLD OF POOK!

TO POOK OR NOT TO POOK, THAT IS THE QUESTION!

IT'S BETTER TO POOK THAN TO BE POOKED!

THE BEST THINGS IN LIFE ARE POOKABLE!

EVERYBODY LOVES A POOKER!

I'D RATHER BE POOKING!

4. D major   B minor (add A♯)

5. B♭ major   G minor (add F♯)

6. A major   F♯ minor (add E♯)

7. E♭ major   C minor (use B♮)

8. E major   C♯ minor (add B♯)

9. A♭ major   F minor (use E♮)

10. B major   G♯ minor (use F𝄪)

11. D♭ major   B♭ minor (use A♮)

12. F♯ major   D♯ minor (use C𝄪)

13. G♭ major...E♭ minor (use D♮)

As just demonstrated, the student follows the POOK order going immediately to the first relative harmonic minor key after the first major key is learned.

When following the polytonal order of keys the first key played is C major. All the chords are played as natural notes as listed in chart #1. As the next key of A harmonic minor is played every G is now played as G♯, changing each quality of the chords which contain a G. The chord changes in chart #1 now change to the qualities in chart #2:

This process of changing chord qualities automatically takes place when following the polytonal order of keys and continues as each new major or minor key signature is applied.

The musical example presented in this article "POOK 7/9" (written for treble and bass clefs instruments) is an exercise based on chord tones starting on the root (C) ascending by thirds up to the ninth (D)

> After writing my first POOK article I realized the possible need to further explain how the chords change when other key signatures are applied. In order to understand how chord qualities change during POOKing, the player must visualize the chord letter names as seventh chords. All seventh chords are built in thirds upward from the root.

with a descending scale to the root of the chord (C) and then an ascending scale starting on the root (C) up to the ninth (D) with descending chord tones ending on the third of the chord (E). Each line thereafter starts on the roots of the chords in the diatonic cycle of fifths. Ex: C F B E A D G (root tones of each diatonic chord).

After practicing the "POOK 7/9" study a student will be better able to hear and play chord tones with its proper mode or scale tying the fingers to the mind's ear.

It should be thoroughly understood that the major diatonic cycle of fifths progression and its chord qualities are the same in all major keys. The qualities of each diatonic chord should be memorized.

In any major key:

- The I Maj7 chord is a major triad with the major seventh.
- The IV Maj7 chord is a major triad with the major seventh.
- The vii half-dim7 chord is a diminished triad with a minor seventh.
- The iiim7 chord is a minor triad with a minor seventh.
- The vim7 chord is a minor triad with a minor seventh.
- The iim7 chord is a minor triad with a minor seventh.
- The V7 chord is a major triad with a minor seventh.

Diatonic Roman numeral symbols in any major key:

IMaj7, IVMaj7, viihalf-dim7, iiim7, vim7, iim7, V7

Examples of diatonic chord symbols in the key of C Major: CMaj7, FMaj7, Bm7♭5, Em7, Am7, Dm7, G7

Likewise, the minor diatonic cycle of fifths progression and its chord qualities are the same in all minor keys.

SEVENTH CHORD CHART #1 (C MAJOR)

SEVENTH	B	C	D	E	F	G	A
FIFTH	G	A	B	C	D	E	F
THIRD	E	F	G	A	B	C	D
ROOT	C	D	E	F	G	A	B
Chord name	*CMaj7*	*Dmi7*	*Emi7*	*FMaj7*	*G7*	*Ami7*	*Bmi7♭5*

SEVENTH CHORD CHART #2 (A MINOR)

SEVENTH	B	C	D	E	F	G#	A
FIFTH	G#	A	B	C	D	E	F
THIRD	E	F	G#	A	B	C	D
ROOT	C	D	E	F	G#	A	B
Chord name	*CMaj7+5*	*Dmi7*	*E7*	*FMaj7*	*G#dim7*	*Ami(Maj7)*	*Bmi7b5*

In any minor key:

- The im(Maj7) chord is a minor triad with the major seventh.

- The ivm7 chord is a minor triad with the minor seventh.

- The vii dim7 chord is a diminished triad with a diminished seventh.

- The III Maj7+5 chord is a augmented triad with a major seventh.

- The VI Maj7 chord is a major triad with a major seventh.

- The ii half-dim7 chord is a diminished triad with a minor seventh.

- The V7 chord is a major triad with a minor seventh.

Diatonic Roman numeral chord symbols in any harmonic minor key: im(Maj7), ivm7, viidim7, IIIMaj7+5, VIMaj7, iim7♭5, V7

Examples of diatonic chord symbols in the key of A harmonic minor are: Am(Maj7), Dm7, G#dim7, CMaj7+5, FMaj7, Bm7♭5, E7

It is easier to understand how the melody changes with signature changes, but difficult to understand how the chords change with each signature change when just a single letter appears. It takes awhile for even the best of musicians to comprehend this.

To aid in understanding how chords change when following The Polytonal order of Keys I will now spell out the changing chord letter names as the student plays through all keys.

The chord letter names of the POOK 7/9 study are: C F B E A D G

When POOKing in the key of C Major the chord qualities become: CMaj7, FMaj7, Bm7♭5, Em7, Am7, Dm7, G7

As the next key signature of A harmonic minor is applied, the raised seventh degree now creates these chord qualities: (add G#) CMaj7+5, FMaj7, Bm7♭5, E7, Am(Maj7), Dm7, G#dim7

When following the Polytonal Order of Keys (POOK) chord qualities change with each applied key signature.

G Major:

CMaj7, F#m7♭5, Bm7, Em7, Am7, D7, GMaj7

E minor:

CMaj7, F#m♭5, B7, Em(Maj7), Am7, D#dim7, GMaj7+5

F Major:

C7, FMaj7, B♭Maj7, Em7♭5, Am7, Dm7, Gm7

D minor:

C♯dim7, FMaj7+5, B♭Maj7, Em7♭5, A7, Dm(Maj7), Gm7

D Major:

C♯m7♭5, F♯m7, Bm7, Em7, A7, DMaj7, GMaj7

B minor:

C♯m7♭5, F♯7, Bm(Maj7), Em7, A♯dim7, DMaj7+5, GMaj7

B♭ Major:

Cm7, F7, B♭Maj7, E♭Maj7, Am7♭5, Dm7, Gm7

G minor:

Cm7, F♯dim7, B♭Maj7+5, E♭Maj7, Am7♭5, D7, Gm(Maj7)

A Major:

C♯m7, F♯m7, Bm7, E7, AMaj7, DMaj7, G♯m7♭5

F♯ minor:

C♯7, F♯m(Maj7), Bm7, E♯dim7, AMaj7+5, DMaj7, G♯m7♭5

E♭ Major:

Cm7, Fm7, B♭7, E♭Maj7, A♭Maj7, Dm7♭5, Gm7

C minor:

Cm(Maj7), Fm7, Bdim7, E♭Maj7+5, A♭Maj7, Dm7♭5, G7

E Major:

C♯m7, F♯m7, B7, EMaj7, AMaj7, D♯m7♭5, G♯m7

C♯ minor:

C♯m(Maj7), F♯m7, B♯dim7, EMaj7+5, AMaj7, D♯m7♭5, G♯7

A♭ Major:

Cm7, Fm7, B♭m7, E♭7, A♭Maj7, D♭Maj7, Gm7♭5

F minor:

C7, Fm(Maj7), E♭m7, Edim7, A♭Maj7+5, D♭Maj7, Gm7♭5

B Major:

C♯m7, F♯7, BMaj7, EMaj7, A♯m7♭5, D♯m7, G♯m7

G♯ minor:

C♯m7, F𝄪dim7, BMaj7+5, EMaj7, A♯m7♭5, D♯7, G♯m(Maj7)

D♭ Major:

Cm7♭5, Fm7, B♭m7, E♭m7, A♭7, D♭Maj7, G♭Maj7

B♭ minor:

Cm7♭5, F7, B♭m(Maj7), E♭m7, Adim7, D♭Maj7+5, G♭Maj7

F♯ Major:

C♯7, F♯Maj7, BMaj7, E♯m7♭5, A♯m7, D♯m7, G♯m7

D♯ minor:

C𝄪dim7, F♯Maj7+5, BMaj7, E♯m7♭5, A♯7, D♯m(Maj7), G♯m7

G♭ Major:

C♭Maj7, Fm7♭5, B♭m7, E♭m7, A♭m7, D♭7, G♭Maj7

E♭ minor:

C♭Maj7, Fm♭5, B♭7, E♭m(Maj7), A♭m7, Ddim7, G♭Maj7+5

Whether in a major or minor key, all styles of music, including jazz and pop tunes, employ all or partials of this diatonic flow of chord changes. Both composers and improvisors add variety and interest to their music by moving from one tonal center to another, thereby creating many different chord progressions.

When a student practices this POOK 7/9 melodic exercise subject to the diatonic cycle of fifths in each tonal center, you will react more easily to chord changes and express more of what one hears in your mind's ear. The key signatures may prevail for the entire study or may be changed to other tonal centers at will, from phrase to phrase or section to section, as the player becomes familiar with more keys. Playing melodic shapes in the context of chord progressions produces quicker ear/instrument response, whether reading music or improvising. This POOK 7/9 shape should be memorized so that the shape can be applied to any chord progression, and specifically to the chord changes of all songs being learned. Using this approach will better connect the mind's ear with the player's fingers.

I hope you will enjoy this unique approach to improvisation as much as my students and I do.

POOK 7/9: TREBLE CLEF INSTRUMENTS

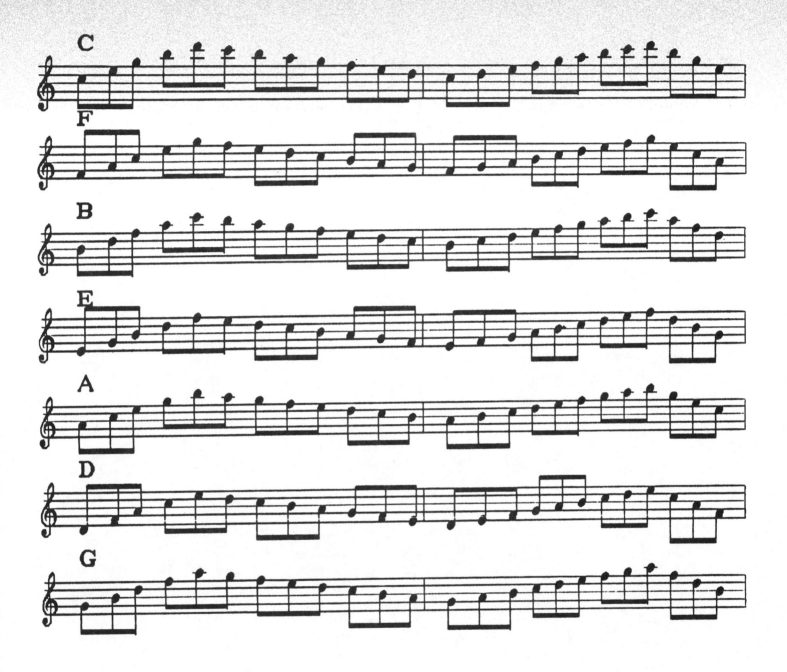

POOK 7/9: BASS CLEF INSTRUMENTS

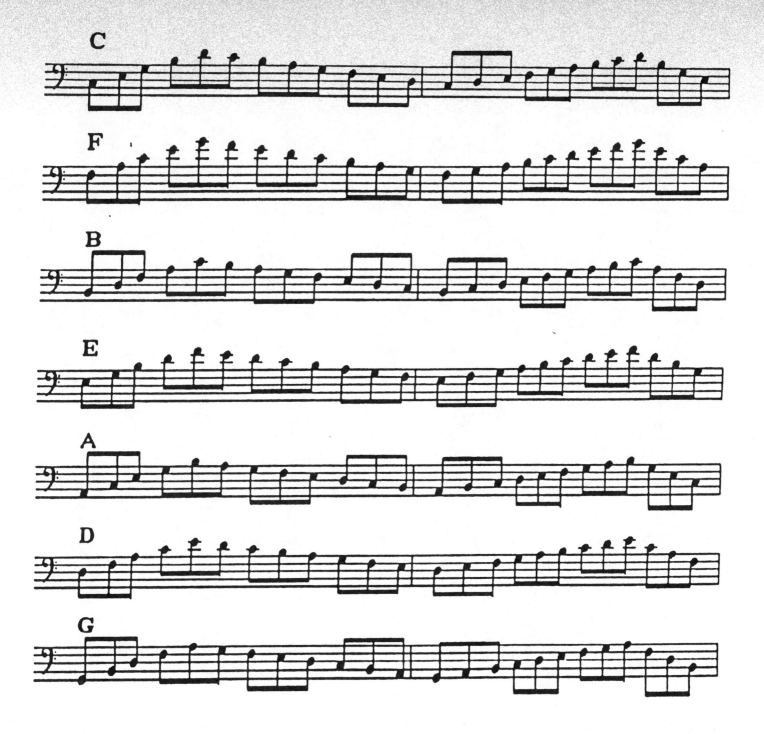

DOWN ACROSSING THE PENTATONIC BLUES SCALE

Playing the blues in every key is difficult, so I decided to introduce my version of the "Pentatonic Blues Scale" as a vehicle for learning and using blues language. Using this exercise students of jazz will also experience my technique of "Down Across" playing.

THE PENTATONIC BLUES SCALE DETAILED

The C blues scale in vogue today is C, E♭, F, F♯, G, B♭, C. A better choice of notes to be used over the blues is what I call the pentatonic blues scale. This blues scale makes use of the pentatonic scale adding a raised second (enharmonically it is the flatted third) to accommodate the flatted seventh of the IV♭7 chord sounding "inside" the key. Example: C, D, D♯, E, G, A, C (ascending)

In reality the C, E♭, F, F♯, G, B♭, C blues scale used by numerous jazz educators is an inversion of an E♭ major pentatonic scale with a raised second spelled E♭, F, F♯, G, B♭, C, E♭ that I call the E♭ pentatonic blues scale. It sounds better over the I♭7 chord when used in its descending form: C, B♭, G, G♭, F, E♭, C.

As a basis for playing over the blues I have chosen a combination of the C pentatonic blues scale (ascending) and the inversion of the E♭ pentatonic blues scale (descending). This gives both a basic "inside" sound and a funky, bluesy "outside" sound when improvising

the blues. To reiterate: C, D, D♯, E, G, A, C (ascending) and C, B♭, G, G♭, F, E♭, C (descending).

The musical example of the pentatonic blues scale included in this chapter is written in every key in both treble and bass clefs which provides a foundation for playing over blues progressions as well as over all dominant seventh chords.

After practicing the pentatonic blues scale in all keys the student will be able to hear and react more easily to the blues progression changes and express more of what he imagines producing quicker ear/instrument response, whether reading or improvising blues.

FORMAT OF DOWN ACROSS PLAYING

Down across playing is an enjoyable and productive non-conventional way of reading music. Down across playing fulfills the needs of the beginning blues instrumentalist which leads to a proficiency of playing jazz blues sounds, jazz blues patterns, and jazz language when improvising over the blues changes in any key.

This is accomplished by reading down the page and across the page in columns as one would when doing a crossword puzzle. Rather than playing the exercise as it would normally be played, across the page reading from left to right, it is played by columns both down and across the page. It will also be broken up into sets of one-note, two-notes, three notes, four notes, etc., up to nine-note groups.

This pentatonic blues exercise is written in both the treble and bass clefs, in all twelve keys, and in descending "Cycle of Fifths." The student will experience, feel and hear the effect of the blues sounds in cycle while playing the page down and across in columns until all sets are completed.

A student rarely sees simple blues melodies in difficult keys (normally the keys and melodies become more difficult as the music becomes more rhythmically complex). The down across method is a way of playing easy blues sounds while experiencing difficult keys that contain more than three sharps or flats.

PROCEDURE OF DOWN ACROSS PLAYING

In order to derive maximum benefit from the exercise, a student should follow this procedure when practicing:

Set 1: Play the first note of the first line of the first column only. Then move down the first column to the second line and again play only the first note. Move down the first column again and play the first note of the third line. Continue playing each first note of each line until you have played the first note of every line. By doing this, the student is playing the first note down the first column in cycle through all the keys.

After playing the first column of notes down the page the student should then proceed to the second column and play the second note of the first line only. Then move down the second column to the second line and again play only the second note. Move down the second column again and play the second note of the third line. Continue playing each second note of each line until you have played the second note of every line down the second column of the pentatonic blues exercise.

The student should then proceed to the third column. Play the third note of the first line only. Then move down to the next line and again play only the

third note. Move down again and play the third note of the third line. Continue playing each third note of each line until you have played the third note of every line in the third column. This procedure should continue until all of the third notes in all fourteen columns have been played.

The following additional sets of notes should be played by columns down the page and then move across the page one note to the right to the next set. Play that set down the page then move across the page one note to the right to the next set of notes. Play that set down the page until all sets of the same number are completed. Then start the next set and follow the same procedure.

In other words, after completing Set 1 (one note) in columns down and across the fourteen columns of the page proceed to Set 2.

Set 2: Play two-note groups down by columns moving across the page.

Set 3: Play three-note groups down by columns moving across the page.

Set 4: Play four-note groups down by columns moving across the page.

Set 5: Play five-note groups down by columns moving across the page.

Set 6: Play six-note groups down by columns moving across the page.

Set 7: Play seven-note groups down by columns moving across the page.

Set 8: Play eight-note groups down by columns moving across the page.

Set 9: Play nine-note groups down by columns moving across the page.

By following these directions, you will have been exposed to one thousand and eighty pentatonic blues sounds or patterns. Now you should be able to improvise over the blues easier and play more melodic jazz lines.

PENTATONIC BLUES SCALE: TREBLE CLEF

Note: All studies in this book can also be played in "Down Across" fashion.

A jazz player has to draw on all musical experiences to improvise creatively. A creative improvisor is only limited by the knowledge of jazz literature which also includes theory, chords, scales, and modes. One should not fall into usual finger patterns or "licks." A creative improvisor is constantly improvising.

Although I have chosen a particular group of notes to play over the blues, no one scale can completely represent a particular form of human expression that has come about in the past one hundred years. A blues scale, consisting of six or more notes cannot encompass the immense range of emotions, tempos, moods, styles, and concepts that this particular form of jazz can convey to an audience. Although it is important to learn the pentatonic blues scale, it is imperative for today's novice jazz student to become familiar and comfortable learning and memorizing many blues melodies, and improvising on the many different blues tunes and blues changes that have developed in the past one hundred years.

A student of jazz should start to work on a repertoire of blues literature, realizing that early jazz improvisors did not have a blues scale or as much literature to work with. The early jazz improvisors learned step by step which notes fit into the blues progression and as they became accustomed to more dissonances, their improvised and composed blues melodies became more altered. A student can learn many of the melodic blues phrases that developed throughout jazz history by playing early blues "roots" and proceeding to more modern blues experiencing and memorizing the blues literature.

Practicing blues literature and the pentatonic blues scale in all keys develops the facility to send out what the ear hears, developing the musical instrument as an extension of the musician's body and connecting it more directly with the mind, thus producing quicker ear/instrument response while improvising over the blues.

PENTATONIC BLUES SCALE: BASS CLEF

CHAPTER 14

THE I MAJOR 7TH CHORD AND THE IONIAN MODE

When this column "Beginning Jazz Improvisation" first appeared in the Dec. 1993, Vol. 1, No. 1 of *Jazz Player* magazine, Frank Bongiorno, the first writer of this column stated, "Obtaining a thorough knowledge of chord structures and scales, as well as their execution, is an important first step for the beginning improviser." This column will present the most "important first step," namely the first mode (or scale) and chord which jazz students need to begin functioning as an improvisor. This study is written combining the ionian mode with its major seventh chord as one sound. After playing the sound it is ingrained in the minds ear for recall during a solo. The musical etudes for this study are written for treble and bass clef instruments. The etude moves in the cycle of fifths progression of the ionian mode using its primary harmony, the major 7th chord.

We will be using a POOK 7/9 pattern of notes. (check *Jazz Player* issue Vol. 2, No. 3 April/May 1995 "How Chords Change A Chording To POOK"). This POOK 7/9 pattern of notes starts on the root of the chord (C). It then continues to ascend in thirds to its third (E) then to the fifth (G) to the major seventh (B) and finally to the ninth (D) which completes a major nine chord. The etude then descends scalewise to its root (C) and continues to ascend in retrograde to the ninth (D), then descends to its final tone (E), the third of the chord. This completes the first line of the etude.

Playing and learning chordal and modal lines through chord changes is a prerequisite for improvising. This skill is expected by most educators and is a requirement for playing all the jazz materials now available as melodies, patterns, and transcribed solos.

THE MAJOR SCALE: SOURCE FOR THE SEVEN DIATONIC MODES

The melodic sound of the major scale surrounds us and is heard many times through the various media: radio, television, records, tapes, CDs, films; it is played by orchestras, concert, marching, jazz, rock, and country bands. Melodies heard today come from varying the succession of musical pitches known as the scale. Each musical pitch that comprises a scale is termed a degree of that scale.

The most common scale used when composing music is the major scale. Derived from this scale are the seven modes: ionian, dorian, phrygian, lydian, mixolydian, aeolian, and locrian. The ionian mode is another term for the major scale. Each major key contains an ionian mode built on the first degree of the scale and uses a major seventh chord for its harmony. A major scale is comprised of two similarly constructed four-note groups of notes called tetrachords using one as a lower tetrachord beginning on the tonic note followed by an upper tetrachord a whole step away from the lower tetrachord.

The term mode is used interchangeably to mean scale; referring to modal steps as opposed to scale steps; referring to the different scale steps as first mode, second mode, third mode, fourth mode, fifth mode, sixth mode, and seventh mode. A mode is determined by its position in the major key. Each mode presents the half steps and whole steps in different positions and creates the difference in character of the seven modes and of music utilizing them. Each mode presents a great source of material when constructing melodies and the specific characteristics of each mode are necessary to conceive well written or improvised modal melodies.

The names of the modes used today came about in 1600 during the time of the church or Medieval modes, however, each individual mode is not constructed in the same manner as the original Greek modes, but some of the modal names given are still in use today.

ACTIVE AND INACTIVE TONES OF THE IONIAN MODE

In the key of C, the ionian mode contains these active and inactive tones:

- The note G, as an active tone, resolves to the root C: (5 to 1) (V to I)

- The note B resolves up a half step to the root C: (7 to 8) (vii to VIII)

- The note F resolves down a half step to the third E: (4 to 3) (IV to iii)

- The note A resolves down a whole step to the fifth G: (6 to 5) (vi to V)

- The note D resolves down a whole step to the root C: (2 to 1) (ii to I)

The remaining tones C, E, and G create a feeling of resolution, repose, or rest when the active tones resolve or, in the case of the note G, can remain stationary.

"Woodshedding" the treble and bass clef exercises included in this chapter, which progresses in cycle through all twelve keys, will put the sound of the ionian mode and its corresponding major seventh chord at the student's fingertips where it belongs for practical application. A student will then be able to hear and react more easily to modal changes and express more of what he imagines producing quicker ear/instrument response, whether reading or improvising modal sounds. Chord symbols have been provided to familiarize the student with the proper chord names and the corresponding keys for the melodic exercises being practiced. With practice, the student's ability to hear and improvise over major seventh chord changes will improve. Practicing the ionian mode will program the student's ears and mind with the basic modal sound of the ionian mode and will identify the notes that sound right over the major seventh chords in all keys or dialects.

In addition to learning modes, scales, and chords, a student should learn as many jazz, standard, and popular songs as possible to acquire an abundance of melodic language and style. These songs, as melodic information stored in the mind's ear, then become part of the total melodic recall to be played in bits or at length when improvising. All great jazz players have hundreds and maybe thousands of jazz tunes at their fingertips that can be used to put together as a puzzle in thousands of different ways over endless chord changes. This process occurs automatically as the improviser reacts to many new tunes and many new sets of chord changes.

The novice player should begin to memorize as many different jazz tunes as possible to expand improvisational fluency and acquire jazz vocabulary and language which should be a continuing process. After memorizing some jazz literature, the student should then practice the tunes in as many different keys as possible to expand the student's jazz language even further.

IONIAN OR MAJOR SCALE TYPE OF POPULAR, STANDARD AND JAZZ TUNES

"Birdlore," Charlie Parker

"Bugle Call Rag," Pattis/Myers

"Butterfly Dreams," Stanley Clarke

"Candy," David/Whitney/cramer

"Concerto for Cootie," Duke Ellington

"Crystal Silence," Chick Corea

"Dear Lord," John Coltrane

"Forest Flower," Charles Lloyd

"Here I'll Stay," Kurt Wiell

"Home Cookin'," Horace Silver

"Hotter than That," Lil Hardin Armstrong

"I Remember You," Johnny Mercer

"Idaho," J. Stone

"If I Were A Bell," Frank Loesser

"In a Silent Way," Josef Zawinul

"It Could Happen To You," Jimmy Van Heusen

"Little Miles," Randy Weston

"Liza," George Gershwin

"Mame," Jerry Herman

"Moonglow," H. Hudson

"Morning Song," Scott Reeves

"Ornithology," Charlie Parker

"Peace Piece," Bill Evans

"Poor Butterfly," R. Hubbell

"Real Live Girl," Cy Coleman

"Singing the Blues," Fields/McHugh

"Something," George Harrison

"Struttin' With Some Barbeque," Louis Armstrong

"Taxi War Dance," Lester Young/Count Basie

"Thembi," Pharaoh Sanders

"Weatherbird," Louis Armstrong

"West End Blues," J. Oliver/C. Williams

IONIAN MODE / I MAJOR 7: TREBLE CLEF

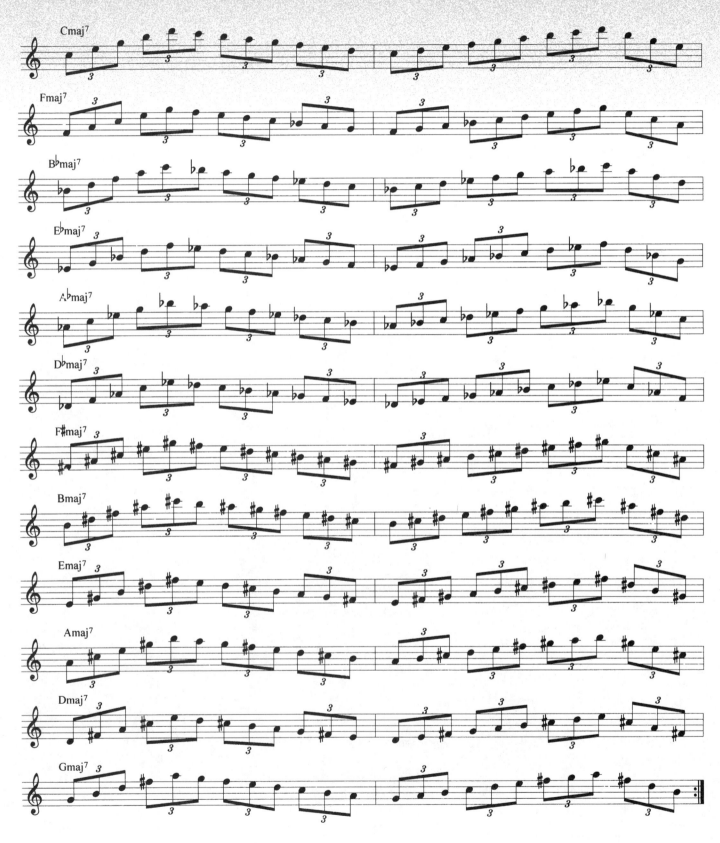

IONIAN MODE / I MAJOR 7: BASS CLEF

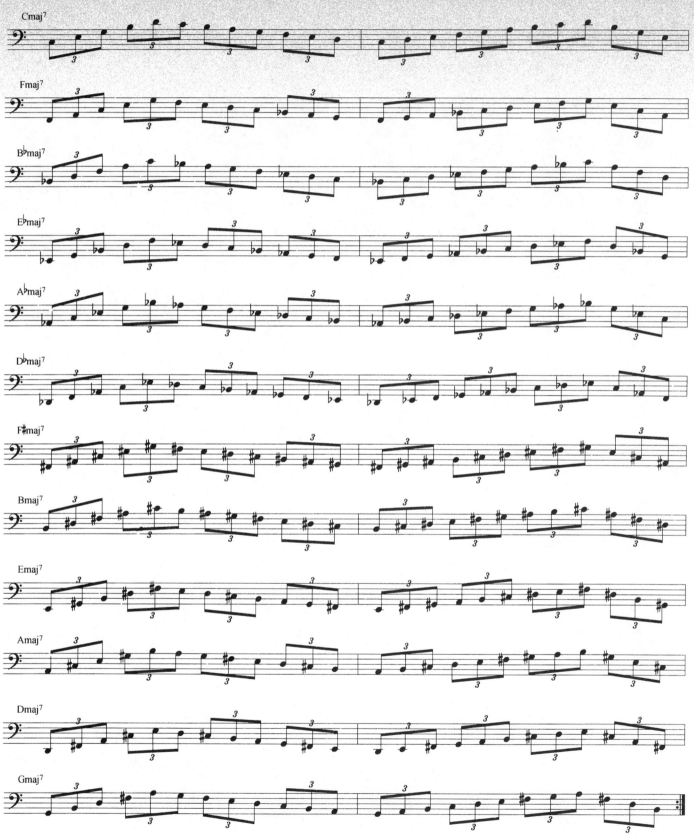

CHAPTER 15

THE ii MINOR 7TH CHORD AND THE DORIAN MODE

The last chapter explained the ionian mode and its harmony and combined the two as an exercise. This chapter will present the second mode (or scale) and the chord used for its harmony. That mode is dorian with a ii minor seventh chord used for its harmony. The etudes for this study are written for treble and bass clef instruments. As in the previous chapter this study is written combining the mode with its chord as one sound. After playing the sound it will be stored in the mind's ear for recall during a solo. This etude moves in the cycle of fifths progression using the minor 7th chord as its primary harmony. It also presents the shape of the POOK 7/9 pattern of notes. This etude is notated with the use of triplets to help with acquiring the swing feel. It also helps the student to gain the facility to play notes faster.

This musical exercise starts on (C), the root of the chord. It then continues to ascend in thirds to its third (E♭), then to the fifth (G), to the minor seventh (B♭), and finally to the ninth (D) which completes the minor ninth chord. The etude then descends scalewise to its root (C) and continues to ascend in retrograde (backwards) to the ninth (D), then descends to its final tone (E♭), the flatted third of the chord, thus completing the first line of the etude.

The most common scale used when composing music is the major scale. Derived from this scale are the seven modes: ionian, dorian, phrygian, lydian, mixoly-dian, aeolian, and locrian. The dorian mode is the term for the notes that appear in every major scale from the second degree ascending or descending through the scale to its octave. Example D is the second note or supertonic tone of the C major scale. The C major scale is composed of the notes: C, D, E, F, G, A, B, C. The D dorian mode uses the notes of the C major scale but starts on the note D: i.e., D, E, F, G, A, B, C, D.

Perceived another way, the dorian mode uses the same key signature as the major scale a major second below. Therefore the dorian mode built from the note D would have the same signature as the major scale a tone below, which is the key of C (no sharps or flats). Harmonically, the dorian mode makes use of the diatonic seventh chord built on the second degree of the major scale which is a minor seventh chord. Next to the mixolydian and ionian modes, the dorian mode is, by far, the most popular and most used mode in modern musical compositions.

A dorian mode is comprised of two similarly constructed four-note groups of notes called tetrachords using one as a lower tetrachord beginning on the second scale degree (D, E, F, G) followed by an upper tetrachord a whole step away from the lower tetrachord (A, B, C, D). The dorian mode consists of scale degrees of two sizes, half steps and whole steps, and occur as: whole step, half step, whole step, whole step, whole step, half step, whole step.

Modal scale degrees are usually numbered using Arabic or Roman numerals and letters to correspond to a specific key.

Dorian Modes in All Keys:

1 2 3 4 5 6 7 1

Roman Numerals:

I II III IV V VI VII I

Modal scale degrees in the key of C:

D E F G A B C D

ACTIVE AND INACTIVE TONES OF THE DORIAN MODE

Playing and learning chordal and modal lines through chord changes is a prerequisite for improvising. This skill is expected by most educators and is a requirement for playing all the jazz materials now available as melodies, patterns, and transcribed solos. By duplicating the way the active and inactive tones of the V7 or dominant chord of all keys resolve, we arrive at the clue to the resolution of all modal steps. By relating the direction of resolution of each tone of the dominant moving to the tones of each mode, the direction or proper resolution for each modal tone is realized. Even though the placement of half steps and whole steps change with each mode, the scale degrees of each mode should resolve in the same direction as when using the dominant chord mode melodically:

- V should resolve to I (as sol resolves to do)

- vii should also resolve to I (as ti resolves to do)

- IV should resolve to iii (as fa resolves to mi)

- vi should resolve to V (as la resolves to sol)

- ii should resolve to I (as re resolves to do)

As stated earlier the dorian mode sounds best when played over the harmony of a minor seventh chord used as the ii min7 chord of the key. The color tones of the dorian mode are the second, third, sixth, and seventh degrees. Melodically, it is better, when improvising, to

As stated earlier the dorian mode sounds best when played over the harmony of a minor seventh chord used as the ii min7 chord of the key. The color tones of the dorian mode are the second, third, sixth and seventh degrees. Melodically, it is better, when improvising, to use the tonic note of the mode at the ending rather than beginning with it. The fifth degree is one of the best notes to precede the modal tonic when starting a solo because it sets up the sound of the dorian mode as heard by the listener.

use the tonic note of the mode at the ending rather than beginning with it. The fifth degree is one of the best notes to precede the modal tonic when starting a solo because it sets up the sound of the dorian mode as heard by the listener.

Along with learning scales, modes, and chords the novice player should begin to memorize as many different jazz tunes as possible to expand improvisational fluency and acquire jazz vocabulary and language. This should be a continuing process. After memorizing some of the jazz literature, the student should then practice the tunes in as many different keys as possible to learn the jazz language.

DORIAN MODAL JAZZ TUNES TO BE LEARNED

"Afro Blue," John Coltrane

"Alabama," John Coltrane

"Atlantis," McCoy Tyner

"Black Narcissus," Joe Henderson

"Blessed Relief," Frank Zappa

"Blue Train," John Coltrane

"Blues To Woody," Scott Reeves

"Butterfly," Herbie Hancock

"C.C.," Stanley Clarke

"Canteloupe Island," Herbie Hancock

"Class B Tavern Serenade," Scott Reeves

"Contemplation," McCoy Tyner

"Crescent," John Coltrane

"De-Liberation," Harold Land

"Eleanor Rigby," John Lennon

"500 Miles High," Chick Corea

"Footprints," Wayne Shorter

"Gary's Waltz," Gary McFarland

"Herzog," Bobby Hutcherson

"I'm So High," Roy Haynes

"Impressions," John Coltrane

"Intrepid Fox," Freddie Hubbard

"Invitiation," Bronislav Kaper

"Like Sonny," John Coltrane

"Litha," Chick Corea

"Little B's Poem," Bobby Hutcherson

"Little Sunflower," Freddie Hubbard

"Live Right Now," Eddie Harris

"Lonnie's Lament," John Coltrane

"Maiden Voyage," Herbie Hancock

"Majoong," Wayne Shorter

"Mile's Mode," John Coltrane

"Milestones," Miles Davis

"Milestones" (new version), Miles Davis

"Morning Song," Scott Reeves

"My Favorite Things," Richard Rodgers

"Mysterious Traveler," Wayne Shorter

"Norwegian Wood," John Lennon/Paul McCartney

"Open Your Eyes You Can Fly," Chick Corea

"Passion Dance," McCoy Tyner

"Pole Vault," Freddie Hubbard

"Portsmouth Figurations," Steve Swallow

"Recordame," Joe Henderson

"Silver's Serenade," Horace Silver

"Sly," Herbie Hancock

"So What," Miles Davis

"Soleil d'Altamira," David Baker

"Son of Mr. Green Genes," Frank Zappa

"Sphering," Jack Peterson

"Spinky," C. Earland

"Spiral Dance," Keith Jarrett

"Summer Social Amenities," John LaPorta

"The Loner," Cedar Walton

"Time Remembered," Bill Evans

"Witch Hunt," Wayne Shorter

DORIAN MODE / II MINOR 7: TREBLE CLEF

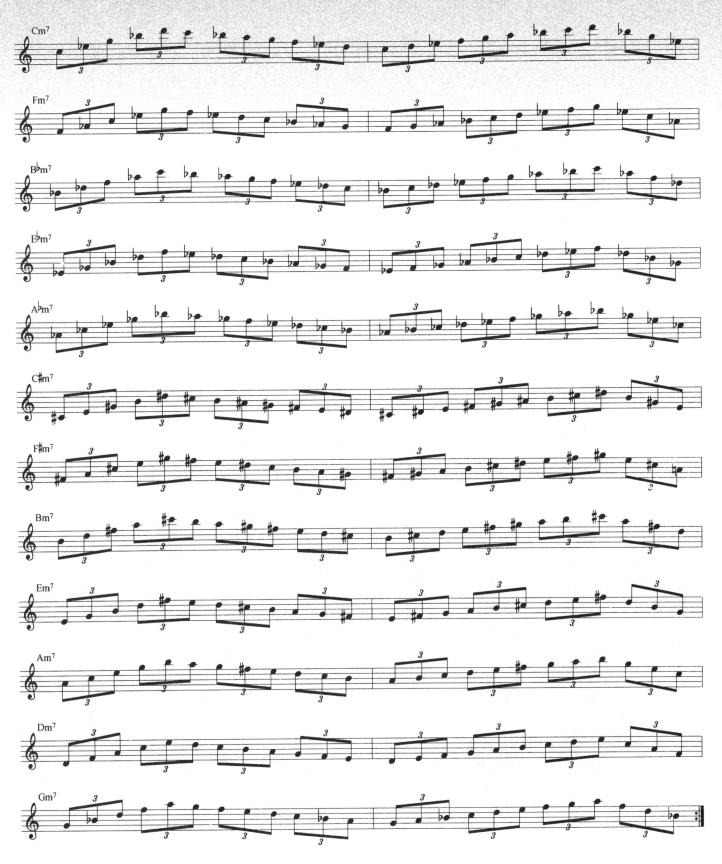

DORIAN MODE / II MINOR 7: BASS CLEF

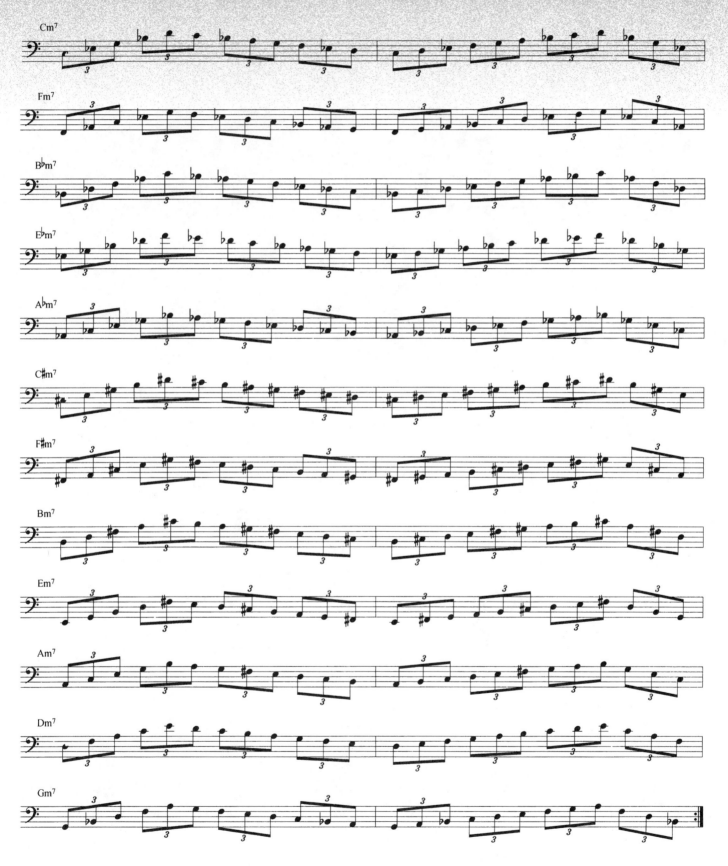

CHAPTER 16

THE iii MINOR 7TH CHORD AND THE PHRYGIAN MODE

I hope you readers are not getting too over moded or over chorded! Hang in there, because there's only four more modes and four more modal chords to go. My last chapter explained the dorian mode and its harmony and combined the two as an exercise. This chapter will present the third mode of the major scale with the chord used for its harmony. This mode is the phrygian mode used over the harmony of a minor seventh chord.

The etudes for this study are written for treble and bass clef instruments. The phrygian mode with its minor seventh chord is combined as one sound. This mode will sound different than the dorian mode because of the placement of whole steps and half steps. There is a half step between the first and second degrees of this mode instead of a whole step. Hopefully, by practicing the new sound, it will be ingrained in the mind's ear for recall during a solo. Also by playing this exercise in "down across" fashion, a great amount of technical prowess will take place. To learn about down across playing refer to my article in Feb/March 1997 issue of *Jazz Player* magazine. (Chapter 13)

Because of the great importance of the cycle of fifths, this etude also moves in cycle progression using the minor 7th chord as its primary harmony while retaining the shape of the POOK 7/9 pattern of notes.

As in the previous articles, this etude is notated with the use of triplets to help feel the swing style. It also helps with the process of playing faster. After playing two notes, the next step to playing faster should be to play three notes instead of the usual four notes.

This POOK 7/9 pattern starts on C, which is the third scale degree in the key of A♭ and becomes the root of the Cmin7 (iiimin7) chord. The study then continues to ascend in thirds to its third (E♭) and continues to the fifth (G), to the minor seventh (B♭), and finally to the flatted ninth (D♭) which completes the ninth chord.

The etude descends scalewise to its root (C) and then ascends in retrograde (backwards) to the flatted ninth (D♭), descends by thirds to its final tone (E♭), the flatted third of the chord, and thus completes the first line of the etude.

THE MAJOR SCALE SOURCE FOR THE PHRYGIAN MODE

The phrygian mode is the term for the notes that appear in every major scale from the third degree ascending through the scale to its octave. The C phrygian mode uses the notes of the A♭ major scale but starts on the note C. Example: C, D♭, E♭, F, G, A♭, B♭, C, which are the Arabic scale numbers 3, 4, 5, 6, 7, 1, 2, 3. The scale tones are then numbered again using Arabic numbers 1, 2, 3, 4, 5, 6, 7, or with Roman numerals I, II, III, IV, V, VI, VII, VIII.

A phrygian mode is comprised of two similarly constructed four-note groups of notes called trachords.. A tetrachord is any succession of four notes used as a basis for constructing a scale.

The lower tetrachord begins on the third scale degree followed by the upper tetrachord a whole step away from the lower tetrachord. The phrygian mode consists of scale degrees of two sizes, half steps and whole steps, and occur as: half step, whole step, whole step, whole step, half step, whole step, whole step.

ACTIVE AND INACTIVE TONES OF THE PHRYGIAN MODE

Playing and learning chordal and modal lines through chord changes is a prerequisite for improvising. This skill is expected by most educators and is a requirement for playing all the jazz materials now available as melodies, patterns, and transcribed solos.

By duplicating the way the active and inactive tones of the V7 or dominant chord of all keys resolve when playing modally, one is better able to play melodically when playing modes. Even though the placement of half steps and whole steps change with each mode, the scale degrees of each mode should resolve in the same direction.

The note G as the fifth (V) should resolve to I (C) the root (as sol resolves to do). The note B♭ as the seventh (vii) should also resolve to I (C) the root (as ti resolves to do). The note F as the fourth (IV) should resolve to iii (E♭) the third (as fa resolves to mi). The note A♭ as the sixth (vi) should resolve to V (G) the fifth (as la resolves to sol). The note D♭ as the second (ii) should resolve to I (C) the root (as re resolves to do).

As stated earlier the phrygian mode sounds best when played over the harmony of a minor seventh chord used as the iii min7 chord of the key. The color tones of the phrygian mode are the second, third, sixth, and seventh degrees. Melodically, it is better, when

improvising, to use the tonic note of the mode (C) at the ending rather than beginning with it. The fifth degree (G) is one of the best notes to precede the modal tonic when starting a solo because it sets up the sound of the phrygian mode as heard by the listener.

The novice player should begin to memorize as many different jazz tunes as possible to expand improvisational fluency and acquire jazz vocabulary and language. This should be a continuing process. After memorizing some of the jazz literature listed above, the student should then practice the tunes in as many different keys as possible to expand the student's jazz language even further.

Following is a list of standard, popular, and jazz tunes that contain the phrygian mode completely or in part. Although it is important to learn the phrygian mode in all keys or dialects, it is imperative for today's novice composer or improvisor to become familiar with the jazz literature that makes use of the phrygian mode. If the student learns, analyses, and memorizes these melodies, improvising on tunes that contain the phrygian mode will be easier.

PHRYGIAN MODAL STANDARD JAZZ TUNES TO BE LEARNED

"Ana Maria," Wayne Shorter

"Dansere," Jan Garbarek

"Bambo," Scott Reeves

"La Fiesta," Chick Corea

"Long as You Know You're Living Yours," Keith Jarrett

"Masqualero," Wayne Shorter

"Song for Shelby," Scott Reeves

"Sweeping Up," Steve Swallow

"What Was," Chick Corea

"Solea," Gil Evans

"Speak No Evil," Wayne Shorter

"Vaskar," Carla Bley

CHAPTER 16: THE iii MINOR 7TH CHORD AND THE PHRYGIAN MODE

> The novice player should begin to memorize as many different jazz tunes as possible to expand improvisational fluency and acquire jazz vocabulary and language. This should be a continuing process. After memorizing some of the jazz literature listed above, the student should then practice the tunes in as many different keys as possible to expand the student's jazz language even further.

As can be seen by the above partial list of jazz literature which contain the phrygian mode in many melodic shapes, a jazz player acquires an abundance of jazz language and style while learning melodies. These tunes, as melodic information stored in the mind's ear, then become part of the total melodic recall to be played in bits or at length when improvising. All great jazz players have hundreds and maybe thousands of jazz tunes at their fingertips that can be put together as a puzzle in thousands of different ways over endless chord changes. This process occurs automatically as the improvisor reacts to many new tunes and many new sets of chord changes. The novice player should begin to memorize as many different jazz tunes as possible to expand improvisational fluency and acquire jazz vocabulary and language which should be a continuing process. After memorizing some of the jazz literature listed above, the student should then practice the tunes in as many different keys as possible to expand the student's jazz language even further.

Practicing the iii min7 and the Phrygian Mode will program the student's ears and mind with the basic modal sound of the phrygian mode, and will identify the notes that sound right over the minor seventh chords in all keys or dialects.

PHRYGIAN MODE / III MINOR 7: TREBLE CLEF

PHRYGIAN MODE / III MINOR 7: BASS CLEF

CHAPTER 17

THE IV MAJOR 7TH CHORD AND THE LYDIAN MODE

The last chapter explained the phrygian mode and its harmony and combined the two as an exercise. This chapter will present the fourth mode of the major scale with the chord used for its harmony. This mode is the lydian mode with a major seventh chord used for its harmony.

The etudes for this study are written for treble and bass clef instruments. As in the previous article this study is written combining the lydian mode with its major seventh chord as one sound. After practicing the sound it will be ingrained in the mind's ear for recall during a solo. This etude moves in the cycle of fifths progression using the major 7th chord as its primary harmony. It again presents the shape of the POOK 7/9 pattern of notes.

As in the previous chapters, this etude is notated with the use of triplets to help feel the swing style. It also helps with the process of playing the notes faster. After playing two notes as eighth notes the next step to playing faster should be to play three notes as triplets instead of four notes as sixteenth notes. This POOK 7/9 pattern starts on C the root of the chord. It then continues to ascend in thirds to its third (E), then to the fifth (G), to the major seventh (B), and finally to the ninth (D), which completes the major ninth chord. The etude then descends scalewise to its root (C) and continues to ascend in retrograde to the ninth (D).

Then it descends to its final tone (E), the third of the chord, thus completing the first line of the etude.

THE MAJOR SCALE SOURCE OF THE LYDIAN MODE

The lydian mode is the term for the notes that appear in every major scale from the fourth degree ascending through the scale to its octave. The C lydian mode uses the notes of the G major scale but starts on the note C. Example: C, D, E, F♯, G, A, B, C, which are the Arabic scale numbers 4, 5, 6, 7, 1, 2, 3, 4. The scale tones are then numbered again using Arabic numbers 1, 2, 3, 4, 5, 6, 7, or with Roman numerals I, II, III, IV, VI, VII, VIII.

A lydian mode is comprised of two different four-note groups of notes called tetrachords. A tetrachord is any succession of four notes used as a basis for constructing a scale. The lower tetrachord begins on the fourth scale degree followed by the upper tetrachord a half step away from the lower tetrachord. The lydian mode consists of scale degrees of two sizes, half steps and whole steps, and occur as: whole step, whole step, whole step, half step, whole step, whole step, half step.

ACTIVE AND INACTIVE TONES OF THE LYDIAN MODE

Playing and learning chordal and modal lines through chord changes is a prerequisite for improvising. This skill is expected by most educators and is a requirement for playing all the jazz materials now available as melodies, patterns, and transcribed solos.

By duplicating the way the active and inactive tones of the V7 or dominant chord of all keys resolve when playing modally, we are better able to play melodically when playing modes. Even though the placement of half steps and whole steps change with each mode, the scale degrees of each mode should resolve in the same direction. The note G as the fifth (V) should resolve to I (C) the root (as sol resolves to do). The note B as the seventh (vii) should also resolve to I (C) the root (as ti resolves to do). The note F♯ as the fourth (IV) should resolve to iii (E) the third (as fa resolves to mi). The note A as the sixth (vi) should resolve to V (G) the fifth (as la resolves to sol). The note D as the second (ii) should resolve to I (C) the root (as re resolves to do).

As stated earlier the lydian mode sounds best when played over the harmony of a major seventh chord used as the IVmaj7 chord of the key. The color tones of the lydian mode are the second, third, sixth, and seventh degrees. Melodically, it is better, when improvising, to use the tonic note of the mode (C) at the ending rather than beginning with it. The fifth degree (G) is one of the best notes to precede the modal tonic when starting a solo because it sets up the sound of the lydian mode as heard by the listener. There has been a greater tendency to use the lydian mode more often. The flavor of the raised fourth degree is found in many jazz compositions of today and creates a bright effect when the note is used or sustained. Many melodies make use of the raised fourth in the ending or final chord.

The lydian mode consists of eight consecutive notes written on the staff ascending or descending, ending on its final note. In the key of C the lydian mode ascending is C, D, E, F♯, G, A, B, C, and in descending order C, B, A, G, F♯, E, D, C. When constructing the lydian mode, half steps occur between the fourth and fifth scale degrees and also between the seventh and eighth scale degrees. All other degrees of the scale are separated by whole steps.

Following is a list of Standard, popular, and jazz tunes that contain the lydian mode completely or in part. Although it is important to learn the lydian mode in all keys or dialects, it is imperative for todays novice composer or improvisor to become familiar with the jazz literature that makes use of the lydian mode. If the student learns, analyses, and memorizes these melodies, improvising on tunes that contain the lydian mode will be easier.

LYDIAN MODAL STANDARD JAZZ TUNES TO BE LEARNED

"April Joy" - Pat Methany
"Black Narcissus" - Joe Henderson
"Brite Piece" - David Liebman
"Coral" - Keith Jarrett
"E.S.P." - Wayne Shorter
"Hold Her Tight" - Marie Osmond
"Inner Urge" - Joe Henderson
"Iris" - Wayne Shorter
"Katrina Ballerina" - Woody Shaw
"Loft Dance" - David Liebman
"Ostinato" - Dan Haerle
"Spiral Dance" - Keith Jarrett
"Bambu" - Scott Reeves
"Bright Yellow" - John LaPorta
"Contemplation" - McCoy Tyner
"Dansre" - Jan Garbarek
"Gary's Waltz" - Gary McFarland
"Icarus" - Ralph Towner

"Intrepid Fox" - Freddie Hubbard

"Jackie-ing" - Thelonious Monk

"Litha" - Chick Corea

"Open Your Eyes You Can Fly" - Chick Corea

"Solea" - Gil Evans

"Tell Me a Bedtime Story" - Herbie Hancock

"The Real Guitarist in the House" - Steve Kuhn

"Think of Me" - George Cables

"Time Remembered" - Bill Evans

"Tomorrow's Destiny" - Woody Shaw

"What Was" - Chick Corea

As can be seen by the length of this partial list of jazz literature containing the lydian mode in many melodic shapes, a jazz player acquires an abundance of jazz language and style while learning melodies. These tunes, as melodic information stored in the mind's ear, then become part of the total melodic recall to be played in bits or at length when improvising. All great jazz players have hundreds and maybe thousands of jazz tunes at their fingertips that can be put together as a puzzle in thousands of different ways over endless chord changes. This process occurs automatically as the improvisor reacts to many new tunes and many new sets of chord changes.

The novice player should begin to memorize as many different jazz tunes as possible to expand improvisational fluency and acquire jazz vocabulary and language. This should be a continuing process. After memorizing some of the jazz literature listed above, the student should then practice the tunes in as many different keys as possible to expand the student's jazz language even further. My next article will explain the mixolydian mode and its dominant seventh harmony, with another POOK 7/9 treble and bass clef etude.

LYDIAN MODE / IV MAJOR 7: TREBLE CLEF

LYDIAN MODE / IV MAJOR 7: BASS CLEF

CHAPTER 18

THE V DOMINANT CHORD AND THE MIXOLYDIAN MODE

The last chapter explained the lydian mode and its harmony. The mode and harmony were combined into an exercise for practice. This article will present the fifth mode and the chord used for its harmony. This mode is the mixolydian with a dominant seventh chord used for its harmony.

The etudes for this study are written for treble and bass clef instruments. As in the previous chapter, this study is written combining the mixolydian mode with the harmony of its dominant seventh chord (V7) as one sound. After playing the sound it will be ingrained in the mind's ear for recall during a solo. This etude moves in the cycle of fifths progression using the dominant seventh chord as its primary harmony. The shape of the POOK 7/9 pattern of notes is continued as in previous articles.

The etude is notated with the use of triplets to help with experiencing the swing feeling. Playing triplets instead of eighth notes helps in gaining technical speed and ability to play sixteenth notes.

This POOK 7/9 pattern starts on C, the root of the chord. It then continues to ascend in thirds to its third (E), then to the fifth (G), to the flatted seventh (B♭) and finally to the ninth (D), which completes the ninth chord. The etude then descends scalewise to its root (C) and continues to ascend in retrograde (backwards) to the ninth (D). It then descends to its final tone (E),

the major third of the chord, thus completing the first line of the etude.

THE MAJOR SCALE: SOURCE FOR THE MIXOLYDIAN MODE

The mixolydian mode is comprised of two different four-note groups of notes called tetrachords. A tetrachord is any succession of four notes used as a basis for constructing a scale. The lower tetrachord begins on the fifth scale degree followed by the upper tetrachord a whole step away from the lower tetrachord. The mixolydian mode consists of scale degrees of two sizes, half steps and whole steps. They occur as: whole-step, whole-step, half-step, whole-step, whole-step, half-step, whole-step.

The mixolydian mode is similar to the major scale, but begins on its fifth degree. It uses the same key signature as any major scale a perfect fifth below. Therefore the mixolydian mode built from the note C would have the same signature as the major scale a fifth below the key of F containing one flat (B♭).

Example: C, D, E, F, G, A, B♭, C, which use the Arabic scale numbers 5, 6, 7, 1, 2, 3, 4, 5. The modal tones are then numbered again using Arabic numbers 1, 2, 3, 4, 5, 6, 7, 8, or Roman numerals I, II, III, IV, V, VI, VII, VIII.

As stated earlier the mixolydian mode sounds best when played over the harmony of a dominant seventh chord used as the V7 chord of the key. The color tones of the mixolydian mode are the second, third, sixth, and seventh degrees. Melodically, it is better, when improvising, to use the tonic note of the mode at the ending rather than beginning with it. The fifth degree is one of the best notes to precede the modal tonic when starting a solo because it sets up the sound of the mixolydian mode as heard by the listener.

Next to the dorian and ionian modes, the mixolydian mode is, by far, the most popular and most used mode in modern compositions.

ACTIVE AND INACTIVE TONES OF THE MIXOLYDIAN MODE

Playing and learning chordal and modal lines through chord changes is a prerequisite for improvising. This skill is expected by most educators and is a requirement for playing all the jazz materials now available as melodies, patterns, and transcribed solos.

By duplicating the way the active and inactive tones of the V7 or dominant chord of all keys resolve, we arrive at the clue to the resolution of all modal steps. By relating the direction of resolution of each tone of the dominant moving to the tones of each mode, the direction or proper resolution for each modal tone is realized.

Even though the placement of half steps and whole steps change with each mode, the scale degrees of each mode should resolve in the same direction as when using the dominant chord mode melodically.

In the key of F the mixolydian mode contains these active and inactive tones: The note C, as an active tone, resolves down or up to the root F (5 to 1)(V to I). The note C can also remain stationary.

The note E, as an active tone, resolves up a half step to the root F (7 to 8) (vii to VIII). The note G resolves down a whole step to the root F (2 to 1) (ii to I). The note B♭ resolves down a half step to the third A (4 to 3) (IV to iii). The remaining tones F, A, and C

create a feeling of resolution, repose, or rest when the active tones resolve.

Woodshedding the exercise included in this article, which progresses in cycle through all twelve keys, will put the sound of the mixolydian mode and its corresponding dominant seventh chord at the student's fingertips, where it belongs for practical application. A student will then be able to hear and react more easily to modal changes and express more of what he/she imagines, producing quicker ear/instrument response, whether reading or improvising modal sounds.

Following is a list of standard, popular and jazz tunes that contain the mixolydian mode completely or in part. The mixolydian mode must be learned in all keys. It is important for today's novice composer or improvisor to become familiar with the jazz literature which makes use of the mixolydian mode. If the student learns, analyses, and memorizes some of these melodies, improvising on tunes that contain dominant harmonies will become easier.

MIXOLYDIAN MODAL STANDARD JAZZ TUNES TO BE LEARNED

"Beauty and the Beast," Wayne Shorter

"Blue Monk," Thelonious Monk

"Boston Marathon," Gary Burton

"Cantaloupe Island," Herbie Hancock

"Cold Sweat," James Brown

"Country Roads," Steve Swallow

"Cuban Mambo," Xavier Cugat

"Evil Ways," S. Henry

"Five Over Five," John LaPorta

"Footprints," Wayne Shorter

"Freddie Freeloader," Miles Davis

"Freedom Jazz Dance," Eddie Harris

"Gemini," Jimmy Heath

"Gypsy Queen," G. Zabor

"Herzog," Bobby Hutcherson

"Inchworm," F. Loesser

"Killer Joe," Benny Golson

"Manteca," Dizzy Gillespie

"Misterioso," Thelonious Monk

"Mr. Clean," Freddie Hubbard

"Norwegian Wood," Lennon/McCartney

"Oliloqui Valley," Herbie Hancock

"Paperback Writer," Lennon/McCartney

"Passion Dance," McCoy Tyner

"Salt Lake Mix," John LaPorta

"Sister Sadie," Horace Silver

"Straight Life," Freddie Hubbard

"The In' Crowd," B. Page

"Sweet Georgia Bright," Charles Lloyd

"Icarus," R. Towner

"The Lonely Bull," Sol Lake

"This Here," Bobby Timmons

"Tommorrow Never Knows," Lennnon/McCartney

"Trancing In," John Coltrane

"Watermelon Man," Herbie Hancock

"Well You Needn't," Thelonious Monk

The above list of jazz literature contains the mixolydian mode in many melodic shapes. An abundance of jazz language and style is acquired while learning melodies. These tunes, as melodic information stored in the mind's ear, then become part of the total melodic recall to be played in bits or at length when improvising. All great jazz players have hundreds and maybe thousands of jazz tunes at their fingertips that can be used to put together as a puzzle in thousands of different ways over endless chord changes. This process occurs automatically as the improvisor reacts to many new tunes and many new sets of chord changes.

The novice player should begin to memorize as many different jazz tunes as possible to expand improvisational fluency and acquire jazz vocabulary and language. After memorizing some of the jazz literature listed above, the student should then practice the tunes in as many different keys as possible to expand the student's jazz language even further.

My next article will explain the aeolian mode and its minor seventh harmony, with another POOK 7/9 treble and bass clef etude.

MIXOLYDIAN MODE / V DOMINANT 7: TREBLE CLEF

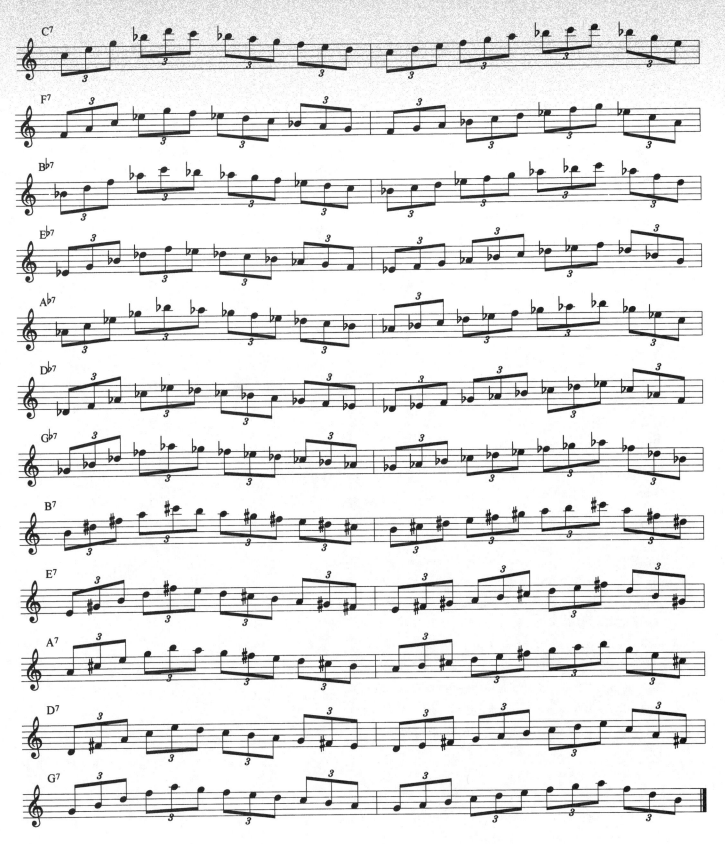

MIXOLYDIAN MODE / V DOMINANT 7: BASS CLEF

CHAPTER 19

THE vi MINOR 7TH CHORD AND THE AEOLIAN MODE

This chapter continues the series of the study of the seven diatonic modes in all keys. The previous mode discussed was the mixolydian mode and its harmony. Each article has included an exercise to practice the subject matter. This chapter will present the sixth mode of the major scale and the chord used for it's harmony. It is the aeolian mode with a minor seventh chord used for its harmony. This mode is also known as the natural minor scale from which all other minor scales are derived.

The etudes for this study are written for treble and bass clef instruments. As in the previous chapters this study is written combining the aeolian mode with its minor seventh chord as one sound. After practicing the sound it will become part of the musical language a student may recall from his/her mind's ear during a solo. This etude moves in the cycle of fifths progression using the minor 7th chord as its primary harmony. Each exercise in this particular series on the diatonic modes uses the shape of the POOK 7/9 pattern of notes.

As in the previous article this etude is notated with the use of triplets to help with getting the swing feeling. It also helps with the process of getting the notes to move along faster. After playing two notes, the next step to playing faster should be to play three notes instead of four notes.

This POOK 7/9 pattern starts on C, the root of the chord. It then continues to ascend in thirds to its third

(E♭), then to the fifth (G), to the minor seventh (B♭), and finally to the ninth (D), which completes the minor nine chord. The etude then descends scalewise to its root (C) and continues to ascend in retrograde (backwards) to the ninth (D). It then descends to its final tone (E♭), the flatted third of the chord, and thus completes the first line of the etude.

ACTIVE AND INACTIVE TONES OF THE AEOLIAN MODE

Playing and learning chordal and modal lines through chord changes is a prerequisite for improvising. This skill is expected by most educators and is a requirement for playing all the jazz materials now available as melodies, patterns, and transcribed solos.

The aeolian mode contains the same notes as the major scale, but begins on its sixth degree, or perceived another way, the aeolian mode uses the same key signature as any major scale a major sixth below. Therefore the aeolian mode built from the note C would have the same signature as the major scale a sixth below: the key of E♭, containing three flats (B♭, E♭, A♭). Harmonically, the aeolian mode makes use of the diatonic seventh chord built on the sixth degree of the major scale which is a minor seventh chord.

By duplicating the way the active and inactive tones of the V7 or dominant chord of all keys resolve, we arrive at the clue to the resolution of all modal steps. By relating the direction of resolution of each tone of the dominant moving to the tones of each mode, the direction or proper resolution for each modal tone is realized.

Even though the placement of half steps and whole steps change with each mode, the scale degrees of each mode should resolve in the same direction as when using the dominant chord mode melodically. The note G as the fifth (V) should resolve to 1 (C) the root (as *sol* resolves to *do*) (V to I). The note B♭ as the seventh (vii) should also resolve up to I (C) (as *ti* resolves to *do*) (vii to I). The note F as the fourth (iv) should resolve to iii (as *fa* resolves to *me*) (iv to iii). The note A♭ as the sixth (vi) should resolve to V (as *la* resolves to *sol*). The note D as the second (ii) should resolve to I (C) (as *re* resolves to *do*) (ii to i).

As stated earlier the aeolian mode sounds best when played over the harmony of a minor seventh chord used as the vimin7 chord of the key. The color tones of the aeolian mode are the second, third, sixth, and seventh degrees. Melodically, it is better, when improvising, to use the tonic note of the mode at the ending rather than beginning with it. The fifth degree is one of the best notes to precede any modal tonic when starting a solo because it sets up the sound of the mode as heard by the listener.

Following is a list of standard, popular, and jazz tunes that contain the aeolian mode completely or in part. Although it is important to learn the aeolian mode in all keys, it is imperative for today's novice composer or improvisor to become familiar with the jazz literature that makes use of the aeolian mode. If the student learns, analyses, and memorizes at least some of these melodies, improvising on tunes that contain the aeolian mode will be easier.

AELOIAN MODAL STANDARD JAZZ TUNES TO BE LEARNED

"Aeolian Man" - John La Porta

"Airegin" - Sonny Rollins

"Alone Together" - Kietz/Schartz

"Angel Eyes" - Dennis/Brent

"Autumn Leaves" - Johnny Mercer

"Beautiful Love" - Victor Young

"Black Orpheus" - Louis Bonfi

"Blue Bossa" - Kenny Dorham

"Conference of the Birds" - Dave Holland

"Django" - John Lewis

"La Lena" - Donovan

"Mr P.C." - John Coltrane

"Legend in Your Own Time" - Carol King

"My Funny Valentine" - Richard Rodgers/Lorenz Hart

"Night and Day" - Cole Porter

"Peace" - Horace Silver

"Portsmouth Figurations" - Steve Swallow

"Round Midnight" - Thelonious Monk

"Sly" - Herbie Hancock

"Some Time Ago" - Chick Corea

"Son of Mr. Green Genes" - Frank Zappa

"Stella by Starlight" - Victor Young

"Vaskar" - Carla Bley

"Yesterdays" - Jerome Kern

As can be seen by the length of the partial list of jazz literature which contain the aeolian mode in many melodic shapes, a jazz player acquires an abundance of jazz language and style while learning melodies. These tunes, as melodic information stored in the mind's ear, then become part of the total melodic recall to be played in bits or at length when improvising. All great jazz players have many jazz tunes at their fingertips to use as part of their musical language while improvising. This process occurs automatically as the improvisor reacts to many new tunes and many new sets of chord changes. The novice player should begin to memorize as many different jazz tunes as possible to expand improvisational fluency and acquire jazz vocabulary and language which should be a continuing process. After memorizing some of the jazz literature listed above, the student should then practice the tunes in as many different keys as possible to expand the student's jazz language even further.

My next article will explain the locrian mode and its minor 7th flat five harmony, with another POOK 7/9 treble and bass clef etude.

AEOLIAN MODE / vi MINOR 7TH: TREBLE CLEF

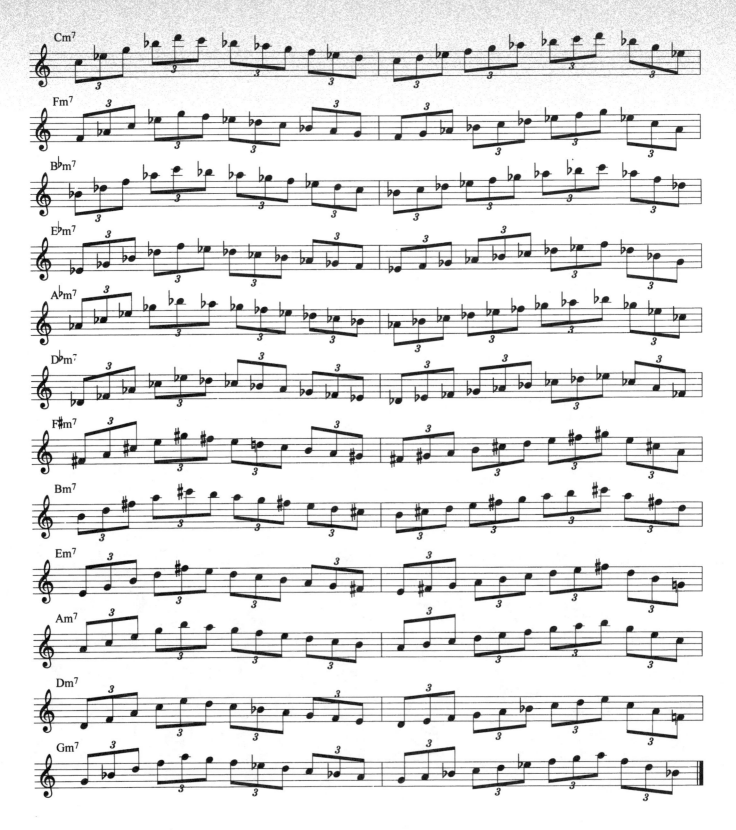

AEOLIAN MODE / vi MINOR 7TH: BASS CLEF

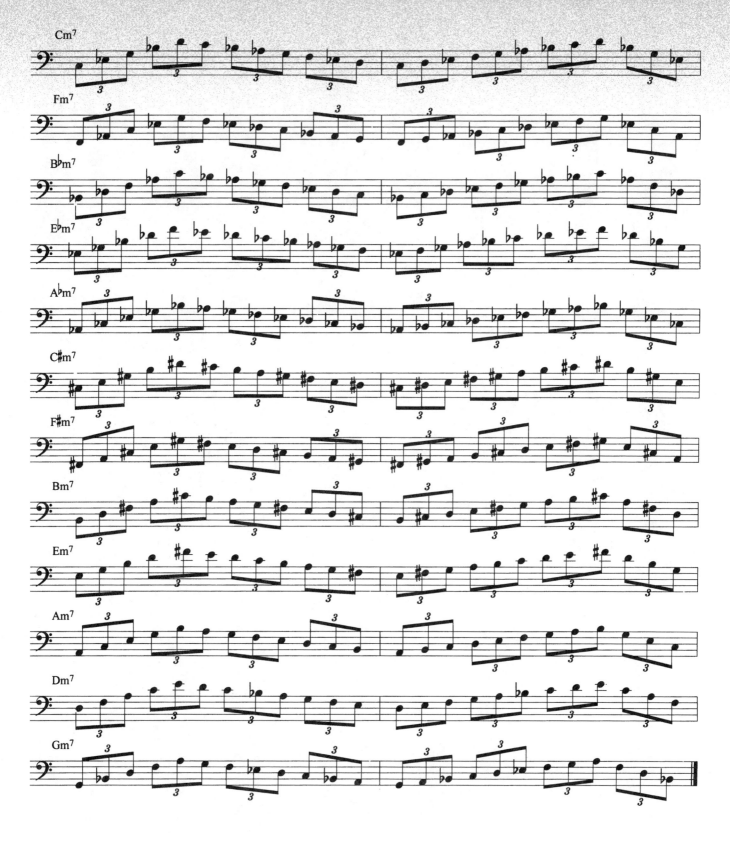

CHAPTER 20

THE VII HALF DIMINISHED CHORD AND THE LOCRIAN MODE

This is the final chapter in the series of diatonic modes. My previous chapter explained the aeolian mode and its minor seventh harmony. This time I will present the seventh mode or last mode built on the seventh degree of the major scale and the chord used for its harmony. That mode is locrian with a half diminished 7th chord used for its harmony. The etudes for this study are written for treble and bass clef instruments. As in the previous chapter this study is written combining the locrian mode with its half diminished seventh chord as a single sound. After practicing the sound it will begin to be ingrained in the mind's ear for recall during a solo. This etude moves in the cycle of fifths progression using the minor 7th flat five chord as its primary harmony. As in all the previous etudes for the diatonic modes it continues the shape of the POOK 7/9 pattern of notes.

Each of the diatonic modes etudes is notated with the use of triplets to help with acquiring the swing feel. It also helps with attaining speed while playing. After playing eighth notes (two-notes groups), the next step to playing faster should be to play triplets (three-note groups), then sixteenth notes (four-note groups).

This POOK 7/9 pattern starts on C the root of the chord. It then continues to ascend in thirds to its third (E♭), then to the fifth (G♭), to the minor seventh (B♭),

and finally to the ninth (D♭), which completes the minor nine chord. The etude then descends scalewise to its root (C) and continues to ascend in retrograde (backwards) to the ninth (D♭). It completes the first line of the etude by descending to its final tone (E♭), the flatted third of the chord.

ACTIVE AND INACTIVE TONES OF THE LOCRIAN MODE

Playing and learning chordal and modal lines through chord changes is a prerequisite for improvising. This skill is expected by most educators and is a requirement for playing all the jazz materials now available as melodies, patterns, and transcribed solos.

The C locrian mode contains the same notes as the D♭ major scale, but begins on its seventh degree. Perceived another way, the locrian mode uses the same key signature as any major scale major seventh below, or a half step below the tonic. Therefore, the locrian mode built from the note C would have the same signature as the major scale a seventh below: the key of D♭ containing five flats (B♭, E♭, A♭, D♭, G♭). Harmonically, the locrian mode makes use of the diatonic seventh chord built on the seventh degree of the major scale which is a minor seventh flat five chord.

By duplicating the way the active and inactive tones of the V7 or dominant chord of all keys resolve, we arrive at the clue to the resolution of all modal steps. By relating the direction of resolution of each tone of the dominant moving to the tones of each mode, the direction or proper resolution for each modal tone is realized.

Even though the placement of half steps and whole steps change with each mode, the scale degrees of each mode should resolve in the same direction as when using the dominant chord mode melodically. The note G♭ as the fifth (V) should resolve to (I) (C) the root (V to I) (as *sol* resolves to *do*). The note B♭ as the seventh (vii) should also resolve up to I (C) (as *ti* resolves to *do*) (vii to I). The note F as the fourth (IV) should resolve to (iii E♭) (as *fa* resolves to *mi*) (iv to iii). The note A♭ as the sixth (VI) should resolve to V (G♭) (as *la* resolves to *sol*) (VI to V). The note D♭ as the second (ii) should resolve to I (C) (as *re* resolves to *do*) (II to I).

As stated earlier the locrian mode sounds best when played over the harmony of a minor seventh flat five chord used as the vii min7♭5 chord of the key. The color tones of the locrian mode are the second, third, sixth, and seventh degrees. Melodically, it is better, when improvising, to use the tonic note of the mode at the ending rather than beginning with it. The fifth degree is one of the best notes to precede the modal tonic when starting a solo because it sets up the sound of the mode as heard by the listener.

The following is a list of standard, popular, and jazz tunes that contain the locrian mode completely or in part. Although it is important to learn the locrian mode in all keys or dialects, it is imperative for today's novice composer or improviser to become familiar with the jazz literature that make use of the locrian mode. If the student learns, analyses, and memorizes these melodies, improvising on tunes that contain the locrian mode will be easier.

LOCRIAN MODAL & STANDARD JAZZ TUNES TO BE LEARNED

"African Flower" - Duke Ellington

"Crescent" - John Coltrane

"Eiderdown" - Steve Swallow

"Gentle Rain" - Louis Bonfi

"Groovitis" - Jamey Aebersold

"I Found a New Baby" - Palmer/Williams

"In Your Own Sweet Way" - Dave Brubeck

"Inner Urge" - Joe Henderson

"Ko Ko" - Duke Ellington

"Lament" - J.J. Johnson

"Minority" - Gigi Gryce

"Napanoch" - David Liebman

"Stampede" - Fletcher Henderson

"Sugar" - Stanley Turrentine

"Taxi War Dance" - Lester Young/Count Basle

"Tones for Jones Bones" - Chick Corea

"Whisper Not" - Benny Golson

As can be seen by the length of the above partial list of jazz literature which contain the locrian mode in many melodic shapes, a jazz player acquires an abundance of jazz language and style while learning melodies. These tunes, as melodic information stored in the mind's ear, then become part of the total melodic recall to be played in bits or at length when improvising. All great jazz players have hundreds and maybe thousands of jazz tunes at their fingertips that can be used to put together as a puzzle in thousands of different ways over endless chord changes. This process occurs automatically as the improvisor reacts to many new tunes and many new sets of chord changes.

The novice player should begin to memorize as many different jazz tunes as possible to expand improvisational fluency and acquire jazz language which should be a continuing process. Memorize some of the jazz literature and play the tunes in many different keys.

LOCRIAN MODE / VII HALF DIM 7TH: TREBLE CLEF

LOCRIAN MODE / VII HALF DIM 7TH: BASS CLEF

CHAPTER 21

THE BYZANTINE SCALE

Now that all the articles concerning the seven diatonic modes are completed I would like to introduce everyone to my wonderful wife Laura. She has been my right arm and co-author during all the writings of articles since my column has appeared in this magazine. I've been trying to give her the credit she deserves for being my co-writer, but she has been content with having editing credits mentioned at the end of each article. I have finally convinced her to change her mind. Soooooooooooooooooooo, Here !!!!! We!!!!! Are!!!!!!

The etudes for this study are written for treble and bass clef instruments. As in all previous articles, this study is written combining the Byzantine scale with the harmony of a dominant seventh chord as a single sound. After practicing the sound it will begin to be ingrained in the mind's ear for recall during a solo. This etude moves in the cycle of fifths progression and as in all the previous etudes for the diatonic modes and continues the shape of the pook 7/9 pattern of notes.

Music of the Western world, which includes all music that has its origin in Europe, differs markedly from music of the Near East, Middle East, and Far East. Western music developed harmonically, and the beginning of Eastern music developed melodically and rhythmically. Eastern scales usually employed pitches not in tune with the chromatic scale, which forms the basis of Western music. The twelve tones within an octave in

Western music is divided into semitones, but the octave in the music of the Orient is divided into quarter tones and other smaller divisions called microtones. Other Oriental music makes use of the five-tone pentatonic scale which is characteristic of primitive music.

Music of the Orient, which includes China, India, Java, Persia, and Iran, not only differs from that of Europe, but varies amongst each other. Music that has been heard in the past from composers such as Tchaikovsky, Puccini, Verdi, etc., may sound Oriental, but should be considered pseudo Oriental—a Western notion of Oriental music, a far cry from the actual music heard by the residents of the Near or Far East.

Early Byzantine music was based on the music of antiquity (1000-605 B.C.) through the music of the Hebrews and music from Assyria, Mesopotamia, Sumaria, Babylonia, and combinations of Oriental sources. Byzantine music was mostly secular until 300 A.D. and was opposed and suppressed by the Orthodox church, disappearing from the records, leaving church music as the music of the court when Constantinople became the seat and symbol of the Byzantine empire (330 A.D.).

In Eli Seigmeister's book *Harmony and Melody, Vol. I The Diatonic Style* he states, "In the chants of Jewish, Hindu, Moslem rituals and in the vast body of folk music created over many centuries melody is the prime mover." "The music of the world's peoples includes a vast number of different modes, each characterized by a different sequence of steps of various kinds. The diversity of scale structures is especially great in the Orient, where the Hindus alone are said to use 70 different modes in their daily music making."

Melodies heard today come from varying the succession of musical pitches known as the scale. Each musical pitch that comprises a scale is termed a degree of that scale. The most common scales used when composing music are the major scale and the three minor scales: the harmonic minor, the melodic minor, and the natural minor. These three minor scales may be used melodically when composing or improvising and provide an abundance of material for melodic ideas within a given harmonic background. Scales in music are man-made and not found in nature, but have been handed or passed down through the centuries either vocally or later on by some type of notation. In *The Nature of Music*, Julius Klauser defines a scale as "a record of tones in use during a certain period of history."

A scale is made up of a group of selected tones arranged in an order of ascending and descending pitches. Many different scales have evolved in different time periods as well as different regions and countries as part of the tradition of folk music.

Early folk music is a vocal expression of people's feelings, character, and interests. Folk music began without the benefit of musical training. As the human race grew vocally from the savage yells, grunts, primitive fragments of time and rhythm the history of music started to take shape. Because there was no notation music was handed down from one generation to another.

THE HARMONIC MINOR SCALE:
Source for Understanding the Construction of the Byzantine Scale

The melodic sound of the harmonic minor scale surrounds us and is heard many times through the various media: radio, television, records, tapes, CDs, films, played by orchestras, concert, marching, jazz, rock, and country bands. In his book, *Harmony Structure and Style*, published by McGraw-Hill Book Co., Inc., 1962, Leonard G. Ratner states, "To Western ears, the major scale is one of the most familiar and convincing musical statements that can be made. This pattern, which we know so well and which we take so much for granted, has values and relationships within it that have tremendous significance for the harmonic procedures of centuries of Western music." "Although the minor mode, by virtue of its borrowed leading tone, has virtually the same structural strength as the major mode, its particular appeal lies in its rich palette of colors." The influence of the major scale has made "the harmonic minor mode a virtual partner in the key-centered harmonic system of Western music."

Harvard Dictionary of Music
Willi Apel, Harvard University Press, 1974
History of Music:

"Nothing certain is known about the music of earliest man, but there is no reason to doubt that some kind of music was practiced even by Stone Age peoples. Some ancient peoples, especially those of Egypt, China, and Mesopotamia, have a musical tradition that can be traced back about three thousand years before the birth of Jesus. No music from these remote times has been preserved, but numerous archaeological findings and pictorial representations of instruments from different periods give evidence of musical activity and development long before the beginning of Western music. Somewhat later, other civilizations e.g., those of Japan and India, developed.

Western music, on the other hand, began at a much later time and, aside from scattered archaeological data, its history is recorded essentially in musical documents supplemented by theoretical writings. Moreover, it is a history that can be continuously traced from c. A.D. 800 to the present. In tracing the history of scales one discovers that constant repetitive simple melodies created by primitive and many folk cultures were in use long before scales came into being."

"The construction of Greek scales developed from the invention by Pythagorus (550 B.C.) of the Pythagorean scale which produces all scale tones by the interval of a fifth. These diatonic tones are obtained by using the circle of fifths. An example of the circle of ascending fifths: C, G, D, A, E, B, F♯ (G♭), D♭, A♭, E♭, B♭, F. By taking five ascending fifths C, G, D, A, E, B and one descending fifth F and rearranging them in stepwise ascending order it produces a major scale. Example: C, D, E, F, G, A, B.

The Byzantine scale, unlike the Byzantine chant used in religious music, evolved from Greek and Persian music and was used in early Greek folk songs."

Harvard Dictionary of Music
Willi Apel
Harvard University Press, 1974.

"Byzantine chant:

The ecclesiastical chant of the Byzantine Empire (founded A.D. 330 by Constantine the Great; destroyed 1453, with the fall of Constantinople). With the exception of a few ceremonial songs, the acclamations, no music other than liturgical chants has been preserved. Although the language of the Byzantine Church was Greek, it has become more and more apparent that Byzantine music was not a continuation of ancient Greek music (as long was assumed) but constituted a new tradition based to some extent on Oriental (Jewish, Syrian) models.

Oriental scales were common in early Greek folk songs and Byzantine music. The Byzantine scale came out of the early Greek chromatic or mixed scales which were really modal or minor scales with added accidentals, which created augmented second intervals. Any scale that contained the augmented second was in ancient meanings called a chromatic interval, thus the name given 'chromatic or mixed scales.' In the folk music of many Oriental peoples there are scales with two such tetrachords which use the augmented second."

GREEK TETRACHORDS

The Greeks first used the tetrachord as a basis for constructing their folk music. The tetrachords were constructed downward. The two outer notes measured an interval of a perfect fourth (D to A).

Notes of various intervals were placed between the two notes. One of their chromatic tetrachords descending was D, C♯, B♭, A. The Byzantine culture reversed the order of this chromatic tetrachord and used it as the upper tetrachord. B♭ and C♯ were placed between A and D to produce A, B♭, C♯, D which is the upper tetrachord of the D harmonic minor scale.

Another similarly constructed tetrachord was added for the lower tetrachord using D and G for the outer notes. The tetrachord was completed by placing the notes E♭ and F♯ between D and G, making the lower tetrachord D, E♭, F♯, and G. When the lower and upper tetrachords are combined they form the complete Byzantine scale: D, E♭, F♯, G, A, B♭, C♯, D.

The two most common Byzantine scales were:

1. D, E♭, F♯, G, A, B♭, C♯, D (Byzantine scale)
   I, II, III, IV, V, VI, VII, I (scale degrees)

2. D, E, F, G♯, A, B♭, C♯, D
   (D Harmonic minor scale with ♯IV)
   I, II, III, IV, V, VI, VII, I (scale degrees)

Scale #1 is the most typical oriental scale and was used in early Greek and early Byzantine folk music. Scale #2 is a D minor harmonic scale with a raised fourth degree which was used for Byzantine melodies that had a smaller or more limited vocal range.

There are many scales from many cultures near Greece that influenced each other. The early Chinese music (3000 B.C.) and the early Egyptian music (4000 B.C.) made use of the pentatonic scale. The early Greeks (700 B.C.) also used the pentatonic scale for the kithara, a five string harp-like instrument.

The kithara used an inversion of the G pentatonic scale for a basis of its tuning: E, G, A, B, D, E which is a forerunner of our present day guitar that uses the same six notes derived from the pentatonic scale starting on E but tuned in ascending fourths: E, A, D, G, to B (a third away) then to E (up a fourth), as shown in Figure 1.

First three strings of the guitar

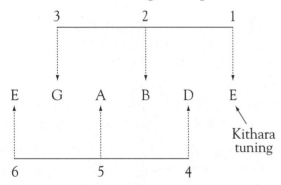

Last three strings of the guitar

Figure 1

Many other cultures throughout history from the near and far East made use of scales that resembled the Byzantine scale. I've listed references to eight such scales in the following text.

1. A pre-Byzantine Jewish scale (400 B.C.) which was used in Hebrew chanting in penitential prayers was called Ahaba-Rabba Mode: E, F, G♯, A, B, C, D, E which is like the beginning of an E Byzantine scale but has a flatted seventh (D♮). It is believed that this chant was adopted in various forms by the Greeks, Armenians, and Byzantines according to the principles of each culture. Many Greek and Gypsy Bulgars and Jewish Frailachs make use of this scale in their melodies and can be found in The Kammen International Dance Folios, arranged by Jack Kammen and William Sher, compiled by Joseph Kammen. Folio #1, c. 1924, Folio #9, c. 1934.

2. The Persian "Chahargh" scale (400 B.C. to 200 A.D.) is similar to the Byzantine scale but has an addition of a flatted fifth degree: C, D♭, E, F, G♭, A♭, B, C.

3. Two scales from the classical system of Hindu scales (200 B.C. to 200 A.D.) are the MA-grama and the SA-grama. The MA-grama scale may be compared to the Western C lydian scale: C, D, E, F♯, G, A, B♭, C, and the SA-grama is like the Western C major scale: C, D, E, F, G, A, B, C.

4. Another scale from the classical period that was considered important in southern India was called the SA-grama altered. This scale is exactly like the C Byzantine scale: C, D♭, E, F, G, A♭, B, C. In 300 A.D. the Spanish scale appeared which was similar to the Jewish scale and the Western F Harmonic minor scale but starting on its fifth degree: C, D♭, E, F, G, A♭, B♭, C.

5. In 328 A.D. the Byzantine scale was used for chants in the music of Byzantine culture which rejected the Greek modal music.

6. The Japanese (300 A.D.) used many different pentatonic scales as a basis for their folk melodies which many times started on the fifth degree of the scale. One of the pentatonic Japanese scales was an inversion of the "semitonal pentatonic" which had a flatted third and a flatted sixth in its construction. This scale was also called the minor pentatonic scale.

Example:

F, G, A♭, C, D♭, F: semitonal pentatonic (minor)

C, D♭, F, G, A♭, C: inversion of semitonal pentatonic

The inversion of the F semitonal pentatonic scale is like the C Byzantine scale with the third (E) and seventh (B) degrees omitted.

7. The scales used by the Gypsies were of many different origins because of the wandering nature of the Gypsy culture. It is unlikely that they possessed any original scales of their own. Most Gypsy music was derived from a combination of Hungarian, Persian, Turkish, Jewish, Greek, Spanish, and Indian scales. One Gypsy scale, identical to the Byzantine scale, became very popular and was used in many Gypsy melodies.

8. There are other scales similar to the Byzantine scale which will be listed but not be discussed. Each of these scales have a slight alteration in scale degrees.
   - Japanese Zokugakusempo scale (descending) C, A♭, G, F, D♭, C
   - Balinese/Indonesia/Javanese scale C, D♭, E♭, G, A♭, C
   - Hungarian Gypsy scale C, D, E♭, F♯, G, A♭, B♭, C
   - Mohammedan scale (similar to harmonic minor) C, D, E♭, F, G, A♭, B, C
   - Oriental scale C, D♭, E, F, G♭, A♭, B♭, C
   - Neapolitan minor scale C, D♭, E♭, F, G, A♭, B, C

CONSTRUCTION OF THE BYZANTINE SCALE

In order to understand the construction of the Byzantine scale the major scale and harmonic minor scales must be detailed and understood. The major scale uses two major tetrachords in its construction (A tetrachord is a group of four tones placed in scalewise succession, usually totaling the interval of a perfect fourth):

1. The lower tetrachord of the C major scale is C, D, E, F.

2. The upper tetrachord of the C major scale is G, A, B, C. The two tetrachords are separated by a whole step resulting in a C major scale.

Example:

A. Lower tetrachord C, D, E, F.

B. Upper tetrachord G, A, B, C.

C. C major scale: C, D, E, F, G, A, B, C.

The harmonic minor scale uses a minor lower tetrachord and an altered major upper tetrachord in its construction:

1. The lower tetrachord of the C harmonic minor scale uses the lower tetrachord of the C major scale (C, D, E, F) but has a flatted third (C, D, E♭, F).

2. The upper tetrachord of the C major scale (G, A, B, C) is used for the upper tetrachord of the C harmonic minor scale but used a flatted sixth (G, A♭, B, C). The two tetrachords are separated by a whole step resulting in a C harmonic minor scale.

Example:

A. Lower tetrachord C, D, E♭, F.

B. Upper tetrachord G, A♭, B, C.

C. C harmonic minor scale: C, D, E♭, F, G, A♭, B, C.

Just as the major scale is constructed using two similar (major) tetrachords, the Byzantine scale uses two similar (minor) tetrachords in its construction. The Byzantine scale (also called the double harmonic scale) uses the harmonic minor scale in its construction:

1. The upper tetrachord of an F harmonic minor scale (C, D♭, E, F) is used for the lower tetrachord of the C Byzantine scale.

2. The upper tetrachord of a C harmonic minor scale (G, A♭, B, C) is used for the upper tetrachord of the C Byzantine scale.

The two tetrachords are separated by a whole step and put together resulting in the C Byzantine scale.

Example:

A. Lower tetrachord C, D♭, E, F.

B. Upper tetrachord G, A♭, B, C.

C. Byzantine scale: C, D♭, E, F, G, A♭, B, C.

Another way of conceiving or composing a Byzantine scale is by interlocking two major seventh chords as illustrated in Figure 2.

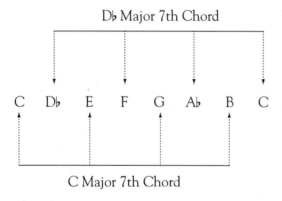

Figure 2

For example: a C Maj7 chord spelled C, E, G, B, and a D♭ Maj7 chord spelled D♭, F, A♭, C when interlocked or dovetailed and written in alternating pitches is spelled as shown in Figure 2.

Because of this interlocking, the Byzantine scale requires a knowledge and an understanding of the construction of major seventh chords. When completed the C Byzantine scale is C, D♭, E, F, G, A♭, B, C and can be played over a C major 7th chord, a D♭ major 7th chord, a C7 chord or a D♭7 chord.

The Byzantine scale is another of the numerous scales which may be used to compose or improvise melodies over dominant seventh chords.

The following is a list of the twelve Byzantine scales and their respective dominant seventh chords in ascending form. The descending scale uses the identical notes:

- C Byzantine scale:
  C, D♭, E, F, G, A♭, B, C uses the C7 chord.
- F Byzantine scale:
  F, G♭, A, B♭, C, D♭, E, F uses the F7 chord.
- B♭ Byzantine scale:
  B♭, C♭, D, E♭, F, G♭, A, B♭ uses the B♭7 chord.
- E♭ Byzantine scale:
  E♭, F♭, G, A♭, B♭, C♭, D, E♭ uses the E♭7 chord.
- A♭ Byzantine scale:
  A♭, B♭♭, C, D♭, E♭, F♭, G, A♭ uses the A♭7 chord.
- D♭ Byzantine scale:
  D♭, E♭♭, F, G♭, A♭, B♭♭, C, D♭ uses the D♭7 chord.
- F♯ Byzantine scale:
  F♯, G, A♯, B, C♯, D, E♯, F♯ uses the F♯7 chord.
- B Byzantine scale:
  B, C, D♯, E, F♯, G, A♯, B uses the B7 chord.
- E Byzantine scale:
  E, F, G♯, A, B, C, D♯, E uses the E7 chord.
- A Byzantine scale:
  A, B♭, C♯, D, E, F, G♯, A uses the A7 chord.
- D Byzantine scale:
  D, E♭, F♯, G, A, B♭, C♯, D uses the D7 chord.
- G Byzantine scale:
  G, A♭, B, C, D, E♭, F♯, G uses the G7 chord.

Note: All of the above Byzantine scales may be used over a dominant seventh chord that is a half step above the chord noted. Example: C7 or D♭7 may be used for the C Byzantine scale.

The Byzantine scale may also be used over major triads. The following is a list of the twelve Byzantine scales and their respective major triads in ascending form. The descending scale uses the identical notes:

- C Byzantine scale:
  C, D♭, E, F, G, A♭, B, C uses the C triad.

- F Byzantine scale:
  F, G♭, A, B♭, C, D♭, E, F uses the F triad.

- B♭ Byzantine scale:
  B♭, C♭, D, E♭, F, G♭, A, B♭ uses the B♭ triad.

- E♭ Byzantine scale:
  E♭, F♭, G, A♭, B♭, C♭, D, E♭ uses the E♭ triad.

- A♭ Byzantine scale:
  A♭, B♭♭, C, D♭, E♭, F♭, G, A♭ uses the A♭ triad.

- D♭ Byzantine scale:
  D♭, E♭♭, F, G♭, A♭, B♭♭, C, D♭ uses the D♭ triad.

- F♯ Byzantine scale:
  F♯, G, A♯, B, C♯, D, E♯, F♯ uses the F♯ triad.

- B Byzantine scale:
  B, C, D♯, E, F♯, G, A♯, B uses the B triad.

- E Byzantine scale:
  E, F, G♯, A, B, C, D♯, E uses the E triad.

- A Byzantine scale:
  A, B♭, C♯, D, E, F, G♯, A uses the A triad.

- D Byzantine scale:
  D, E♭, F♯, G, A, B♭, C♯, D uses the D triad.

- G Byzantine scale:
  G, A♭, B, C, D, E♭, F♯, G uses the G triad.

All the tones of the Byzantine scale are active when used melodically. When used harmonically, the first, third, and fifth degrees form a major triad. The second, fourth and sixth degrees also form a major triad. Therefore, these tones, when sounded as chords, can also be considered non active tones.

Diatonic chords produced from the C Byzantine scale include:

- The chord on the first degree is a major seventh. (CMaj7)

- The chord on the second degree is a major seventh. (D♭Maj7)

- The chord on the third degree is a minor seventh. (Emin7)

- The chord on the fourth degree is a minor triad with a major seventh. (Fm♯7)

- The chord on the fifth degree is a dominant seventh with a flatted fifth. (G7♭5)

- The chord on the sixth degree is a major seventh with a raised fifth. (A♭Maj7+5)

- The chord on the seventh degree is a diminished seventh. (Bdim7)

Songs which use the Byzantine scale include:

1. The melody of "Miserlou" c. 1941, title and music by N. Roubanis, English words by Fred Wise, Milton Leeds, S.K. Russell, Spanish Words by J. Pina is a perfect example of the use of the Byzantine scale.

2. "Temptation," c. 1933, words by Arthur Freed, music by Nacio Herb Brown.

3. "Caravan," c. 1937, words by Irving Mills, music by Duke Ellington and Juan Tizol.

4. "Hungarian Rhapsody."

5. "The Girl Friend of The Whirling Dervish," c. 1938, words by Al Dubin and Johnny Mercer, Music by Harry Warren.

6. "Hajji Baba," from the movie *Hajji Baba*, c. 1954, words by Ned Washington, music by Dimitri Tiomkin.

7. "Amar Y Vivir," c. 1944 by C. Velazquez.

8. "Anatevka," c. 1964 by Allied Music Corp., Inc., words by Sheldon Harnick, music by Jerry Bock. Other songs from the Broadway show *Fiddler on the Roof* have a similar Middle Eastern flavor.

9. "Malaquena (At The Crossroads)" c. 1929, by Ernesto Lecuona.

10. "Carioca," c. 1933, words by Gus Kahn and Edward Eliscu, music by Vincent Youmans.

11. *Strange Enchantment* c. 1939, by Hollander.

12. "My Heart Belongs To Daddy," c. 1938, Cole Porter.

13. "March Slav," by Peter Ilich Tchaikovsky.

14. "Nardis," c. 1958, by Miles Davis. This melody was composed using the E Byzantine scale. In his *Kind of Blue* album, 1959, Miles Davis plays an improvisation using a partial of the Byzantine scale on the song "Flamenco Sketches." Cannonball Adderley's improvisation later in the same song uses the complete Byzantine scale throughout the solo.

As stated earlier, the C Byzantine scale sounds best when played over the harmony of a C or a D♭ dominant seventh chord used as the ♭7 of the key. The following list of standard, popular, and jazz tunes that contain the Harmonic minor scale completely or in part has been included because the harmonic minor scale is so closely related to the Byzantine scale. Although it is important to learn the Harmonic minor scale in all keys or dialects, it is imperative for today's novice composer or improviser to become familiar with the jazz literature that makes use of the Harmonic minor scale. The Byzantine scale can be used as an alternative choice while improvising on tunes with minor progressions. If the student learns, analyses, and memorizes these minor melodies, improvising on tunes that contain the harmonic minor scale will become easier.

The following is a list of standard jazz tunes to be learned that use the sound of the harmonic minor scale melodically:

"Airegin" - Sonny Rollins

"Bikini" - Dexter Gordon

"Blue Serge" - Duke Ellington

"East St. Louis Toodle-oo" - Duke Ellington

"In a Sentimental Mood" - Duke Ellington

"Lament" - J.J.Johnson

"Besame Mucho" - C. Velazguez

"My Funny Valentine" - Richard Rodgers/Lorenz Hart

"Nica's Dream" - Horace Silver

"Shutterbug" - J.J.Johnson

"Sky Dive" - Freddie Hubbard

"Solar" - Miles Davis

"Somebody Loves Me" - MacDonald/Gershwin/DeSylva

"Summertime" - George Gershwin

"Yesterdays" - Jerome Kern

As can be seen by the length of the above partial list of jazz literature which contain the harmonic minor scale in many melodic shapes, a jazz player acquires an abundance of jazz language and style while learning melodies. These tunes, as melodic information stored in the mind's ear, then become part of the total melodic recall to be played in bits or at length when improvising. All great jazz players have hundreds and maybe thousands of jazz tunes at their fingertips that can be used to put together as a puzzle in thousands of different ways over endless chord changes. This process occurs automatically as the improvisor reacts to many new tunes and many new sets of chord changes. The novice player should begin to memorize as many different jazz tunes as possible to expand improvisational fluency and acquire jazz vocabulary and language which should be a continuing process. After memorizing some of the jazz literature listed above, the student should then practice the tunes in as many different keys as possible to expand the student's jazz language even further.

POOK 7/9 BYZANTINE SCALE: TREBLE CLEF

POOK 7/9 BYZANTINE SCALE: BASS CLEF

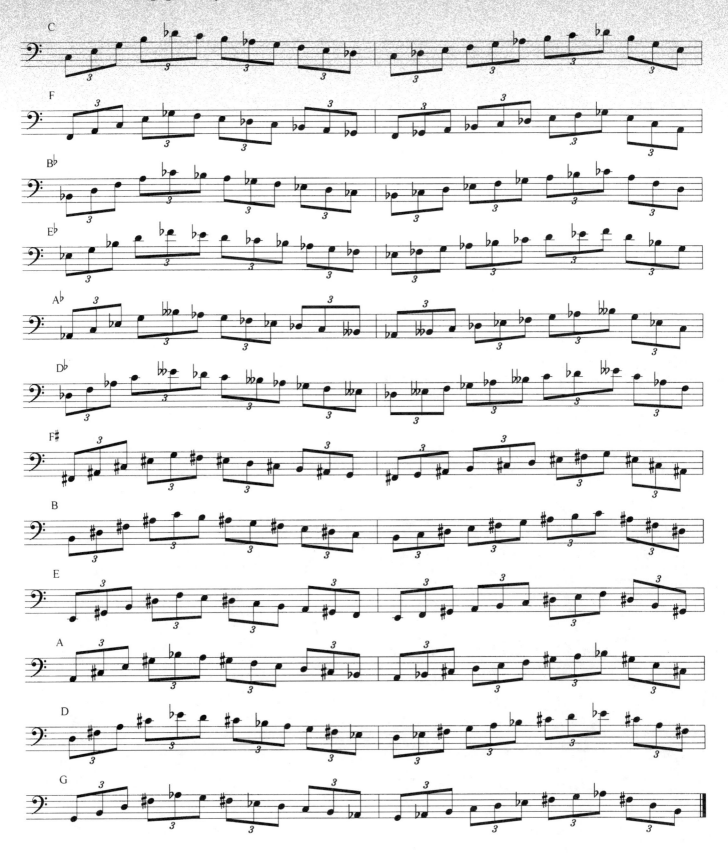

CHAPTER 22

THE AUGMENTED ELEVENTH SCALE

The progressive sound of the augmented eleventh scale surrounds us and is heard many times through the various media: radio, television, records, tapes, CDs, films. Just as a C mixolydian mode (C, D, E, F, G, A, Bb, C) creates a linear sound for the C7 chord (C, E, G, Bb), we find that a melodic minor ascending scale starting from the fifth (G of the C7 chord) (G, A, Bb, C, D, E, F#, G) named the augmented eleventh scale, provides a linear sound for the upper partials of the C7 chord derived from the overtone series.

The etudes for this study are written for treble and bass clef instruments. As in all previous articles, this study is written combining the augmented eleventh scale with the harmony of a dominant ninth chord as a single sound. After practicing this sound it will begin to be ingrained in the mind's ear for recall during a solo. This etude also moves in the cycle of fifths progression and continues the shape of the POOK 7/9 pattern of notes. In fact the sound of the overtones built on the fundamental C produces a dominant thirteenth chord with an added augmented eleventh.

Example:

C, E, G, Bb, D, F#, A which is a C13+11 chord.

The Augmented 11th Scale POOK 7/9 exercise begins with the C augmented eleventh scale using the C7 chord and proceeds through the remaining eleven augmented eleventh scales and their corresponding dominant 9th chords. In order to understand the augmented eleventh scale, we must first take a look at the overtone series.

OVERTONES: UPPER PARTIALS & HARMONICS

The harmonic, partial, or overtone series is a sequence of notes produced when any tone or chord is played, which are audible in accordance with a universal principle of nature, as fundamental to music as gravity is to motion. Fifths (V) fall to tonics (I), just as physical objects fall to the earth. For example, if C is played, the ear actually hears not only the C but the series of overtones C, E, G, Bb, thus, the first six overtones produce a dominant 7th chord. The remaining overtones from the seventh to the fifteenth partial are actually sounding a highly altered dominant seventh chord from which the augmented eleventh scale originates.

Inclusion of overtones beyond the first six intensify the gravitational pull toward resolution, especially as the diminished fifth, augmented fifth, the ninth and the augmented eleventh occur. Notice, that due to tempered tuning, the diminished fifth and augmented eleventh are synonymous.

THE OVERTONE SERIES FROM THE FUNDAMENTAL TONE

Overtones:

|F | F | C | F | A | C | E♭ | F | G | A | B | C | D | E♭ | E | F

Partials:

| 1 | 2 | 3 | 4 | 5 | 6 | 7 | 8 | 9 | 10 | 11 | 12 | 13 | 14 | 15 | 16

The overtone series from the fundamental tone F can be seen as the origin of the theoretical information as follows:

- F triad = F, A, C
- F seventh chord = F, A, C, E♭
- F ninth chord = F, A, C, E♭, G
- F thirteenth + augmented eleventh chord = F, A, C, E♭, G, B, D
- C minor sixth chord = C, E♭, G, A
- A half-diminished or A minor seventh flat five = A, C, E♭, G
- Lower tetrachord from the F whole tone scale = F, G, A, B
- C melodic minor scale ascending = C, D, E♭, F, G, A, B, C
- F overtone scale = F, G, A, B, C, D, E♭, F
- G major lower tetrachord = G, A, B, C
- G seventh chord = G, B, D, F
- G mixolydian mode = G, A, B, C, D, E, F, G
- G ninth chord = G, B, D, F, A
- G thirteenth chord= G, B, D, F, A, C, E
- A minor tetrachord = A, B, C, D
- B half diminished seventh chord = B, D, F, A
- C pentatonic blues scale = C, D, E♭, E, G, A, C
- One third of the chromatic scale from D = D, D♯, E, F
- Two tritones = F to B and A to E♭

Each new fundamental tone produces a new set of theoretical information.

Alexander Scriabin's famous "Mystic Chord" that was used in his *Prometheus Symphony Opus* 60, of 1910 and the seventh *Piano Sonata, Opus* 64 contained tones taken from partials of the overtone series. The Mystic Chord was built in intervals of fourths instead of thirds (C, F♯, B♭, E, A, D). Scriabin's chord has the sound of a dominant seventh containing the augmented eleventh and the thirteenth and was created to reject tonality.

In contrast to Scriabin's original intention the Mystic Chord veritably demands a resolution to tonality just as the overtone series of any fundamental demands a resolution to a tone a fifth below. Most of Scriabin's music made use of chords of the eleventh and thirteenth. Many jazz players listen to his music to gain knowledge of the sounds of the eleventh and thirteenth chords.

While famous jazz alto saxophonist Charlie Parker (b.1920, d.1955) was playing at a jam session, he became bored with the standard chord changes being used. The song being played was Ray Noble's standard "Cherokee." While he was improvising, in his mind's ear he could hear other sounds based on the upper partials of dominant chords. Instead of playing on the roots, thirds, fifths, and sevenths he decided to play melodies using the upper partials of the overtones that were heard in his mind's ear. He began to explore, compose, and improvise new melodies using these very upper partials. In this way he began playing on top of the chord changes instead of inside the changes. This style of playing was new to jazz and became the beginning of bebop. Charlie Parker was inspired to experiment with the upper partials after listening to many great modern composers such as Paul Hindemith, Maurice Ravel, Claude Debussy, Arnold Schoenberg, Bela Bartok, Edgard Varese, Alban Berg, and Igor Stravinsky.

After bebop gave way to hardbop, and then to funk, many musicians used the sound of the augmented

THE AUGMENTED ELEVENTH SCALE

eleventh melodically in their compositions. One such musician/composer was Horace Silver who wrote many songs, among them "Barbara," "Summer in Central Park," "Ecaroh," "Strollin'," "Nica's Dream" and "Mayreh." Another famous jazz musician who used the sound of the augmented eleventh scale extensively in his improvisations over hundreds of standard tunes in the 1960s was John Coltrane. One of today's contemporary jazz musicians, Michael Brecker, continues to use this progressive sound in his music.

THE AUGMENTED ELEVENTH SCALE

The overtone series from the fundamental tone F produces the following tones: F, A, C, Eb, F, G, A, B, C, D, Eb, E, F. This is also known as "Nature's Chord." If we construct a scale using no repeated notes from the overtone series we arrive at a scale with eight tones: F, G, A, B, C, D, Eb, E. By using the first seven tones, including the octave we arrive at what is called the overtone scale: F, G, A, B, C, D, Eb, F. The overtone series, when observed as a highly altered dominant seventh chord, is the basis of the augmented eleventh scale. If we begin a scale from the fifth (C) of the fundamental F the resulting scale is a melodic minor ascending scale: C, D, Eb, F, G, A, B, C. This scale is called the C augmented eleventh scale.

One of the main problems that confront today's musician is the use of confusing nomenclature by music educators, composers, and arrangers in explaining theories of chords, scales, and modes in music. This confusion is perpetuated by students and musicians. The simplest way of naming scales is to use the name of the chord from which it originates. Therefore the augmented eleventh scale is named according to the augmented eleventh chord from which it is derived. The augmented eleventh scale should not be confused with the augmented scale which is comprised of two augmented chords one half step apart. The B augmented chord: B, D#, F# and the C augmented chord: C, E, G# creates the

B augmented scale: B, C, D#, E, G, Ab.

OTHER NAMES GIVEN TO THE AUGMENTED ELEVENTH SCALE

1. Lydian Augmented: The third diatonic mode of the C melodic minor ascending scale starting from the third degree of the scale (Eb, F, G, A, B, C, D, Eb).

2. Lydian Flat Seven: A fourth diatonic mode of the C melodic minor ascending scale starting on the fourth degree of the scale (F, G, A, B, C, D, Eb, F). Some educators say that the Lydian Flat Seven is an altered modal scale starting on the root of the F13+11 chord.

3. Lydian Dominant: (Same as Lydian flat seven)

4. Lydian Mixolydian Scale: (Same as Lydian flat seven)

5. Overtone Scale: (Same as Lydian flat seven)

6. Locrian #2: The sixth diatonic mode of the C Melodic Minor ascending scale (A, B, C, D, Eb, F, G, A).

7. Jazz Minor Scale (sometimes called the jazz melodic minor scale): This scale is used in songs in a minor key or minor blues when the chord changes go to the iv7 chord. This scale is the melodic minor scale ascending starting on the root.

8. Diminished Whole Tone: same as the jazz minor scale.

THE SEVEN AUGMENTED ELEVENTH MODES AND THEIR RESPECTIVE CHORDS
(using the C augmented eleventh scale)

- The First mode contains the notes: C, D, Eb, F, G, A, B, C. The diatonic seventh chord used harmonically is the Cmi (maj7).

- The Second mode contains the notes: D, Eb, F, G, A, B, C, D. The diatonic seventh chord used harmonically is the Dmi7.

- The Third mode contains the notes: Eb, F, G, A,

B, C, D, E♭. The diatonic seventh chord used harmonically is the E♭maj7+5.

- The Fourth mode contains the notes: F, G, A, B, C, D, E♭, F. The diatonic seventh chord used harmonically is the F7.

- The Fifth mode contains the notes: G, A, B, C, D, E♭, F, G. The diatonic seventh chord used harmonically is the G7 or G dominant seventh.

- The Sixth mode contains the notes: A, B, C, D, E♭, F, G, A♭. The diatonic seventh chord used harmonically is Ami7♭5.

- The Seventh mode contains the notes: B, C, D, E♭, F, G, A, B. The diatonic seventh chord used harmonically is the Bmi7♭5.

By making use of the way the active tones of the augmented eleventh scale degrees move and relating the direction each one of these tones resolve to each modal degree of the key, the proper resolution for each modal tone is realized.

The C augmented eleventh scale sounds best when played over the harmony of the V7 (C7) or V13+11 (C13+11) chord. The color tones of the augmented eleventh scale are the second (D), third (E♭), sixth (A), and seventh (B) degrees. Melodically, it is better, when improvising, to use the tonic note (C) of the mode at the ending rather than beginning with it. The fifth degree (G) is one of the best notes to precede the tonic when starting a solo because it sets up the sound of the augmented eleventh scale as heard by the listener.

DETAILS OF
THE AUGMENTED ELEVENTH SCALE

The augmented eleventh scale is comprised of two four-note groups of notes called tetrachords. It has a lower minor tetrachord beginning on the tonic minor note followed by an upper major tetrachord a whole step away from the lower tetrachord. The augmented eleventh scale ordinarily consists of scale degrees of two sizes, half steps and whole steps, and occur as: whole step, half step, whole step, whole step, whole step, whole step, and half step.

The augmented eleventh scale consists of eight consecutive notes written on the staff ascending and descending, using the same notes, and then ending on the tonic note. When constructing the augmented eleventh scale, half steps occur between the second and third scale degrees and also between the seventh and eighth scale degrees. All other degrees of the scale are separated by whole steps. Scale degrees are usually numbered using Arabic or Roman numerals and letters to correspond to a specific key.

THE ASCENDING AND DESCENDING SCALE DEGREES FOR ALL AUGMENTED ELEVENTH SCALES AND THEIR RESPECTIVE CHORDS

1 2 3 4 5 6 7 1

I II III IV V VI VII I

- Aug 11th scale used for C9 chord: C D E F♯ G A B♭ C

- Aug 11th scale used for F9 chord: F G A B C D E♭ F

- Aug 11th scale used for B♭9 chord: B♭ C D E F G A♭ B♭

- Aug 11th scale used for E♭9 chord: E♭ F G A B♭ C D♭ E♭

- Aug 11th scale used for A♭9 chord: A♭ B♭ C D E♭ F G♭ A♭

- Aug 11th scale used for D♭9 chord: D♭ E♭ F G A♭ B♭ C♭ D♭

- Aug 11th scale used for G♭9 chord: G♭ A♭ B♭ C D♭ E♭ F♭ G♭

- Aug 11th scale used for B9 chord: B C♯ D♯ E♯ F♯ G♯ A B

- Aug 11th scale used for E9 chord: E F♯ G♯ A♯ B C♯ D E

- Aug 11th scale used for A9 chord: A B C♯ D♯ E F♯ G A

- Aug 11th scale used for D9 chord: D E F♯ G♯ A B C D

- Aug 11th scale used for G9 chord: G A B C♯ D E F G

As stated earlier, the C augmented eleventh scale sounds best when played over the harmony of a C dominant seventh chord (C7) or dominant thirteenth sharp eleventh chord (C13+11). For a more "outside" sound, the G♭ augmented eleventh scale starting from C (the flatted fifth substitute of the C augmented eleventh scale) can be played over the C7 chord. This "outside" sound is called the altered scale (C, D♭, E♭, F♭, G♭, A♭, B♭, C).

FLATTED FIFTH SUBSTITUTES IN JAZZ

The progressive jazz players of the late 1940s and 1950s such as Charlie Parker, Dizzy Gillespie, and the bebop school of players altered the chord changes of many of the tunes played. Along with the altered chords, they used many of these altered sounds in their melodic lines. The most common altered sound from the bebop school of music was the flatted fifth, or enharmonically the sharp fourth. Examples: C to G♭ = flatted fifth, C to F♯ = augmented fourth. Many jazz pieces of that era ended on the flatted fifth. In fact, there was a bebop greeting that gave the flatted fifth sign: a raised open hand with the other hand placed horizontally at the wrist.

In Reese Markewich's book *Inside Outside* he notes: "Ever since the birth of modern jazz the term flatted fifth has been bandied about. Musicians used to make the sign of the flatted fifth when greeting each other in humorous ritual." The flatted fifth or augmented fourth is contained in the upper partials of the overtone series, where the jazz players discovered it.

THE FLATTED FIFTH CONCEPT AND ITS TRADITIONAL HARMONIC ROOTS

Any chord of any species or quality can have for its harmonic substitute a similar type chord built a flatted fifth away from its root called the flatted fifth or tritone substitution. In other words any two similar type chords whose roots are located a tritone apart can substitute for each other.

NEAPOLITAN, FRENCH & GERMAN SIXTH

This concept can be traced to its roots in traditional harmony, where augmented sixth chords were used as a type of chromatic harmony and named: Neapolitan, French, and German sixths.

The Neapolitan or Italian sixth, introduced in the seventeenth century, was an altered ii chord of a minor key that sounded like a major triad which resolves to its tonic.

- D♭ major triad resolving to C minor triad, D♭, F, A♭ resolving down to C, E♭, G. It could also resolve to the dominant seventh chord of that minor key first and then to its tonic.

- D♭ major triad, D♭, F, Ab resolving to a G dominant triad G, B, D, then to its tonic C minor

- D♭ major triad resolving to a G dominant 7th chord, D♭, F, A♭ resolving to G, B, D, F and then to its tonic C minor.

The D♭ root of the triad is the flatted fifth of the G7 chord. The interval created between the root of the G7 chord and the root of the D♭ triad is a tritone or the flatted fifth relationship.

GERMAN SIXTH & FRENCH SIXTH

The German sixth is a complete dominant seventh chord, for instance, D♭, F, A♭, C♭ that resolves a half-step lower to a C major chord, C, E, G or from a D♭7 chord to a G7 chord and then to its tonic C major chord. Example: D♭7 to G7 to C Major

The French sixth is a dominant seventh with a flatted fifth, for instance, D♭, F, A♭♭, C♭ that resolves a half step lower to a C Major chord, C, E, G or from a D♭7♭5 chord to a G7 chord and then to its tonic. Example: D♭7♭5 to G7 to C Major

The two most important notes of a dominant seventh chord are its third and seventh, creating a tritone which demands resolution. The tritone divides an octave in half; therefore, when a tritone is inverted it becomes another tritone. The D♭7 chord contains the tritone from its third, F, to its seventh, C♭ or (B). The G7 chord contains a tritone from its third, B, to its seventh, F. The third, F, and the seventh, C♭, of the D♭7 chord when inverted become the seventh, F, and the third, B, of the G7 chord. The roots of the D♭7 chord and the G7 chord are also a tritone apart thus completing the three tritones in the flatted fifth substitution. The three tritones present in the flatted fifth substitution cause an overwhelming demand for its resolution to a chord one half-step lower from the root of the D♭7 chord (D♭) or to the root of the G7 chord (G).

Example:

The D♭7 chord containing the tritone from F to C♭ wants to resolve to a CMaj7 chord. The G7 chord containing the tritone from B to F wants to resolve to a G♭Maj7 chord. The tonics of these two keys D♭ and G are also a flatted fifth or a tritone apart. The basic Diatonic Cycle of Fifths can supply the harmonic flow during a progression. Flatted fifth chord, scale and mode substitutions are frequently inserted in this diatonic flow by composers and improvisers. Any standard, pop, rock, or jazz tune can be embellished by using flatted fifth substitutions of standard chords, modes, and scales. Interesting progressions can be accomplished with the use of the flatted fifth (tritone) substitution. Knowing how to handle any type of tune along with its many substitutions is a prerequisite for the contemporary jazz player. Any chord, mode, or scale can be substituted by a same species or different type chord, mode, or scale built a flatted fifth away from the chord, mode, or scale for which it is substituting by applying this concept.

SPECIES OF CHORDS AND THEIR FLATTED FIFTH SUBSTITUTES

- A CMaj7 would have a G♭Maj7 as its substitution.
- A C7 (dominant seventh) would have a G♭7 as its substitution.

- A Cmin7 would have a G♭min7 as its substitution.
- A C7min7♭5 would have a G♭min7♭5 as its substitution.
- A Cdim7 would have a G♭dim7 as its substitution.

MODES AND THEIR FLATTED FIFTH SUBSTITUTES

- A C Ionian Mode would have a G♭ Ionian Mode as its substitute.
- A C Dorian Mode would have a G♭ Dorian Mode as its substitute.
- A C Phrygian Mode would have a G♭ Phrygian Mode as its substitute.
- A C Lydian Mode would have a G♭ Lydian Mode as its substitute.
- A C Mixolydian Mode would have a G♭ Mixolydian Mode as its substitute.
- A C Aeolian Mode would have a G♭ Aeolian Mode as its substitute.
- A C Locrian Mode would have a G♭ Locrian Mode as its substitute. (This would include all modes in all major and minor keys and their flatted fifth substitutes.)

SCALES AND THEIR FLATTED FIFTH SUBSTITUTES

- A C Major scale would have a G♭ Major scale as its substitute.
- A C melodic minor scale would have a G♭ melodic minor as its substitute.
- A C harmonic minor scale would have a G♭ harmonic minor scale as its substitute.
- A C diminished scale would have a G♭ diminished scale as its substitute.

THE AUGMENTED ELEVENTH SCALE AND ITS FLATTED FIFTH SUBSTITUTE: THE ALTERED SCALE

The altered scale can be traced back to 1907 in *Sketch of a New Esthetics of Music*, by Ferruccio Busoni (b. 1866, d. 1924). He states, "There is a significant difference between the sound of the scale C, D♭, E♭, F♭, G♭, A♭, B♭, C when C is taken as tonic, and the scale of D♭ minor. By giving it the customary C-major triad as a fundamental harmony, a novel harmonic sensation is obtained."

VARIOUS NAMES USED FOR THE FLATTED FIFTH SUBSTITUTE OF THE AUGMENTED ELEVENTH SCALE

All these scales are used over the flatted fifth substitute of the F7 chord (B7 chord). Each scale starts from the seventh degree of the C melodic minor scale: B, C, D, E♭, F, G, A, B.

1. Altered Scale
2. Super Locrian Mode
3. Pomeroy Scale
4. Diminished Whole Tone Scale

THE ASCENDING AND DESCENDING SCALE DEGREES FOR ALL ALTERED SCALES AND THEIR RESPECTIVE CHORDS

1 2 3 4 5 6 7 1

I II III IV V VI VII I

Altered scale used for B7 chord: B C D E♭ F G A B

Altered scale used for E7 chord: E F G A♭ B♭ C D E

Altered scale used for A7 chord: A B♭ C D♭ E♭ F G A

Altered scale used for D7 chord: D E♭ F G♭ A♭ B♭ C D

Altered scale used for G7 chord: G A♭ B♭ C♭ D♭ E♭ F G

Altered scale used for C7 chord: C D♭ E♭ F♭ G♭ A♭ B♭ C

Altered scale used for E♯7 chord: E♯ F♯ G♯ A B C♯ D♯ E♯

Altered scale used for A♯7 chord: A♯ B C♯ D E F♯ G♯ A♯

Altered scale used for D♯7 chord: D♯ E F♯ G A B C♯ D♯

Altered scale used for G♯7 chord: G♯ A B C D E F♯ G♯

Altered scale used for C♯7 chord: C♯ D E F G A B C♯

Altered scale used for F♯7 chord: F♯ G A B♭ C D E F♯

In 1941 a hit song called "Autumn Nocturne" was composed by lyricist Kim Gannon with music by Josef Mirow. Within a single measure Mirow used the sound of both the augmented eleventh scale and the altered scale. This measure is repeated three times during the length of one chorus: twice in the beginning A section and once in the last A section. In 1945 singer Frankie Laine wrote lyrics for a song called "We'll Be Together Again" (music composed by Carl Fischer). The song contains many flatted fifth and augmented eleventh sounds. Jazz composer Tadd Dameron wrote a piece called "Hot House" (made famous by Charlie Parker and Dizzy Gillespie) based on the chord changes of "What Is This Thing Called Love" which contains numerous examples of the augmented eleventh and altered scales. A popular title song from the 1965 Broadway musical "On a Clear Day You Can See Forever" by lyricist Alan Jay Lerner and composer Burton Lane contains an excellent example of the use of the augmented eleventh sound in the second chord change. An interesting side note is that a famous jazz lick named after the song that it comes from, "Cry Me A River," c. 1955 by Arthur Hamilton is the retrograde melodic fragment for the opening notes in the composition "A Night in Tunisia," c. 1944 by Frank Paparelli and Dizzy Gillespie.

The following list of standard, popular, and jazz tunes contain ninth, eleventh, sharp eleventh, and thirteenth chords, augmented eleventh scale sounds completely, or in part. Although it is important to learn the augmented eleventh scale in all keys or dialects, it is imperative for today's novice composer or improvisor to become familiar with the jazz literature. If the student learns, analyses, and memorizes these melodies, improvising on tunes using the augmented eleventh scale will become easier.

Standard Jazz Tunes to be Learned that use the Sound of the Augmented Eleventh Scale Melodically or Harmonically

"A Night in Tunisia" - Dizzy Gillespie/Frank Paparelli

"Algo Bueno" - Dizzy Gillespie

"Autumn Nocturne" - Kim Gannon/Josef Mirow

"Au Privave" - Charlie Parker

"Barbara" - Horace Silver

"Bloomdido" - Dizzy Gillespie/Charlie Parker

"Blue Seven" - Sonny Rollins

"Boomerang" - Clark Terry

"Boplicity" - Cleo Henry

"Chelsea Bridge" - Billy Strayhorn

"Cry Me a River" - Arthur Hamilton

"Dizzy Atmosphere" - Dizzy Gillespie

"Donna Lee" - Miles Davis

"Donna" - Jackie McLean

"Early Autumn" - Ralph Burns

"Ecaroh" - Horace Silver

"Emanon" - Gillespie/Shaw

"Gary's Waltz" - Gary McFarland

"Girl From Ipanema" - Antonio Carlos Jobim

"Gregory is Here" - Horace Silver

"Groovin High" - Dizzy Gillespie

"Hamburger Helper" - Scott Reeves

"Heaven" - Duke Ellington

"Hot House" - Tadd Dameron

"Iris" - Wayne Shorter

"Jody Grind" - Horace Silver

"Kampala" - Ralph Towner

"Katrina Ballerina" - Woody Shaw

"Killer Joe" - Benny Golsen

"Limehouse Blues" - Braham

"Little Willie Leaps" - Miles Davis

"Lucifer's Fall" - Ralph Towner

"Mayreh" - Horace Silver

"M.D." - Dave Liebman

"Midnight Sun" - Sunny Burke/Lionel Hampton/ Johnny Mercer

"Morning Song" - Scott Reeves

"Motion" - Jimmy Raney

"Move" - Denzil Best

"Nica's Dream" - Horace Silver

"O Go Mo" - Kai Winding

"October 10th" - Richard Beirach

"On a Clear Day You Can See Forever" - Lerner/Lane

"One Note Samba" - Antonio Carlos Jobim

"Paper Butterflies" - Ruben Rada

"Pee Wee" - Tony Williams

"Pensativa" - Claire Fischer

"Pirana" - Hugo Fattoruso

"Prince of Darkness" - Wayne Shorter

"Scrapple from the Apple" - Charlie Parker

"Serenity" - Scott Reeves

"Signal" - Jimmy Raney

"Soul Eyes" - Mal Waldron

"Stella By Starlight" - Victor Young

"Strollin" - Horace Silver

"Summer In Central Park" - Horace Silver

"Take the A Train" - Duke Ellington

"That's What I'm Talking About" - Shorty Rogers

"The Fruit" - Bud Powell

"Thriving on a Riff" - Charlie Parker

"Travisimo" - Al Cohen

"Trumpet Blues" - Roy Eldridge/Dizzy Gillespie

"We'll Be Together Again" - Carl Fischer/Frankie Laine

As can be seen by the length of this partial list of jazz literature which contain the Augmented Eleventh Scale in many melodic shapes, a jazz player acquires an abundance of jazz language and style while learning melodies. These tunes, as melodic information stored in the mind's ear, then become part of the total melodic recall to be played in bits or at length when improvising. All great jazz players have hundreds and maybe thousands of jazz tunes at their fingertips that can be used to put together as a puzzle in thousands of different ways over endless chord changes. This process occurs automatically as the improviser reacts to many new tunes and many new sets of chord changes. The novice player should begin to memorize as many different jazz tunes as possible to expand improvisational fluency and acquire jazz vocabulary and language which should be a continuing process. After memorizing some of the jazz literature listed above, the student should then practice the tunes in as many different keys as possible to expand the student's jazz language even further.

Practicing this exercise will program the student's ears and mind with the sound of the augmented eleventh scale which will lead to greater freedom of expression when improvising. Adding the augmented eleventh scale to a student's jazz repertoire will give the student an important melodic "tool" for improvising. Therefore it will enable the student to express more of what is heard in the mind's ear, thus producing quicker ear instrument response while improvising.

THE AUGMENTED ELEVENTH SCALE: TREBLE CLEF

164

THE AUGMENTED ELEVENTH SCALE: BASS CLEF

CHAPTER 23

THE ARABIAN SCALE

We will now take a look at the Arabian scale, a Middle Eastern scale.

According to what has been passed down in history by etchings in stone and written in scriptures, most ancient nations had some form of music in religious and secular life.

The Arabs, because of their numerous conflicts and conquests of nations such as Egypt, Morocco, ancient Greece, and Persia from 500 B.C. to 800 A.D., became one of the most cultured people of their day.

Syria and Palestine were conquered by the Arabs between 635 A.D. and 638 A.D. Syrian history and culture dates as far back as 3000 B.C., when it was inhabited by the Semites.

The Arabs began dominating Spain in the 8th century. Early Spanish music was influenced by the "Arab element," as was all European music; however, it is difficult to prove this.

Persian music again influenced Arabian music in the 9th and 10th centuries. In the 11th century, some of the intervals in the Arabian modes were made smaller and the 17-note Arabian scale was created in the 13th century.

Later, during the Crusades (1095–1271 A.D.), the knowledge that was gained by the Arabs through their conquests was learned and absorbed by the young European nations. This included science, music, architecture, design, and manufacturing.

Arabian influence ended in the year 1256 A.D., with the fall of Baghdad by Hulegu, the Mughal conqueror who was the grandson of Genghis Khan, the barbarian. Many cultural treasures that the Arabs accumulated during five centuries of pillaging—such as music, art, and literary and scientific translations from the Greeks—were destroyed by a fire known as The Caliph of Baghdad and 800,000 inhabitants were slaughtered.

Harvard Dictionary of Music, Willi Apel, Harvard University Press, 1974.

Arab music: The music of the Arab nations and tribes of Arabia, North Africa, and the Near East.

Our knowledge of the history of this music is derived chiefly from theoretical treatises, since there are very few examples of notated compositions, and none prior to the 13th century. Among the most important treatises are those of Al-Kini (c. 796–873), Al-Farabi (872–950), Ibn Sina ((Avicenna, 980–1037), Safi al-Din (d. 1294), and Abd al-Qadir (d. 1435).

New Oxford Companion to Music, General Editor Denis Arnold, Middle Eastern Music Vol. 2 K–Z.

Middle East: A meeting point of people and cultures. Heir to ancient civilizations, like Mesopotamia and Egypt, and with the expansion of Islam from the 7th century, has three great modern peoples: the Iranians, the Arabs, and the Turks.

Persia–predominance of instrumental music.

Arabia–predominance of voice.

Turks–synthesis of the two.

Arabic, Persian, Turkish–united by Islam.

The Arabic script survived as a basis for the writing of the Iranian and Turkish languages and later works on music. Conflicting claims have resulted, such as the nationality of the famous Al Farabi (the "Alfarabius" of the Middle Ages), considered Arab by the Arabs, Iranian by the Persians, and Turkish by the Ottomans.

Source of the Twelve Arabian Modes Derived from Tonal Systems: "A Systematic Order of Pitches Particular to a Certain Society."

The following twelve modes show the musical knowledge gained through the Arabian paths of conquest of various nations. Knowledge was also found in the music of scholars of Europe by the treatises on the science of music by Al Farabi and other Arabian writers.

Melodies of Arabic and Persian art songs are derived from the twelve modes or "maquam." In Egypt, they are called "naghma," in Tunis, called "taba," and in Algeria they are called "sana'a." All these modes are equivalent to the Hindu raga. The modes were based on a melodic order, each mode being essentially a short melodic formula, making frequent use of the augmented second.

Uschak: A, B, C♯, D, E, G♭, G, A (A Mixolydian mode)

Neva: A, B, C, D, E, F, G, A (A Aeolian mode)

Abu-selik: A, A♯, D, D♯, F, G, A (enharmonically spelled A, B♭, D, E♭, F, G, A, is like the Dorian mode of the G harmonic minor scale minus the fourth degree of the scale)

Rasd: A, A♯, C, D, E, F♯, G, A (G melodic minor ascending starting on A)

Arak: A, B♭, C♯, D, E♭, F, F♯, G♯, A (first four notes are the upper tetrachord of D harmonic minor; last five notes are the beginning of the E♭ diminished scale)

Ispahan: A, B♭, C♯, D, E, F, G, A (first four notes are the D harmonic minor starting on A)

Zirefkend: A, B♭, C, D, D♯, F, F♯, G♯, A (first four notes are the F major scale staring on A; last five notes are a partial of the diminished scale)

Buzurg: A, B♭, C♯, D, D♯, E, G♭, G♯, A (first four notes are the D harmonic minor scale starting from A; last five notes are the E major scale staring on the seventh D♯)

Zenkla: A, B, C♯, D, D♯, F♯, G, A (first four notes are the upper tetrachord of the D major scale; last five notes are the D Byzantine scale)

Rhaoui: A, A♯, C♯, D, D♯, F, G, A (first four notes are the upper tetrachord of the D harmonic minor scale; last four notes are the lower tetrachord of the D♯ whole-tone scale)

L'sain: A, A♯, C, D, D♯, F, G, A (first four notes of B♭ Locrian mode; last four notes are D♯ whole-tone scale)

Hidschaf: A, A♯, C, D♯, F♯, G, A (G harmonic minor starting on A, omitting the fifth (D))

These scales or modes show the musical mixture of the many other nations that were conquered by the Arabs.

CHRONOLOGICAL HISTORY OF THE CONQUERED NATIONS AND THEIR CONQUERORS

4000 B.C. – Mesopotamia—Sumerians

3300 B.C. – Egypt

2350 B.C. – Akkadians

2000 B.C. – Hittites

1792 B.C. – Hammurabi—Assyrians

1600 B.C. – Phoenicians

1200 B.C. – Discovery of the whole-tone scale by the Chinese

550 B.C. – Pythagoras derives the major scale from the Greek diatonic modes

525 B.C. – Egypt conquered by Persia

500 B.C. to 300 A.D. – Persian and Greek political and cultural wars

200 B.C. to present – Hindu scale (some authorities claim 200 A.D., and some even say 500 A.D.)

226–641 A.D. – Persian reign of the Seleucids, who had strong nationalistic feelings and an anti-Greek sentiment

328 A.D. – Byzantine scale

635–638 A.D. – Palestine and Syria conquered by the Arabs

641 A.D. – Egypt conquered by the Arabs

700 A.D. – Arab conquest of Spain

800 A.D. – Oriental scale influences Arabian music

800–900 A.D. – Persia again influences Arabian music

900–950 A.D. – Al Farabi, through the influence of Greek music, presents a scale constructed on the interval of a fourth. The most popular Arabian instruments—the oud and the tanbur—tuned in fourths

1000 A.D. – The intervals of the Arabian modes made smaller

1085 A.D. – Arabs continue domination of Spain

1200 A.D. – The 17-tone Arabian scale comes into prominence

ARABIAN INSTRUMENTS

The Arabian lute was called the "oud," which means "wood from trees." The first Arabian lute was tuned C, D, G, A.

The Persian lute, which was adopted by the Arabs, was tuned A, D, G, C. In the 9th century, a fifth string was added, and the tuning became A, D, G, C, F.

The oud or tanbur was tuned in fourths: G, C, F, B♭.

VARIOUS SCALES THAT INFLUENCED THE DEVELOPMENT OF THE ARABIAN SCALE

Many other cultures throughout history, from the Near and Far East, made use of scales. Partials of various other cultures' scales were used to create Arabian scales.

There are five scales somewhat similar to the Arabian scale, which will be listed, but not discussed. Each of these scales has slight alterations in scale degrees.

Hungarian Gypsy scale: C, D, E♭, F♯, G, A♭, B♭, C

Oriental scale: C, D♭, E, F, G♭, A♭, B♭, C

Natural minor scale: C, D, E♭, F, G, A♭, B♭, C

Minor Arabian scale: C, D, E♭, F, G♭, A♭, B♭, C

Hindu Scale: C, D, E, F, G, A♭, B♭, C

CONSTRUCTION OF THE ARABIAN SCALE

In order to understand the construction of the Arabian scale, the major, chromatic, and whole-tone scales must be understood.

The construction of Greek scales developed from the invention by Pythagoras (550 B.C.) of the Pythagorean scale, which produces all scale tones by the interval of a fifth. These diatonic tones are obtained by using the Circle of Fifths, and are used to construct the diatonic C major scale.

Example: circle of ascending fifths: C, G, D, A, E, B, F♯/G♭, D♭, A♭, E♭, B♭, F.

Example: circle of descending fifths: C, F, B♭, E♭, A♭, D♭, G♭/F♯, B, E, A, D, G.

By taking five ascending fifths, C, G, D, A, E, B, and one descending fifth, F, and rearranging them in stepwise ascending order, it produces a C major scale.

Example: C, D, E, F, G, A, B. If we take the lower tetrachord of the C major scale and combine it with the lower tetrachord of a G♭ whole-tone scale, we arrive at the Arabian scale.

The major scale uses two major tetrachords in its construction (a tetrachord is a group of four tones placed in scale-wise succession, usually totaling the interval of a perfect fourth):

The lower tetrachord of the C major scale is C, D, E, F.

The upper tetrachord of the C major scale is G, A, B, D.

The two tetrachords are separated by a whole step, resulting in a C major scale.

Example:

a. Lower tetrachord C, D, E, F

b. Upper tetrachord G, A, B, C

c. C major scale: C, D, E, F, G, A, B, C

THE CHROMATIC SCALE: SOURCE FOR THE TWO WHOLE-TONE SCALES

Chinese music influenced the use of the chromatic scale by the Greeks, and is probably the oldest musical system in existence. Its chromatic scale is composed of twelve "Lus," which correspond to the notes in the Circle of Fifths; used by "yellow" Emperor Huang-ti in 2697 B.C. Each note used signified a particular month and hour of day.

The word "chromatic" is a derivative of the Greek "chromos." The Greeks had three types of scales: diatonic, chromatic, and enharmonic. Pythagoras, who invented the tetrachord, considered the 4th, 5th, and the octave as perfect intervals. The outer notes of inter-

vals were fixed, but the inner notes were moveable, and were used as embellishments.

CHROMATIC SCALE THEORY

1 2 3 4 5 6 7 8 9 10 11 12: twelve tones

C C♯ D D♯ E F F♯ G G♯ A A♯ B: chromatic tones

By skipping every other chromatic tone, we arrive at the C whole-tone scale:

C D E F♯ G♯ A♯

The C whole-tone scale represents yang, sun, or masculine tones.

The remaining chromatic tones produce the C♯ whole-tone scale.

C♯ D♯ F G A B

The C♯ whole-tone scale represents yin, moon, or feminine tones.

Both whole-tone scales are considered an arpeggio of the chromatic scale by many composers.

Example: chromatic scale

C, C♯, D, D♯, E, F, F♯, G, G♯, A, A♯, B, C

C D E F♯ G♯ A♯   C = C whole-tone scale

C♯ D♯ F G A B = C♯ whole-tone scale

The whole-tone scale, which is comprised of six tones a whole step apart, has been associated with French impressionistic composer, Claude Debussy. The whole-tone scale is made up of one half of the chromatic scale, also known as the "duodecuple," or "dodecuple scale." Even though Debussy made use of this scale more than any other composer of his time, the Chinese discovered it in 1200 B.C.

The first mode of the Arabian twelve modes (Uschak) is A, B, C♯, D, which is the lower tetrachord of the A major scale. The third mode of the Arabian twelve modes (Abu-selik) is E♭, F, G, A. These notes are the first four notes of the E♭ whole-tones scale. The Arabs combined the first four notes of the Uschak mode and the first four notes of the Abu-selik mode to produce the Arabian scale. When transposed to C, the scale becomes C, D, E, F (Uschak transposed), G♭, A♭, B♭, C (Abu-selik transposed).

In other words, the Arabian scale, built on the note C, can be constructed by using the first four notes (lower tetrachord) of the C major scale, whose construction is similar to the first four notes of the Uschak mode. The Uschak mode is the first mode of the twelve primary Arabian/Persian modes called "maqamat." Then, by adding the last four notes of the third mode, called "Abu-selik," the notes are similar to the last four notes of the C whole-tone scale (G♭, A♭, B♭, C). This completes the Arabian scale. The two tetrachords are separated by a half step.

Example:

    a. Lower tetrachord: C, D, E, F

    b. Upper tetrachord: G♭, A♭, B♭, C

    c. Arabian scale: C, D, E, F, G♭, A♭, B♭, C

The Arabian scale may use a dominant seventh chord or a minor I chord as its harmony. The Arabian scale is another of the numerous scales that may be used to compose or improvise melodies over dominant seventh minor chords. The following is a list of the twelve Arabian scales and their respective chords. The scale ascends and descends using the identical notes.

C Arabian scale: C, D, E, F, G♭, A♭, B♭, C; uses the C7 or the F minor chord

F Arabian scale: F, G, A, B♭, C♭, D♭, E♭, F; uses the F7 or the B♭ minor chord

B♭ Arabian scale: B♭, C, D, E♭, F♭, G♭, A♭, B♭; uses the B♭7 or the E♭ minor chord

E♭ Arabian scale: E♭, F, G, A♭, B♭, C♭, D♭, E♭; uses the E♭7 or the A♭ minor chord

A♭ Arabian scale: A♭, B♭, C, D♭, E♭♭, F♭, G♭, A♭; uses the A♭7 or the D♭ minor chord

D♭ Arabian scale: D♭, E♭, F, G♭, A♭♭, B♭♭, C♭, D♭; uses the D♭7 or the G♭ minor chord

F♯ Arabian scale: F♯, G♯, A♯, B, C, D, E, F♯; uses the F♯7 or the B minor chord

B Arabian scale: B, C♯, D♯, E, F, G, A, B; uses the B7 chord or the E minor chord

E Arabian scale: E, F♯, G♯, A, B♭, C, D, E; uses the E7 chord or the A minor chord

A Arabian scale: A, B, C♯, D, E♭, F, G, A; uses the A7 chord or the D minor chord

D Arabian scale: D, E, F♯, G, A♭, B♭, C, D; uses the D7 chord or the G minor chord

G Arabian scale: G, A, B, C, D♭, E♭, F, G; uses the G7 chord or the C minor chord

All the tones of the Arabian scale are active when used melodically. When used harmonically, the first, third, fifth, and seventh degrees form a dominant seventh chord with a flatted fifth. The second, fourth, sixth, and eighth degrees form a half diminished chord (minor 7th ♭5). Therefore, these tones, when sounded as chords, can also be considered active tones.

The two treble and bass clef studies are presented in the next two pages.

DIATONIC CHORDS PRODUCED FROM THE C ARABIAN SCALE

(C, D, E, F, G♭, A♭, B♭, C)

The chord on the first degree is a dominant seventh with a flatted fifth (C7♭5).

The chord on the second degree is a minor seventh with a flatted fifth (Dmin7♭5).

The chord on the third degree is an inversion of the dominant seventh with a sharp fifth (G♭7♯5).

The chord on the fourth degree is a minor triad with a major seventh (FmMaj7).

The chord on the fifth degree is a major seventh with a sharp fifth (G♭Maj7♯5).

The chord on the sixth degree is a dominant seventh with a sharp fifth (A♭7♯5).

The chord on the seventh degree is a dominant seventh (B♭7).

JAZZ SONGS CONTAINING WHOLE-TONE SCALES AND/OR AUGMENTED CHORDS

Leonard Feather, noted jazz historian, critic, author, and composer since the early '30s, best known for his volumes of "Encyclopedia of Jazz" reference books, has written a blues song entitled "12-Tone Blues," using the two whole-tone scales (c. 1960).

"One Up, One Down" - John Coltrane

"Spanning" - Charles Tolliver

"Criss Cross" - Thelonious Monk

"Gregory Is Here" - Horace Silver

"Ju-Ju" - Wayne Shorter

"Queer Notions" - Coleman Hawkins

"Take The A-Train" - Billy Strayhorn

"Our Man Higgins" - Lee Morgan

"Cappuccino" - Chick Corea

"Evidence" - Thelonious Monk

"Jody Grind" - Horace Silver

"Le Roi" - David Baker

"Stella By Starlight" - Victor Young

The Arabian scale sounds good when played over the harmony of a dominant seventh chord built on the root of the scale, to a minor chord a fifth below used as the I chord of the key, or a dominant triad with an augmented and flatted fifth.

As can be seen by the length of the above partial lists of jazz literature, which contain many major and whole-tone scale sounds in melodic shapes, a jazz player acquires an abundance of jazz language and style while learning melodies. These tunes, as melodic information stored in the mind's ear, then become part of the tonal melodic recall to be played in bits or at length when improvising. All great jazz players have hundreds, and maybe thousands, of jazz tunes at their fingertips that can be used to put together, as a puzzle, in a thousand different ways over endless chord changes. This process occurs automatically as the improvisor reacts to many new tunes and many new sets of chord changes. The novice player should begin to memorize as many different jazz tunes as possible to expand improvisational fluency, and acquire jazz vocabulary and language, which should be a continuing process. After memorizing some of the jazz literature listed above, the student should then practice the tunes in as many different keys as possible to expand the student's jazz language even further.

THE ARABIAN SCALE — TREBLE CLEF INSTRUMENTS

treble clef

Emile De Cosmo

Music Graphics by Kevin Hagen

THE ARABIAN SCALE — BASS CLEF INSTRUMENTS

Emile De Cosmo

CHAPTER 24

THE CHROMATIC MINOR 7TH PROGRESSION

In the beginning of the jazz era most of the tunes played or used as vehicles of improvisation were composed with the use of simple chord changes. Usually these tunes included cycle of fifths chord changes which were progressions typically used for the church or religious music of the day.

Chromatic progressions appeared later in the history of jazz music and are an outgrowth of the cycle of fifths. Therefore they should be learned after one has immersed oneself in the cycle of fifths and the diatonic cycle of fifths and all its dialects (keys).

In the past and present jazz educators instruct students to reproduce everything they play chromatically on their instruments. This is usually ignored because of its difficulty. Practicing this way was suggested because most of the educators were either pianists, instrumentalists who possessed piano skills, composers, or theorists.

As the piano is a visual instrument, practicing chromatically is accomplished more easily. Most other instruments that are played are not as visual. The cycle of fifths was understood thoroughly by those who were able to play the piano because most early musical literature made use of the cycle of fifths in part or completely.

When harmonic or chord progressions appear in melodic situations they are constructed with the use of five types of movement.

1. Cycle of Fifths: natural harmonic progression of music.

2. Diatonic Cycle of Fifths: natural progression within any key.

3. Whole Steps Ascending or Descending: whole tone scales.

4. Minor Thirds Ascending or Descending: diminished thirds.

5. Minor Seconds Ascending or Descending: chromatic scale.

OVERTONAL INFLUENCE

Although heard as single tones, each individual pitch consists of a fundamental tone and a series of overtones referred to as either harmonics or partials. The fundamental and all of its overtones produce a highly altered dominant seventh chord containing tensions extending to diminished or flatted fifth, augmented fifth, ninth, augmented eleventh, and thirteenth.

The fundamental and its subsequent overtones or partials, create a magnetic or gravitational force that puts the fundamental in motion causing it to resolve or fall to another fundamental a fifth below that contains another set of overtones. This is due to the fact that there are two tritones in the partials of the overtone series. Each new set of overtones create the cadential flow of the Dominant cycle of fifths.

THE TRITONE

The tritone, an interval of an augmented fourth, was called the "devil's interval" (diabolus in musica) during the Middle Ages and avoided melodically, but when used harmonically is the most powerful force of harmonic action within the musical universe. When heard harmonically the augmented fourth creates a tremendous need for resolution and is more properly to be regarded instead as the "Angel of Resolution." (author's term). The tritone provides the most distinctive characteristic of the dominant seventh chord creating individual tension and unrest; increasing the tonal magnetism; causing a greater need for resolution to another chord a fifth below. The tritone resolves or moves inwardly or outwardly depending on its interval, whether it's a flatted fifth or augmented fourth, to the first and third degrees of its related chord.

The fact that the strongest pull in music is from a dominant chord to another dominant chord known as the chain of dominants cannot be over emphasized, because this relationship is the musical doorway to understanding the harmonic movement or delay of resolutions, of all progressions in all music. This includes classical, popular, jazz, rock, and folk. Delay of resolution to the final or tonic chord creates the interesting forward motion of music. When resolution to the tonic is effected the motion comes to rest and the piece is heard as having reached a conclusion.

THE CHAIN OF DOMINANTS

The cycle of fifths serves as the magnetic vehicle of all cadential movement. The fundamental bass moves in descending fifths (C, F, B♭, E♭, A♭, D♭, G♭ (F♯), B, E, A, D, G). Because of the overtonal influence discussed earlier, the cycle of fifths is in reality a cycle of dominant sevenths moving in an endless harmonic spiral of descending fundamentals producing dominant sevenths. The cycle of fifths chain of dominants establishes the force of gravity of the musical universe, the strongest and most natural harmonic progression in music.

RELATIONSHIP OF THE CYCLE OF FIFTHS TO THE CHROMATIC SCALE

Because of the V to I relationship which exists between each chord in the chain of dominants the term "cycle of fifths" is employed and established; each note is the fifth of the note it precedes. When you substitute a flatted fifth for every other note in the cycle you arrive at the chromatic scale.

Descending cycle of fifths:

- Example: C F B♭ E♭ A♭ G♭ B E A D G C

  Substituting a flatted fifth for every other note creates the descending chromatic scale:

- Example: C B B♭ A A♭ G G♭ F E E♭ D D♭ C

Ascending cycle of fifths:

- Example: C G D A E B G♭ D♭ A♭ E♭ B♭ F C

  Substituting a flatted fifth for every other note creates the ascending chromatic scale:

- Example: C D♭ D E♭ E F G♭ G A♭ A B♭ B C

  This chart shows that the chromatic scale is the "disguised cycle of fifths," a substitute of the cycle of fifths either in descending or ascending form which can be used whenever cycle changes are being used.

UPPER PARTIALS OF DOMINANT CHORDS USED IN JAZZ

While famous jazz alto saxophonist Charlie Parker (b.1920, d.1955) was playing at a jam session, he became bored with the standard chord changes being used. The song being played was Ray Noble's standard *Cherokee*. While he was improvising, in his mind's ear he could hear other sounds based on the upper partials of dominant chords.

Instead of playing on the roots, thirds, fifths and sevenths he decided to play melodies using the upper partials of the overtones that were heard in his mind's ear. He began playing more chromatically and explored, composed and improvised new melodies using the very chromatic upper partials of the overtone series.

In this way he began playing on top of the chord changes instead of inside the changes. This style of playing was new to jazz and became the beginning of bebop. Charlie Parker was inspired to experiment with the upper partials after listening to many great modern composers such as Paul Hindemith, Maurice Ravel, Claude Debussy, Arnold Schoenberg, Bela Bartok, Edgard Varese, Alban Berg, and Igor Stravinsky.

After bebop gave way to hardbop and then to funk, many musicians used the sound of the upper partials melodically while playing their improvisations. One such musician/composer was Horace Silver who wrote many songs among them *Barbara, Summer In Central Park, Ecaroh, Strollin, Nica's Dream,* and *Mayreh.* John Coltrane was another famous jazz musician who used the sound of upper partials extensively in his improvisations over hundreds of standard tunes in the 1960s. One of today's contemporary jazz musicians, Michael Brecker continues to use ColtraneÕs progressive sound in his music.

FLATTED FIFTHS IN JAZZ

The progressive jazz players of the late 1940s and 1950s such as Charlie Parker, Dizzie Gillespie and the bebop school of players altered the chord changes of many of the tunes played. Along with the altered chords, they used many of these altered sounds in their melodic lines. The most common altered sound from the bebop school of music was the flatted fifth (or enharmonically the augmented fourth).

• Examples: C to G♭ = Flatted Fifth

C to F♯ = Augmented Fourth

Many jazz pieces of that era ended on the flatted fifth. In fact, there was a bebop greeting that gave the

flatted fifth sign: a raised open hand with the other hand placed horizontally at the wrist.

In Reese Markewich's book *Inside Outside* he notes, "Ever since the birth of modern jazz the term flatted fifth has been bandied about. Musicians used to make the sign of the flatted fifth when greeting each other in humorous ritual." Reese Markewich also created the term "disguised cycle of fifths" known as the chromatic scale. In the tune Cool, written by Howard McGhee the progression Dmin7, D♭min7, Cmin7, F7, appears in measures eight, nine and the first half of the tenth measure.

In the composition "Contours" by Shorty Rodgers the eleventh measure finds this harmonic progression: Cmin7, F7, B♭min7, E♭7, a set of ii7 V7 progressions that has perfect chords which can be changed to a minor chromatic progression, namely Cmin7, Bmin7, B♭min7, A7. As a matter of fact, whenever any set of ii7, V7 chord changes appear in a song a tritone substitution may be inserted for the ii7 chord.

Charlie Parker used this progression of chords in the composition "Barbados:" Amin7, D7, Gmin7, C7. Flatted fifth or tritone substitutions can be used to change the qualities of some chords to arrive at this:

Original chords: Amin7 D7 Gmin7 C7.

Tritone substitutions: Amin7 A♭min7 Gmin7 F♯7.

Anytime you have a iii7, vi7, ii7, V7 diatonic cycle progression that is changed by tritone substitution the roots of the chords that were in cycle will now move down chromatically.

Chord Progressions in Roman Numerals: iii7 vi7 ii7 V7

Original chords in the key of C: Emin7 Amin7 Dmin7 G7.

Tritone substitutions of vi7 and V7: Emin7 E♭min7 Dmin7 D♭7.

Reese Markewich sums it up beautifully in his book *Inside Outside* by stating, "This half step chromatic progression of the roots, or of the II-7s or the V7s, for the matter, is really the cycle of fifths in disguise, a substitution for the original root progression. Thus the chromatic scale, which contains all intervals and chords, is really the cycle of fifths in disguise."

The flatted fifth or augmented fourth is contained in the upper partials of the overtone series where the jazz players discovered it. In fact, the sound of the overtones built on the fundamental C produces a dominant thirteenth chord with an added augmented eleventh.

- Example: C, E, G, Bb, D, F#, A, C which is a C13+11 chord.

THE FLATTED FIFTH CONCEPT AND ITS TRADITIONAL HARMONIC ROOTS

Any chord of any species or quality can have for its harmonic substitute a similar type chord built a flatted fifth away from its root called the flatted fifth or tritone substitution. In other words any two similar type chords whose roots are located a tritone apart can substitute for each other. This concept can be traced to its roots in traditional harmony, where augmented sixth chords were used as a type of chromatic harmony and named: Neapolitan, French and German sixths. The Neapolitan or Italian sixth, introduced in the seventeenth century, was an altered ii chord of a minor key that sounded like a major triad which resolves to its tonic.

- Example: Db major triad resolving to C minor triad, Db, F, Ab resolving down to C, Eb, G.

  The Db major triad could also resolve to the dominant seventh chord of that minor key first and then to its tonic.

- Example: Db major triad, Db, F, Ab resolving to a G dominant triad G, B, D, then to its tonic C minor, or Db major triad resolving to a G dominant chord, Db, F, Ab resolving to G, B, D, F and then to its tonic C minor.

The Db root of the triad is the flatted fifth of the G7 chord. The interval created between the root of the G7 chord and the root of the Db triad is a tritone or the flatted fifth relationship.

THE GERMAN SIXTH

The German sixth is a complete dominant seventh chord, for instance, Db, F, Ab, Cb that resolves a half-step lower to a C major chord, C, E, G or from a Db7 chord to a G7 chord and then to its tonic C major chord.

- Example: Db7 to G7 to C Major

THE FRENCH SIXTH

The French sixth is a dominant seventh with a flatted fifth, for instance, Db, F, Abb, Cb that resolves a half step lower to a C Major chord, C, E, G or from a Db7b5 chord to a G7 chord and then to its tonic.

- Example: Db7b5 to G7 to C Major

The two most important notes of a dominant seventh chord are its third and seventh creating a tritone which demands resolution. The tritone divides an octave in half, therefore, when a tritone is inverted it becomes another tritone.

The Db7 chord contains the tritone from its third, F to its seventh, Cb or (B). The G7 chord contains a tritone from its third, B to its seventh, F. The third, F and the seventh, Cb of the Db7 chord when inverted become the seventh, F and the third, B of the G7 chord. The roots of the Db7 chord and the G7 chord are also a tritone apart thus completing the three tritones in the flatted fifth substitution.

The three tritones present in the flatted fifth substitution cause an overwhelming demand for its resolution to a chord one half-step lower from the root of the Db7 chord (Db) or to the root of the G7 chord (G).

The Db7 chord containing the tritone from F to Cb wants to resolve to a CMaj7 chord. The G7 chord containing the tritone from B to F wants to resolve to a

G♭Maj7 chord. The tonics of these two keys D♭ and G are also a flatted fifth or a tritone apart.

CHORD SUBSTITUTIONS MAKING USE OF THE FLATTED FIFTH CONCEPT

Any Standard, Pop, Rock or Jazz tune can be embellished by using flatted fifth substitutions of standard chord changes. Interesting turnarounds can be accomplished with the use of the flatted fifth (tritone) substitution. Knowing how to handle any type of turnaround along with its many substitutions is a prerequisite for the contemporary jazz player.

Any chord can be substituted by a same species or different type chord built on the same root a flatted fifth away from the root of the chord for which it is substituting by applying this concept.

The chromatic minor seventh progression is a perfect example of this type of substitution. Normally, in the key of C the iii min7 chord is the Emin7th chord. The iii7 chord would progress down by steps diatonically iii7-ii7-V7-I, or Emin7-Dmin7-G7-CMaj7. By using the diatonic cycle the progression would now become iii7-vi7-ii7-V7-I. Applying the flatted fifth concept and changing the vi7 (Amin7) to its flatted fifth substitute ♭iii7 (E♭min7) we arrive at this chromatic minor seventh progression: iii7-♭iii7-ii7-V7 or Emin7-E♭min7-Dmin7-G7.

Following is a list of these minor seventh progressions.

- In the key of C: iii7-♭iii7-ii7-V7 or Emin7-E♭min7-Dmin7-G7.
- In the key of F: iii7-♭iii7-ii7-V7 or Amin7-A♭min7-Gmin7-C7.
- In the key of B♭: iii7-♭iii7-ii7-V7 or Dmin7-D♭min7-Cmin7-F7.
- In the key of E♭: iii7-♭iii7-ii7-V7 or Gmin7-G♭min7-Fmin7-B♭7.
- In the key of A♭: iii7-♭iii7-ii7-V7 or Cmin7-Bmin7-B♭min7-E♭7.
- In the key of D♭: iii7-♭iii7-ii7-V7 or Fmin7-Emin7-E♭min7-A♭7.
- In the key of G♭: iii7-♭iii7-ii7-V7 or B♭min7-Amin7-A♭min7-D♭7.
- In the key of B: iii7-♭iii7-ii7-V7 or D♯min7-Dmin7-C♯min7-F♯7.
- In the key of E: iii7-♭iii7-ii7-V7 or G♯min7-Gmin7-F♯min7-B7.
- In the key of A: iii7-♭iii7-ii7-V7 or C♯min7-Cmin7-Bmin7-E7.
- In the key of D: iii7-biii7-ii7-V7 or F♯min7-Emin7-Emin7-A7.
- In the key of G: iii7-biii7-ii7-V7 or Bmin7-B♭min7-Amin7-D7.

The flatted fifth substitution may be employed in any piece of music when the harmony moves in cycle through the iii7-vi7-ii7-V7 of any key. This can work with any quality of chords: major sevenths, minor sevenths, dominant sevenths, minor sevenths ♭5s, diminished sevenths, etc. The quality of each chord may also change at the will of the improviser or composer.

QUALITIES OR TYPES OF CHORDS AND THEIR FLATTED FIFTH SUBSTITUTES

CMaj7 would have a G♭Maj7 as its substitution.

C7 would have a G♭7 as its substitution.

Cmin7 would have a G♭min7 as its substitution.

Cmin7♭5 would have a G♭min7♭5 as its substitution.

Cdim7 would have a G♭dim7 as its substitution.

CMaj7♯5 would have a G♭Maj7♯5 as its substitution.

CMaj7♭5 would have a G♭Maj7♭5 as its substitution.

C7♭5 would have a G♭7♭5 as its substitution.

C7♯5 would have a G♭7♯5 as its substitution.

Cmin(maj7) would have a G♭min(maj7 as its substitution.

C7min7♭5 would have a G♭min7♭5 as its substitution.

Cdim7 would have a G♭dim7 as its substitution.

As can be seen by this list any type chord can be substituted by the same type chord a flatted fifth away for any harmonic progression.

MODES AND THEIR FLATTED FIFTH SUBSTITUTES

- A C ionian mode would have a G♭ Ionian Mode as its substitute.
- A C dorian mode would have a G♭ dorian mode as its substitute.
- A C phrygian mode would have a G♭ phrygian mode as its substitute.
- A C lydian mode would have a G♭ lydian mode as its substitute.
- A C mixolydian mode would have a G♭ mixolydian mode as its substitute.
- A C aeolian mode would have a G♭ aeolian mode as its substitute.
- A C locrian mode would have a G♭ locrian mode as its substitute.

(This would include all modes in all major and minor keys and their flatted fifth substitutes).

VARIOUS SCALES AND THEIR FLATTED FIFTH SUBSTITUTES

- A C Major scale would have a G♭ Major scale as its substitute.
- A C Melodic minor scale would have a G♭ Melodic minor as its substitute.
- A C Harmonic minor scale would have a G♭ Harmonic minor scale as its substitute.
- A C Diminished scale would have a G♭ Diminished scale as its substitute.
- A C Augmented eleventh scale would have a G♭ Augmented scale as its substitute.
- A C Blues scale would have a G♭ Blues scale as its substitute.

- A C Byzantine scale would have a G♭ Byzantine as its substitute.
- A C Arabian scale would have a G♭ Arabian scale as its substitute.
- A C Altered scale would have a G♭ Altered scale as its substitute.
- A C augmented eleventh scale would have a G♭ augmented scale as its substitute.

The basic Diatonic Cycle of Fifths can supply the harmonic flow during any progression. Flatted fifth chord substitutions are frequently inserted in this diatonic flow by composers or improvisors.

We've included a list of standard, popular, and jazz tunes containing Cycle of Fifths changes. (Cycle of Fifth changes are usually found in the bridge or B section of many AABA tunes and many begin with cycle changes.)

The list of tunes we've included is just a partial list of jazz literature which contains cycle of fifth changes. The flatted fifth concept can be applied when improvising on these tunes. These tunes are melodic information to be stored in the mind's ear, which then becomes part of the total melodic recall to be played in bits or at length when improvising. All great jazz players have hundreds and perhaps thousands of jazz tunes at their fingertips which can be used to put together as a puzzle in thousands of different ways over endless chord changes. This process occurs automatically as the improvisor reacts to many new tunes and many new sets of chord changes. After memorizing some of the jazz literature above, the student should then transpose the tunes into as many different keys as possible to expand the student's jazz vocabulary even further.

After getting familiar with and memorizing as many tunes as possible the novice improvisor or composer should try to apply some flatted fifth substitutions to the tunes when encountering cycle changes.

Standard, Popular and Jazz Tunes Containing Cycle of Fifths Changes

"All Blues" - Miles Davis

"Anthropology" - C. Parker/D. Gillespie.

"Blue Monk" - Thelonious Monk

"Broadway" - Wood/McCrae/Bird

"Celebrity" - Charlie Parker

"Chasin' the Bird" - Charlie Parker

"Dewey Square" - Charlie Parker

"Dig" - Miles Davis

"Doxy" - Sonny Rollins

"Four Brothers" - Jimmy Guiffre

"Freddy Freeloader" - Miles Davis

"I've Got Rhythm" - George Gershwin

"Jordu" - Duke Jordon

"Killer Joe" - Benny Golson

"Kim" - Charlie Parker

"Leap Frog" - Charlie Parker

"Lil' Darlin'" - Neil Hefti

"Misterioso" - Thelonious Monk

"Moose the Mooche" - Charlie Parker

"Perdido" - J. Tizol

"Sermonette" - Cannonball Adderley

"Sister Sadie" - Horace Silver

"Skippy" - Thelonious Monk

"Straight Life" - Freddie Hubbard

"Watermelon Man" - Herbie Hancock

"Well You Needn't" - Thelonious Monk

"A Night in Tunisia" - Dizzy Gillespie/Frank Paparelli

"Algo Bueno" - Dizzy Gillespie

"Au Privave" - Charlie Parker

"Barbara" - Horace Silver

"Bloomdido" - Dizzy Gillespie/Charlie Parker

"Blue Seven" - Sonny Rollins

"Boomerang" - Clark Terry

"Boplicity" - Cleo Henry

"Chelsea Bridge" - Billy Strayhorn

"Dizzy Atmosphere" - Dizzy Gillespie

"Donna Lee" - Miles Davis

"Donna" - Jackie McLean

"Eb-Bob" - Fats Navarro/Leo Parker

"Ecaroh" - Horace Silver

"Emanon" - Gillespie/Shaw

"Gregory is Here" - Horace Silver

"Groovin High" - Dizzy Gillespie

"Hot House" - Tadd Dameron

"Iris" - Wayne Shorter

"Jody Grind" - Horace Silver

"Katrina Ballerina" - Woody Shaw

"Killer Joe" - Benny Golsen

"Little Willie Leaps" - Miles Davis

"Mayreh" - Horace Silver

"M.D." - Dave Liebman

"Motion" - Jimmy Raney

"Move" - Denzil Best

"Nica's Dream" - Horace Silver

"One Note Samba" - Antonio Carlos Jobim

"Prince of Darkness" - Wayne Shorter

"Scrapple from the Apple" - Charlie Parker

"Signal" - Jimmy Raney

"Soul Eyes" - Mal Waldron

"Strollin" - Horace Silver

"Summer In Central Park" - Horace Silver

"The Fruit" - Bud Powell

"Thriving on a Riff" - Charlie Parker

"Travisimo" - Al Cohen

"We'll Be Together Again" - Carl Fischer/Frankie Laine

CHROMATIC MINOR SEVENTH PROGRESSION: TREBLE CLEF

Emile DeCosmo

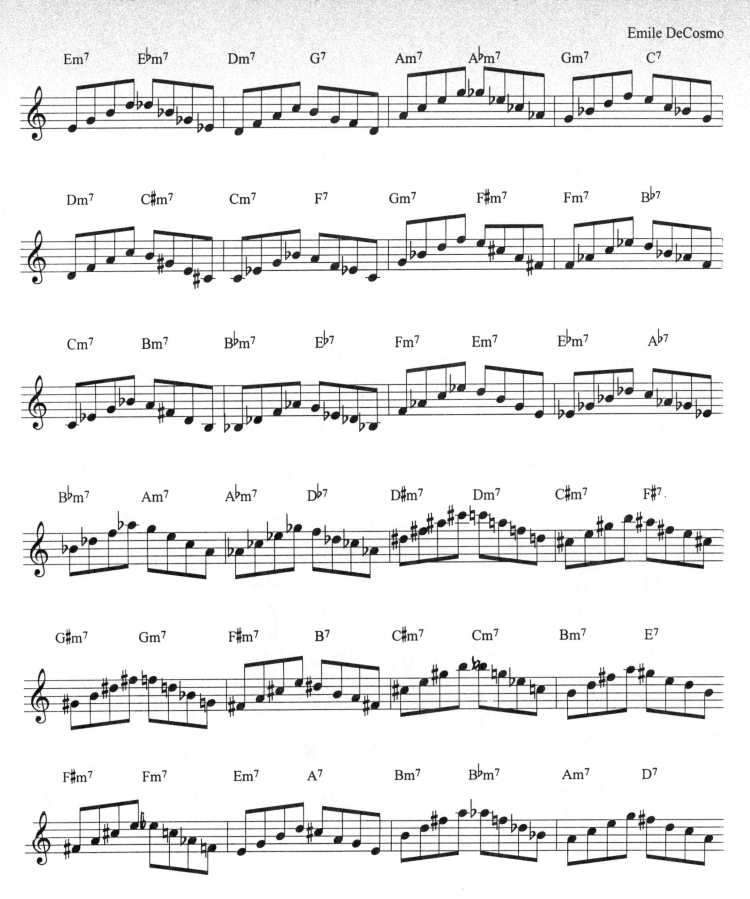

CHROMATIC MINOR SEVENTH PROGRESSION: BASS CLEF

Emile DeCosmo

CHAPTER 25

THE WHOLE-TONE SCALE

The whole-tone scale is usually associated with the music of Claude Debussy, who used it more than any other composer. In a book written by William Hugh Miller, entitled *Introduction to Music Appreciation*, published by Chilton Book Company, 1970, the author states, "The whole-tone scale was an innovation of the last decade of the nineteenth century. This new movement was called 'impressionism,' and its originator in the field of music was Debussy." In the early twentieth century, the whole-tone scale, comprised of six tones all separated by whole steps, was used occasionally by other French impressionistic composers. The whole-tone scale is made up of one half of the chromatic scale, also known as the "duodecuple," or "dodecuple scale," in the twelve-tone system of composition. In 1889, Javanese gamelan players (generic term for an Indonesian orchestra) came to Paris, France and played a scale that was similar to the whole-tone scale. When heard by Debussy, the scale caught his fancy, and by his use of it, brought the scale to its highest development.

In classical circles, Russian composer Dargomyzhsky was one of the earliest composers who made use of this scale in his opera *The Stone Guest*, which was based on the Don Juan legend.

The whole-tone scale consists of all whole steps lacking two fundamental intervals of traditional music—the perfect fifth or the perfect fourth—and has neither a dominant nor a leading tone. Having little gravitational pull, it lacks a true tonic. Because of the way this scale is constructed, it was extremely suitable for impressionistic composing, which was very vague and restless, but at the same time, its use was limited for other styles of music. Using the whole-tone scale can become monotonous. A composer must switch from one scale to another, or use other tonalities to break the monotony. In order to understand the whole-tone scales, we must first trace the discovery and history of the chromatic scale. Even though Debussy made use of the whole-tone scale more than any other composer of his time, the scale was first discovered in 1200 B.C. by the Chinese.

The Western world's chromatic scale can be traced back to the twelve *Lus* that evolved out of the Chinese Empire, and are the source for two whole-tone scales. The chromatic scale and the whole-tone scale are closely related. Chinese music influenced the use of the chromatic scale by the Greeks, and is probably the oldest musical system in existence. Its chromatic scale is composed of twelve Lus, which correspond to the notes in the Circle of Fifths, used by the "yellow" Emperor Huang-ti in 2697 B.C. Each note signified a particular month and hour of day.

The word "chromatic" is a derivative of the Greek "chromos." The Greeks had three types of scales: diatonic, chromatic, and enharmonic. Pythagoras, who invented the tetrachord, considered the 4th, 5th, and the octave as perfect intervals. The outer notes of intervals were fixed, but the inner notes were moveable, and were used as embellishments.

CHROMATIC SCALE THEORY

1   2   3   4   5   6   7   8   9   10   11   12:
twelve tones

C   C♯   D   D♯   E   F   F♯   G   G♯   A   A♯   B:
chromatic tones

By skipping every other chromatic tone, we arrive at the C whole-tone scale:

C   D   E   F♯   G♯   A♯

The C whole-tone scale represents yang, sun, or masculine tones.

The remaining chromatic tones produce the C♯ whole-tone scale.

C♯   D♯   F   G   A   B

The C♯ whole-tone scale represents yin, moon, or feminine tones.

Many composers consider both whole-tone scales an arpeggio of the chromatic scale.

Example: chromatic scale

C, C♯, D, D♯, E, F, F♯, G, G♯, A, A♯, B, C

C   D   E   F♯   G♯   A♯   C = C whole-tone scale

C♯   D♯   F   G   A   B = C♯ whole-tone scale

Each whole-tone scale produces six augmented triads, six tritones, and six dominant seventh chords that contain flatted fifths and raised fifths. The six tritones of the C whole-tone scale are C–F♯, D–G♯, E–A♯, F♯–C, G♯–D, A♯–E. The six tritones of the D♭ whole-tone scale (C♯ enharmonically) are D♭–G, E♭–A, F–B, G–D♭, A–E♭, B–F. All triads are augmented in this scale, causing an

absence and a lack of harmonic variety. When used in brief passages, composers may interweave modes, or major or minor scales, which create a kaleidoscopic effect. Also by using parallel seconds, fourths, fifths, and ninths moving over a pedal, Debussy's music became very stylish.

The C whole-tone scale produces scale tones C, D, E, F♯, G♯, A♯, augmented triads, and six dominant seventh chords build on each tone of the scale. The C♯ whole-tone scale produces scale tones C♯, D♯, E♯, F, G, A, augmented triads, and six dominant seventh chords built on each tone of the scale. Any tone of a whole-tone scale can be used as its tonic or final note, and any tone can be used to produce a whole-tone dominant chord (a dominant chord that contains all notes of the whole-tone scale, including the augmented eleventh and minor thirteenth with the fifth raised or lowered fifth). When the whole-tone scale is used for composing music, the melody becomes vague and weakened and seems to wander.

In summation, constructed entirely of whole steps, this scale tends to:

(a) lack a usual tonic (any tone can be used as a tonic)

(b) contain the same quality chords on each step of its scale

(c) have certain special harmonies

(d) have very little gravitational pull

(e) contain melodies that have a floating effect

(f) have no tension or release

(g) cause little or no forward drive

(h) have a very repetitive sound

(i) lack a dominant or leading tone

(j) have a feeling of vagueness and restlessness

(k) not have any rules of harmonic progression

Claude Debussy was not the only composer who used the whole-tone scale in his compositions. Other composers who made use of this interesting sound were Modest Moussorgsky, Ferruccio Busoni, Alexander Scriabin, Ernst Toch, Bela Bartok, Alban Berg, Paul Hindemith, Jacques Ibert, Charles Ives, Maurice Ravel, and Igor Stravinsky. The American composer Wallingford Riegger experimented with both whole-tone scales, using them as two halves of a twelve-tone row. Composers after 1900 lost interest in using the whole-tone scale.

In addition to the great classical composers that made use of the whole-tone scale, jazz composers were led by the "high priest of bebop": Thelonious Monk (born October 10, 1920, died February 17, 1982), who began a renewal of the use and overuse of the whole-tone and chromatic scales more than any other jazz player/composer in his improvisations. Monk, also known as the "Mad Monk," was one of the many pianist/composers who made a distinctive contribution to the music of the bebop era. He wrote very angular melodies using sudden chord progressions and chromatic changes that were difficult to improvise over. Thelonious would play and insert whole-tone motives and chromatic colors anywhere and whenever the urge was felt. An excellent example of this is in the song by Monk called "Skippy." Because of the relationship of the chromatic scale and the whole-tone scale, Monk used progressions of chromatic dominant seventh chords moving down or up. He also made use of the cycle of fifths progressions or augmented chords, while composing the melody using the two whole-tone scales. Steve Lacy recorded this rendition of "Skippy" on his *Reflections* album.

To quote from the *Downbeat* magazine article written by Steve Griggs (who also transcribed Lacy's solo), he states, "Lacy has made a career of studying, performing, and recording Monk tunes. To learn [Monk tunes], I listened to Monk's records hundreds of times, and learned a lot more in the process of listening and prac-

ticing than merely the tunes themselves. The harmony, melody, and rhythm are all interesting in Monk tunes. I like their shapes and the way they interlock—the harmony gives the shapes colors."

Another idiosyncrasy of Monk's playing was told to me by Al Lukas, a famous bass player and friend of mine who once played with Monk: "At times during improvisations, Monk would stay on a few measures or sections of the song and improvise over and over until he had exhausted his ideas and then continued with the piece." The late, great trumpeter Ray Copeland told me that when he played with Thelonious Monk, the same things would also take place, especially on intros and bridges.

An example of this type of playing/composing is in the melody of "Straight, No Chaser." The melody consists of a repetitive chromatic theme in a different part of each measure. The reason this works is because the song is a blues song and the progression holds the song together. Another reason that this type of playing works is because the repeating melody acts like a pedal tone over the moving progression. This is the opposite of using a bass pedal under a moving melody. Monk inserted or used the whole-tone scale abruptly whenever he felt the urge, but also wrote vertical melodies with a few notes using chords with no resolution, and playing two-part intervals or chord clusters.

In Dave Gelly's book entitled *The Giants of Jazz*, published by Schirmer Books (1986), he states:

"His parents can't have known it at the time, but they gave Thelonious Sphere Monk a name which was to match his music to perfection; the sound of the one instantly calls the other to mind. In the course of his life, his public reputation went through three distinct phases—from harmless lunatic to fashionable, eccentric artist to revered, elder statesman. It is entirely probable that Monk himself noticed none of this, except for the fact that he was working more regularly during the last two periods, and that the pianos were in tune. He arrived on the scene with the bebop movement of the '40s; in a sense, he was the most through-going bebopper of them all."

Leonard Feather, noted jazz historian, critic, author, and composer since the early '30s, best known for his volumes of "Encyclopedia of Jazz" reference books, has written a blues song entitled "12-Tone Blues," using the two whole-tone scales (c. 1960 by Model Music Co.).

The following is a list of jazz tunes that contain whole-tone scales, augmented chords, partials of whole-tone scales, chromatically ascending and descending seventh chords, chromatically ascending and descending ii7V7 chords, and chromatic bass lines against stagnant or angular melodies. As many of these tunes as possible should be played and memorized.

"One Up, One Down" - John Coltrane

"Our Man Higgins" - Lee Morgan

"Spanning" - Charles Tolliver

"Cappuccino" - Chick Corea

"Criss Cross" - Thelonious Monk

"Evidence" - Thelonious Monk

"Gregory Is Here" - Horace Silver

"Jody Grind" - Horace Silver

"Ju-Ju" - Wayne Shorter

"Le Roi" - David Baker

"Queer Notions" - Coleman Hawkins

"Stella By Starlight" - Victor Young

"Skippy" - Thelonious Monk

"Take The A-Train" - Billy Strayhorn

"52 Street Theme" - Thelonious Monk

"Bye Ya" - Thelonious Monk

"Played Twice" - Thelonious Monk

"Well, You Needn't" - Thelonious Monk

"Rhythm-A-Ning" - Thelonious Monk

"Straight, No Chaser" - Thelonious Monk

"Mysterioso" - Thelonious Monk

"Epistrophy" - Thelonious Monk

"Brilliant Corners" - Thelonious Monk

"Monk's Mood" - Thelonious Monk

"Ask Me Now" - Thelonious Monk

"Little Rootie Tootie" - Thelonious Monk

"In Walked Bud" - Thelonious Monk

"'Round Midnight" - Thelonious Monk

"Off Minor" - Thelonious Monk

"Let's Cool One" - Thelonious Monk

"Monkish" - Thelonious Monk

"Ruby, My Dear" - Thelonious Monk

"Thelonious" - Thelonious Monk

"Introspection" - Thelonious Monk

The whole-tone scale sounds best when played over the harmony of a dominant seventh chord with an augmented and/or flatted fifth.

As can be seen by the length of the above partial list of jazz literature, which contains many whole-tone scale sounds in melodic shapes, a jazz player acquires an abundance of jazz language and style while learning melodies. These tunes, as melodic information stored in the mind's ear, then become part of the total melodic recall to be played in bits or at length when improvising. All great jazz players have hundreds, and may thousands, of jazz tunes at their fingertips that can be used to put together, as a puzzle, in thousands of different ways over endless chord changes. This process occurs automatically as the improvisor reacts to many new tunes and many new sets of chord changes. The novice player should begin to memorize as many different jazz tunes as possible to expand improvisational fluency, and acquire jazz vocabulary and language, which should be a continuing process. Playing jazz tunes through the cycle of fifths, chromatically (ascending and descending), can do this. Doing this will eventually enable the student to play any song in any key.

POOK 7/9 WHOLE-TONE SCALE — TREBLE CLEF INSTRUMENTS

treble clef

Emile De Cosmo

Music Graphics By Louis De Cosmo

POOK 7/9 WHOLE-TONE SCALE — BASS CLEF INSTRUMENTS

bass clef

Emile De Cosmo

CHAPTER 26

THE TRITONE CYCLE

A turnaround usually consists of a set of chords used in the first ending that end a phrase and then leads back to the repeat of the first phrase. It also helps to lead from one chorus to another or sometimes in the second ending after a second chorus leading to a bridge. The turnaround is also used to create an interesting progression when chord changes are stagnant or are the same for two, four, or more measures.

The turnaround may consist of many different species, types, or qualities of chords, such as a major seven, minor seven, dominant seven, minor seven flat five (half-diminished chord), diminished, or combinations of these chords, sometimes including the upper partials such as ninths, elevenths, and thirteenths. After many years of improvising a jazz player may encounter thousands of variant types of this progression.

The **Sample List of Turnarounds** (see top of next page) I've included in a graphics box is a partial list of turnaround progressions that relate to The Tritone Cycle progression. There are many other turnarounds in existence that have not been mentioned here, but the novice jazz player would do well to learn these.

The tritone cycle exercise used in this article uses this turnaround progression:

CMaj7 | E♭Maj7 | A♭Maj7 | D♭Maj7 |

IMaj7 | ♭IIIMaj7 | ♭VIMaj7 | ♭IIMaj7 |

DEFINITIONS OF TURNAROUNDS

Definitions of Turnarounds: also known as Turnbacks, Turnabouts, and Vamps:

From *Melody and Harmony in Contemporary Songwriting* by Daniel A. Ricigliano, published by Donato Music Publishing Co., N.Y., copyright 1978:

A chord pattern which occurs at the end of a section and prepares for the repeat of a section is referred to as a turnaround pattern.

Examples:

1. | C Ami | F G7 |

2. | Cmi A♭Maj | G7sus G7 |

As stated by Mark C. Gridley in *Jazz Styles, A History and Analysis* published by Prentice-Hall, Inc, N.J., copyright 1978:

A short progression just prior to the point at which the player must "turnaround" to begin another repetition of the larger progression. Turnarounds are the chord progressions occurring in the seventh, eighth, fifteenth, and sixteenth, thirty-first and thirty-second bars of a thirty-two bar chord progression and in the eleventh and twelfth bars of a twelve bar blues progression. Some turnarounds occupy more or less than two measures, however. Turnarounds provide an opportunity for

Sample List of Turnarounds in the Key of C										
Expressed as: **Chord Progression Symbols**					**Expressed as:** **Roman Numerals**					
C	Ami7	Dmi	G7	....	I	vi7	ii7	V7		
C	E♭mi7	Dmi7	G7	....	I	♭iii7	ii7	V7		
C	Ami7	A♭mi7	G7	....	I	vi7	♭ii7	V7		
C	Ami7	Dmi7	D♭7	....	I	vi7	ii7	♭II7		
C	E♭mi7	A♭mi7	G7	....	I	♭iii7	♭vi7	V7		
C	E♭mi7	A♭mi7	D♭7	....	I	♭iii7	♭vi7	♭II7		
C	Ami7	A♭mi7	D♭7	....	I	vi7	♭vi7	♭II7		
C	E♭mi7	Dmi7	D♭7	....	I	♭iii7	ii7	♭II7		
C	A7	D7	D♭7	....	I	VI7	II7	♭II7		
C	A7	D7	G7	....	I	VI7	II7	V7		
C	E♭7	D7	D♭7	....	I	♭III7	II7	♭II7		
C	E♭7	D7	G7	....	I	♭III7	II7	V7		
C	E♭7	A♭7	G7	....	I	♭III7	♭VI7	V7		
C	E♭7	A♭7	D♭7	....	I	♭III7	♭VI7	♭II7		
C	A7	A♭7	D♭7	....	I	VI7	♭VI7	♭II7		
C	A7	A♭7	G7	....	I	VI7	♭VI7	V7		

numerous variations, which depend on the preferences and era of soloist and rhythm section.

Examples:

| G7 | G7 |

| Dmi7 | G7 | C |

| Dmi7 | A♭mi7 D♭7 | C |

| Dmi7 | Fmi7 | C |

| Fmi7 | B♭7 | C |

| Dmi E♭7 | A♭ B7 | E G7 | C |
  (similar to *Giant Steps* changes)

In *Jazz Theory*, by Andrew Jaffe, published by Wm. C. Brown Company Publishers, Iowa, 1983, Jaffe defines the Turnaround as:

Repeating progression of three or four chords usually ending on an unresolved dominant seventh. These serve as the basis for many improvised endings and introductions and become a part of the actual progressions of many tunes. Turnaround is a simple, often repeating, progression, usually involving three or four chords, that has the effect of reinforcing the tonic chord by moving slightly away from it and then implying a resolution to it; often used as the harmonic basis for improvised introductions and endings.

From *Jazz Improvisation*, by David Baker, Frangipani Press, second edition, 1983.

The term turnback usually refers to a two-measure progression consisting of four chords. This progression serves a number of purposes. First, it helps define the form of a composition. For instance, in a Blues the last two measures of each chorus consists of a I chord. The first four measures also consist of a I chord; consequently, the listener hears six measures of a tonic chord. These six measures could be divided 1+5, 5+1, 4+2, 2+4, or 3+3. By using the turnback the performer is able to clearly indicate the correct division 2+4. Secondly, it serves the purpose of providing a link from one chorus to another. A third purpose served is that of preventing staticness. For example, it provides the possibility for harmonic motion where no motion exists. A fourth purpose served is that of providing rhythmic and melodic interest at the ends of sections within compositions.

DEFINITION OF VAMP

Handbook of Music Terms, by Parks Grant, The Scarecrow Press, 1967.

A short introductory passage, usually two measures in length, and normally enclosed in repeat signs. It is often marked "until ready" and may be repeated as often as desired. Vamps are found in many popular songs.

A simple, improvised accompaniment to a simple melody.

DEFINITIONS OF TRITONE

Harvard Dictionary of Music, Willi Apel, Harvard University Press, 1974.

The interval of the augmented fourth (C-F♯) or diminished fifth (C-G♭), so called because it spans three whole tones. It has always been considered a dangerous interval, to be avoided or treated with great caution [see Diabolus in musica]. As a melodic progression it was rarely used before 1900, except in combinations such as

C-F♯-G, where F♯ is the leading tone before G. In modern music, however, it is a legitimate interval, e.g., in the whole-tone scale or in various experimental devices based on the fact that the tritone is exactly one-half of the octave.

Handbook of Music Terms, by Parks Grant, The Scarecrow Press, 1967:

A term applied to either the augmented fourth or the diminished fifth (see intervals). The name is derived from the fact that this interval contains three tones or whole-steps.

Harmony and Structure, Leonard G. Ratner, McGraw-Hill Book Co., 1962:

The tritone is by far the most powerful agent of harmonic action or instability within our traditional harmonic system, exactly because it creates such an urgent need for resolution to a specific harmonic point. In music of the eighteenth and nineteenth centuries, whenever the tritone is heard, a need for its resolution is generated.

OTHER USES OF THE TURNAROUND PROGRESSION

A turnaround can be also similar to a deceptive cadence, where the dominant triad or seventh chord moves to another chord instead of to a tonic chord in a surprising, evasive, or interrupted way. The turnaround cannot close a composition, but can be used at the end of a piece as a "fade" (to die out gradually). The turnaround constitutes an excellent device whereby a piece can be kept moving and a premature end avoided.

Many jazz players will, at the end of a tune, often stay on the turnaround and improvise for an extended period of time until the conclusion of the solo. This turnaround can be also used as a deceptive introduction that is repeated many times before the "head" (melody) begins. The deceptive turnaround can also be used between soloists as an interlude before the next soloist. The next soloist can then pick up that interlude and improvise until deciding to play on the chord changes of the melody.

Turnarounds can be added to a piece of music to keep the music moving when the motion has stopped in the melody or the harmony. Sometimes when both melody and harmony are stagnant a composer will use motion in the rhythm. Many times when the melody is constantly moving the composer will write stagnant harmony to balance out the motion in the melody, e.g. *Perpetual Motion*, by Paganinni.

When a melody of a song is stagnant the composer will balance the melody by having many chords that move in the harmony, e.g. *The One Note Samba*, by Antonio Carlos Jobim.

Traditional Folk, Country Western, Ragtime, Dixieland, and Rock use the simplest of turnarounds. Pop tunes, Swing tunes, and Blues contain turnarounds that are a bit more interesting. Jazz tunes use the most complex turnarounds generally utilizing chromatic harmony and odd chord progressions. The turnaround is a common device used in all types of music. There are countless variations of turnarounds and possibly many yet undiscovered and unwritten.

THE TRITONE

The tritone, an interval of an augmented fourth, called the devil's interval (diabolus in musica) during the Middle Ages, is the most powerful force of harmonic action within the musical universe. The augmented fourth when heard harmonically creates a tremendous need for resolution and is more properly to be regarded as the "angel of resolution." The tritone provides the most distinctive characteristic of the dominant seventh chord creating individual tension and unrest, increasing the tonal magnetism, causing a greater need for resolution to a tonic chord whose root is a fifth below the root

of the dominant seventh chord. This interval is naturally found between the fourth and seventh degrees of the major scale. The dominant seventh chord (V7) contains both of these scale degrees which create forward motion pressing for resolution to the tonic (I) chord making the dominant seventh to tonic the most prevalent chord progression.

The seventh of the V7 chord in the key of F, i.e.: the B♭ in the C7chord: C, E, G, B♭, moves down a half-step to the third of the I chord (Fa to Mi), A of the F, A, C chord, while the third of the V7, the E of the C, E, G, B♭, in the key of F, moves up a half-step to the tonic of the I chord (Ti to Do), the F of the F, A, C chord. The tritone moves inwardly or outwardly depending on its interval whether its a flatted fifth or augmented fourth, to the first and third degrees of its related tonic chord. The direction of these tones determines the movement or voice leading of the chord as a whole making the V7 to I progression almost inevitable.

FLATTED FIFTHS IN JAZZ:

The progressive jazz players of the late 1940's and 1950's such as Charlie Parker, Dizzie Gillespie and the Bebop school of players altered the chord changes of many of the tunes played. Along with the altered chords, they used many of these altered sounds in their melodic lines. The most common altered sound from the Bebop school of music was the flatted fifth or enharmonically the sharp fourth.

Examples:

1. C to G♭ = Flatted Fifth

2. C to F♯ = Augmented Fourth:

Many jazz pieces of that era ended on the flatted fifth. In fact, there was a bebop greeting that gave the flatted fifth sign: a raised open hand with the other hand placed horizontally at the wrist.

In Reese Markewich's book *Inside Outside* he notes:

"Ever since the birth of modern jazz the term flatted fifth has been bandied about. Musicians used to make the sign of the flatted fifth when greeting each other in humorous ritual."

The flatted fifth or augmented fourth is contained in the upper partials of the overtone series where the jazz players discovered it. In fact the sound of the overtones built on the fundamental C produces a dominant thirteenth chord with an added augmented eleventh.

Example:

C, E, G, B♭, D, F♯, A, C which is a C13+11 chord.

THE FLATTED FIFTH CONCEPT AND ITS TRADITIONAL HARMONIC ROOTS

Any chord of any species or quality can have for its harmonic substitute a similar type chord built a flatted fifth away from its root called the flatted fifth or tritone substitution. In other words any two similar type chords whose roots are located a tritone apart can substitute for each other.

This concept can be traced to its roots in traditional harmony, where augmented sixth chords were used as a type of chromatic harmony and named: Neopolitan, French and German sixths. The Neopolitan or Italian sixth, introduced in the seventeenth century, was an altered ii chord of a minor key that sounded like a major triad which resolves to its tonic.

Example: D♭ major triad resolving to C minor triad, D♭, F, A♭ resolving down to C, E♭, G.

The D♭ major triad could also resolve to the dominant seventh chord of that minor key first and then to its tonic.

Example: D♭ major triad, D♭, F, A♭ resolving to a G dominant triad G, B, D, then to its tonic C minor, or D♭ major triad resolving to a G dominant chord, D♭, F, A♭ resolving to G, B, D, F and then to its tonic C minor.

The D♭ root of the triad is the flatted fifth of the G7 chord. The interval created between the root of the G7 chord and the root of the D♭ triad is a tritone or the flatted fifth relationship.

The **German sixth** is a complete dominant seventh chord, for instance, D♭, F, A♭, C♭ that resolves a half-step lower to a C major chord, C, E, G or from a D♭7 chord to a G7 chord and then to its tonic C major chord. Example: D♭7 to G7 to C Major

The **French sixth** is a dominant seventh with a flatted fifth, for instance, D♭, F, A♭♭, C♭ that resolves a half step lower to a C Major chord, C,E,G or from a D♭7♭5 chord to a G7 chord and then to its tonic. Example: D♭7♭5 to G7 to C Major

The two most important notes of a dominant seventh chord are its third and seventh creating a tritone which demands resolution. The tritone divides an octave in half, therefore, when a tritone is inverted it becomes another tritone.

The D♭7 chord contains the tritone from its third, F to its seventh, C♭ or (B). The G7 chord contains a tritone from its third, B to its seventh, F. The third, F and the seventh, C♭ of the D♭7 chord when inverted become the seventh, F and the third, B of the G7 chord. The roots of the D♭7 chord and the G7 chord are also a tritone apart thus completing the three tritones in the flatted fifth substitution.

The three tritones present in the flatted fifth substitution cause an overwhelming demand for its resolution to a chord one half-step lower from the root of the D♭7 chord (D♭) or to the root of the G7chord (G).

Example: The D♭7 chord containing the tritone from F to C♭ wants to resolve to a CMaj7 chord. The G7 chord containing the tritone from B to F wants to resolve to a G♭Maj7 chord. The tonics of these two keys D♭ and G are also a flatted fifth or a tritone apart.

The title of this article, *The Tritone Cycle*, is a term coined by the author and was chosen because of the tritone substitution of the roots of the vi7, ii7, V7 of the basic I7, vi7, ii7, V7 progression.

In *The Tritone Cycle* exercise the turnaround used in the key of C is CMaj7, E♭Maj7, A♭Maj7, D♭Maj7, which is composed using the flatted fifth substitutes of the roots of the basic vi7, ii7, V7 chords. In the key of C the progression used is CMaj7, Ami7, Dmi7, G7 as the basic turnaround; then substituting major seventh chords built on a root a flatted fifth above the basic vi7, ii7, V7 chords of the I7, vi7, ii7, V7 progression.

Example: CMaj7 is the IMaj7 chord in the key of C and the first chord change in the tritone cycle turnaround.

Ami7, the second chord change in the tritone cycle turnaround, is the vi7 chord in the key of C. A flatted fifth above the root of the Ami7 chord is E♭ and upon this E♭ root a major seventh chord is built which is an E♭Maj7 chord. Now the partial progression is CMaj7 to E♭Maj7.

Dmi7, the third chord change in the tritone cycle turnaround, is the ii7 chord in the key of C. A flatted fifth above the root of the Dmi7 chord is A♭ and upon this A♭ root a major seventh chord is built which is an A♭Maj7 chord. Now the partial progression is CMaj7 to E♭Maj7 to A♭Maj7.

G7, the fourth chord change in the tritone cycle turnaround, is the V7 chord in the key of C. A flatted fifth above the root of the G7 chord is D♭ and upon this D♭ root a major seventh chord is built which is an D♭Maj7 chord. Now the complete progression is CMaj7 (I7) to E♭Maj7 (♭IIIMaj7), to A♭Maj7 (♭VIMaj7), to D♭Maj7 (♭IIMaj7).

In the tritone cycle exercise we will be working with just one turnaround, the I7, ♭IIIMaj7, ♭VIMaj7, ♭IIMaj7, which will progress through the twelve keys making use of the cycle of fifths harmonic progression.

When improvising on any major seventh chord improvise using the notes and diatonic chords using the key of tonic of the major seventh chord. Example: For an A♭Maj7 chord improvise using the notes of the A♭ major scale with all or partials of the diatonic seventh chords staying in the key of A♭ major: A♭Maj7, B♭min7, Cmin7, D♭Maj7, E♭7, Fmin7, Gmin7♭5.

After learning this turnaround a good improvisor should memorize several other turnarounds, to have at his fingertips and later insert into a progression to add variety and interest in his improvisations.

The basic diatonic cycle of fifths can supply the harmonic flow during a turnaround progression. Flatted fifth chord substitutions are frequently inserted in this diatonic flow by composers or improvisers.

CHORD SUBSTITUTIONS MAKING USE OF THE FLATTED FIFTH CONCEPT

Any standard, pop, rock or jazz tune can be embellished by using flatted fifth substitutions of standard chord changes. Interesting turnarounds can be accomplished with the use of the flatted fifth (tritone) substitution. Knowing how to handle any type of turnaround along with its many substitutions is a prerequisite for the contemporary jazz player.

Any chord can be substituted by a same species or different type chord built a flatted fifth away from the chord for which it is substituting by applying this concept.

- A CMaj7 would have a G♭Maj7 as its substitution.
- A C7 (dominant seventh) would have a G♭7 as its substitution.
- A Cmin7 would have a G♭min7 as its substitution.
- A C7min7♭5 would have a G♭min7♭5 as its substitution.
- A Cdim7 would have a G♭dim7 as its substitution.

The term "The Tritone Cycle" used in this concept is "the tritone substitution" turnaround, a flatted fifth substitute of the I7, vi7, ii7, V7 progression, a common turnaround found in "The Diatonic Cycle" of fifths which has been used as a vamp in hundreds of songs written in the 1950's and in many songs prior to the 1950's.

Famous Standard Songs Pre-1950's Using the I7 vi7 ii7 V7 Progression

- 1927 "Can't Help Lovin' Dat Man"
  music by Jerome Kern
  lyrics by Oscar Hamerstein II

- 1930 "I Got Rhythm," from *Girl Crazy*
  music by George Gershwin
  lyrics by Ira Gershwin

- 1934 "Blue Moon"
  music by Richard Rodgers
  lyrics by Lorenz Hart

- 1935 "I Can't Get Started"
  music by George Gershwin
  lyrics by Ira Gershwin

- 1938 "Heart and Soul," from *A Song is Born*
  music by Hoagy Carmichael
  lyrics by Frank Loesser, Famous Music Corp.

- 1939 "Perfidia"
  music and lyrics by Alberto Dominguez.

- 1945 "These Foolish Things Remind Me of You"
  music by Jack Strachey and Harry Link
  lyrics by Holt Marvell

- 1949 "My Foolish Heart,"
  from the movie *My Foolish Heart*
  music by Victor Young
  lyrics by Ned Washington

Famous Songs From The 1950's Using the I7 vi7 ii7 V7 Progression

- "All I Have to Do is Dream"
  recorded by The Everly Brothers.

- "Book of Love"
  written by Warren Davis, George Malone and Charles Patrick

- "Come Go with Me"
  recorded by The Del Vikings

- "Diana" written and recorded by Paul Anka.

- "Do You Want to Dance?" by Robert Freeman

- "Earth Angel" by Dootsi Williams, Gaynell Hodge, Jesse Belvin

- "Ebb Tide"
  music by Robert Maxwell, lyrics by Carl Sigman

- "Eddie My Love" by Collins, David, and Ling

- "Hey Paula" by Ray Hilderbrand.

- "Little Darlin'" by Maurice Williams

- "Lollipop" by Beverly Ross and Julius Dixon

- "One Summer Night" by Danny Webb

- "Please Mr. Sun" by Ray Getzov

- "Put Your Head On My Shoulder"
  written and recorded by Paul Anka.

- "Sh-Boom, Sh-Boom (Life Could Be a Dream)"
  recorded by the Crew Cuts

- "Sherry"
  recorded by The Four Seasons

- "Silhouttes" by Frank C. Slay, Jr. and Bob Crewe

- "Stagger Lee"
  recorded by Lloyd Price

- "There Goes My Baby"
  recorded by The Drifters

- "Why Do Fools Fall in Love"
  Frankie Lyman and The Teenagers

- "The Wonder of You"
  recorded by Elvis Presley

There are countless other songs written in the 50's that use the I7, vi7, ii7, V7 progression. In fact, one particular song from the music score of the movie *Grease*, music and lyrics written by Warren Casey and Jim Jacobs, 1976, contained a rock and roll song written whose title was "Those Magic Changes" which used chord names as part of the lyric. Those magic changes were, in fact a variation of the I, vi7, ii7, V7 progression, which was the I7, vi7, iv7, V7 progression. The iv chord with an added sixth is spelled similar to an inversion of the ii7chord.

The following is a list of standard popular jazz tunes that contain the I7, vi7, ii7, V7 turnaround progression completely or in part. Although it is important to learn the I7, vi7, ii7, V7 progression in all keys or dialects, it is imperative for today's novice composer or improviser to become familiar with the jazz literature that makes use of the I7, vi7, ii7, V7 progression. If the student learns, analyzes, and memorizes these melodies, improvising on I7, vi7, ii7, V7 turnaround and the tritone cycle turnaround will become easier.

The tunes listed can be used as a vehicle for superimposing tritone cycle chord changes when improvising. Example: in the key of C when improvising on I7, vi7, ii7, V7 (Cmaj7, Amin7, Dmin7, G7) changes the keys or dialects of the tritone cycle chord changes (Cmaj7, E♭maj7, A♭maj7, D♭maj7) can be played as a tritone substitution instead of using the basic chord changes.

Many great jazz players improvise over the basic chord changes of a tune and superimpose the tritone cycle changes to make the jazz improvisation more interesting. Clifford Brown was one great jazz player who substituted the tritone changes often in a composition. The jazz piece "Brownie Speaks," written by Clifford Brown, uses the tritone cycle changes for the beginning two measures of every eight measures of the A section as a substitute for basic rhythm changes.

The chord changes of the first eight measures are as follows:

| C E♭ | A♭ D♭ | C E♭ | A♭ G | C C/B♭ | F/A A♭
| C G | Dm7 D♭7 |

Chord changes of the second eight measure are:

| C E♭ | A♭ D♭ | C E♭ | A♭ G | C C/B♭ | F/A A♭
| C G7 | C |

The Bridge, or B Section, is the same as "I Got Rhythm" changes.

The last eight measures are the same as the first eight measures of the A section except for the last measure which ends on the tonic C chord.

List of Standard Jazz Tunes That Use the I7 vi7 ii7 V7 Turnaround Progression

"An Oscar for Treadwell," Charlie Parker

"Anthropolgy," Charlie Parker

"Apple Honey," Recorded By Woody Herman

"Blue Moon," Richard Rodgers/ Lorenz Hart

"Celerity," Charlie Parker

"Chasin The Bird," Charlie Parker

"Crazeology," Bud Powell

"Dexterity," Charlie Parker

"Don't Be That Way," Benny Goodman/Sampson

"Dot's Groovy," Jack Montrose

"EB POB," Fats Navarro/Leo Parker

"Eternal Triangle," Dizzy Gillespie/Sonny Rollins/ Sonny Stitt

"52nd Street Theme," Thelonious Monk

"Five," Bill Evans

"Get Happy," Ted Koehler/Harold Arlen

"Good Bait," Tad Dameron

"Ham Fat," Scott Hamilton

"I Got Rhythm," George Gershwin/Ira Gershwin

"I Can't Get Started," George Gershwin/Ira Gershwin

"Into It," Stan Getz

"Jeepers Creepers," Harry Warren/Johnny Mercer

"Jumpin at the Woodside," recorded By Count Basie

"Kim," Charlie Parker

"Lemon Drop," recorded By Woody Herman

"Lester Leaps In," Lester Young

"Mack the Knife," Kurt Wiell/Marc Blitzstein

"Mambo Bounce," Sonny Rollins

"The Man with a Horn," Eddie DeLange

"Merry Go Round," Charlie Parker

"Miles Theme," Miles Davis

"Moose the Mooche," Charlie Parker

"My One and Only Love," Wood/Mellin

"Oleo," Sonny Rollins

"On the Scene," Lou Donaldson

"One Bass Hit," Dizzy Gillespie

"Ow," Blue Mitchell

"Parisian Thoroughfare," Bud Powell

"Passport," Charlie Parker

"Red Cross," Charlie Parker

"Rhythm-a-ning," Thelonious Monk

"Salt Peanuts," Dizzy Gillespie

"Senor Mouse," Chick Corea

"Shaw Nuff," Dizzy Gillespie/Charlie Parker

"Sonny Side," Sonny Stitt

"Steeplechase," Charlie Parker

"The Stopper," Sonny Rollins

"Stranger in Paradise," Robert Wright/George Forest

"The Theme," Miles Davis

"The Serpents Tooth," Miles Davis

"Thriving on a Riff," Charlie Parker

As can be seen by the length of the partial list of jazz literature which contain the I7, vi7, ii7, V7 progression, a jazz player acquires an abundance of jazz language and style while learning melodies. In fact, there are thousands of jazz tunes, which contain the diatonic cycle of fifths progression completely or partially. The tunes listed above, as melodic information stored in the mind's ear, then become part of the total melodic recall to be played in bits or at length when improvising. All great jazz players have hundreds and maybe thousands of jazz tunes at their fingertips that can be used to put together as a puzzle in thousands of different ways over endless chord changes. This process occurs automatically as the improvisor reacts to many new tunes and many new sets of chord changes. The novice player should begin to memorize as many different jazz tunes as possible to expand improvisational fluency and acquire jazz vocabulary and language which should be a continuing process. After memorizing some of the jazz literature listed above, the student should then practice the tunes in as many different keys as possible to expand the student's jazz language even further. The jazz language learned in twelve keys can be taken another step further by using the bits of language as flatted fifth substitutes to be used when played over the basic I7, vi7, ii7, V7 chord progression.

HARMONIC BACKGROUND

Chord symbols have been provided to familiarize the student with the proper chord names and the corresponding keys for the arpeggios being practiced. The chords also allow the studies to be played as duets. The teacher should play the chord accompaniment as the student plays the exercise, or the chord progressions may be prerecorded for practicing alone. Playing over the chords will enable the student to hear the sound of each study against its proper harmonic background. With practice, the student's ability to hear and improvise over major seventh chord changes will improve.

The exercise in this article comes from *The Tritone Cycle* by Emile De Cosmo, which can be used as a guide for theory, ear training, and harmony, and covers the I7 chords through the cycle of fifths in all major keys.

The Tritone Cycle is endorsed by leading educators and instrumentalists including Arnie Lawrence, Clark Terry, Bill Watrous, Clem DeRosa, John Faddis and Slide Hampton, Vincent Bell, Trade Martin, Jack Grassel, Eddie Bert, Joe Cinderella, Leon Russianoff, Friday the 13th film composer Harry Manfredini, and conductor Gerard Schwarz.

THE TRITONE CYCLE: TREBLE CLEF

THE TRITONE CYCLE: BASS CLEF

CHAPTER 27

THE DIMINISHED SCALE

The diminished scale is a rather arbitrary and sometimes ambiguous, but extremely useful organization of notes that may be conceived and constructed in various ways. It is composed in several different ways (listed here numerically 1-4).

1. By placing two minor tetrachords a tritone apart as one scale. A tetrachord is a group of four tones placed in scale wise succession, usually totaling the interval of a perfect fourth.

Example:

A. Lower C minor tetrachord C, D, E♭, F.

B. Upper F♯ minor tetrachord F♯, G♯, A, B.

When completed the C diminished scale is C, D, E♭, F, F♯, G♯, A, B, C and sounds the most "inside" when played over a C diminished chord.

2. Composed of alternating whole and half steps or major and minor seconds and called an octatonic or eight tone scale.

Example:

C, D, E♭, F, F♯, G♯, A, B, C.

C-D whole step or major second; D-E♭ half step or minor second; E♭-F whole step or major second; F-F♯ half step or minor second; F♯-G♯ whole step or major second;

G♯-A half step or minor second; A-B whole step or major second; B-C half step or minor second.

3. When used against a dominant seventh chord the diminished scale is constructed in alternating half and whole steps or minor and major seconds.

Example:

B7 uses a B, C, D, E♭, F, F♯, G♯, A, B scale.

B-C half step or minor second; C-D whole step or major second; D-E♭ half step or minor second; E♭-F whole step or major second; F-F♯ half step or minor second; F♯-G♯ whole step or major second; G♯-A half step or minor second; A-B whole step or major second.

Twelve Dominant Seventh Chords and their Respective Diminished Scales:

- B7 or B dominant seventh chord uses a B half, whole diminished scale:

  B, C, D, E♭, F, F♯, G♯, A, B.

- D7 or D dominant seventh chord uses a D half, whole diminished scale:

  D, E♭, F, F♯, G♯, A, B, C, D.

- F7 or F dominant seventh chord uses a F half, whole diminished scale:

  F, F♯, G♯, A, B, C, D, E♭, F.

- G#7 or G# dominant seventh chord uses a G# half, whole diminished scale:

  G#, A, B, C, D, E♭, F, F#, G#.

- C7 or C dominant seventh chord uses a C half, whole diminished scale:

  C, D♭, E♭, E, F#, G, A, B♭, C.

- E♭7 or E♭ dominant seventh chord uses an E♭ half, whole diminished scale:

  E♭, E, F#, G, A, B♭, C, D♭, E♭.

- F#7 or F# dominant seventh chord uses a F# half, whole diminished scale:

  F#, G, A, B♭, C, D♭, E♭, E, F#.

- A7 or A dominant seventh chord uses an A half, whole diminished scale:

  A, B♭, C, D♭, E♭, E, F#, G.

- C#7 or C# dominant seventh chord uses a C# half, whole diminished scale:

  C#, D, E, F, G, A♭, B♭, B, C#.

- E7 or E dominant seventh chord uses an E half, whole diminished scale:

  E, F, G, A♭, B♭, B, C#, D, E.

- G7 or G dominant seventh chord uses a G half, whole diminished scale:

  G, A♭, B♭, B, C#, D, E, F, G.

- B♭7 or B♭ dominant seventh chord uses a B♭ half, whole diminished scale:

  B♭, B, C#, D, E, F, G, A♭, B♭.

The half step, whole step diminished scale is most effective when improvising over dominant seventh chords and offers the improvisor or composer an excellent choice of altered notes to use. This scale provides the best altered sounds when used while improvising over a B7 chord, D7 chord, F7 chord, A♭7 chord, producing the following alterations of each dominant seventh chord: The root, flatted ninth, raised ninth, third, fifth, flatted fifth, thirteenth, flatted seventh of the B7, D7, F7, A♭7, and as a more outside sound may be played over a C7, E♭7, F#7, A7. This means that a dominant seventh chord whose root is any one of the eight scale

tones of a diminished scale may be used harmonically for that scale.

4. Another way of conceiving or composing a diminished scale is by interlocking two diminished seventh chords as illustrated below.

For example:

A C dim7 chord spelled C, E♭, F#, A, and a D dim7 chord spelled D, F, G#, B when interlocked or dovetailed and written in alternating pitches is spelled:

C, D, E♭, F, F#, G#, A, B, C

C DIMINISHED 7TH CHORD SCALE

Because of this interlocking, the diminished scale requires a knowledge and an understanding of the construction of diminished seventh chords.

The twelve diminished seventh chords are:

C–E♭–F#–A–E♭–F#–A–C–F#–A–C–E♭–A–C–E♭–F#

C#–E– G–B♭–E–G–B♭–D♭–G–B♭–D♭–E–B♭–D♭–E–G

D–F–A♭–B–F–A♭–B–D–G#–B–D–F–B–D–F–A♭

The diminished scale has been in existence since the mid nineteenth century, and was often referred to as the "Bolshevik" scale, which means scale of the Russian people, and was favored by many Russian composers. Rimsky-Korsakov, b.1844- d.1908, a famous Russian composer, used the diminished scale in many of his compositions.

In the introduction of *Thesaurus of Scales and Melodic Patterns*, by Nicolas Slonimsky, published in 1947, Coleman Ross Co., inc., he states:

"In his Chronicle of My Musical Life, Rimsky-Korsakov mentions the use he made of an 8 tone scale, formed by alternating major and minor seconds."

Some early works by Rimsky-Korsakov, found in *Chronicle of My Musical Life, and Principles of Orchestration*, which include the diminished scale are:

Sadko, a tone poem composed July 14, 1867, which uses a B♭ diminished scale descending in the woodwind section in measure 119.

Antar, composed in 1868, first named *Second Symphony* and renamed many years later *Symphonic Suite*, which uses a D diminished scale ascending in the woodwind section at measure 52.

Mlada, an opera-ballet, completed July 15, 1889, which uses a G diminished scale descending, used as a Glissando in measure 39 of the woodwind section.

Olivier Messiaen, a French composer, organist, and teacher wrote a text book published in 1944 titled *Technique de mon language musical*. In his book he derives new scales from the chromatic scale by applying mathematical methods to music. Messiaen does not base his scales on the seven-note normal scale but groups his tones into scales of six and ten notes, naming these scales "modes of limited transposition" and numbering them from one to seven. Mode two of Messiaen's scales is the C diminished scale which can be transposed onto two other degrees or tones: C♯ and D. There are only three diminished scales which are C, C♯, and D. Inversions of these three scales are only duplications.

The notes of a C diminished scale—C, D, E♭, F, F♯, G♯, A, B, C—do not make an authentic scale. This fact causes the diminished scale to be termed an artificial or symmetric scale. In an authentic scale any scale tone cannot appear twice as different notes. For example, in a D♭ scale the notes are D♭, E♭, F, G♭, A♭, B♭, C, D♭. Each tone has a different letter name. If a D♭ scale were written D♭, E♭, F, F♯, A♭, B♭, C, D♭ it would not be considered an authentic scale because of the use of the F and F♯ instead of the correct F and G♭.

Each diminished chord uses a choice of four scales that contain the identical notes. The basic scale difference is the starting note which is the root of the scale and diminished chord used.

Notes of the diminished scale may be used with its corresponding diminished chord that contains the same root beginning with the first set of diminished seventh chords: C, E♭, G♭ (F♯), A.

Example:

- C dim7 chord, C, E♭, G♭, A, uses a C diminished scale which is:
  C, D, E♭, F, F♯, G♯, A, B, C.
- E♭ dim7 chord, E♭, F♯, A, C, uses the same diminished scale starting
  E♭, F, F♯, G♯, A, B, C, D, E♭.
- F♯ dim7 chord, F♯, A, C, E♭, uses the same diminished scale starting
  F♯, G♯, A, B, C, D, E♭, F, F♯.
- A dim7 chord, A, C, E♭, F♯ uses the same diminished scale starting
  A, B, C, D, E♭, F, F♯, G♯, A.

Second set of diminished seventh chords: C♯, E, G, B♭.

- C♯ dim7 chord, C♯, E, G, B♭ uses a C♯ diminished scale which is:
  C♯, D♯, E, F♯, G, A, B♭, C, C♯.
- E dim7 chord, E, G, B♭, C♯, uses the same diminished scale starting
  E, F♯, G, A, B♭, C, C♯, D♯, E.
- G dim7 chord, G, B♭, C♯, E, uses the same diminished scale starting
  G, A, B♭, C, C♯, D♯, E, F♯, G.
- B♭ dim7 chord, B♭, C♯, E, G uses the same diminished scale starting
  B♭, C, C♯, D♯, E, F♯, G, A, B♭.

Third set of diminished seventh chords: D, F, A♭, B (C♭).

- D dim7 chord, D, F, A♭, B, uses a D diminished scale which is:
  D, E, F, G, A♭, B♭, B, C♯, D.
- F dim7 chord, F, A♭, B, D uses the same diminished scale starting
  F, G, A♭, B♭, B, C♯, D, E, F.

- A♭ dim7 chord, A♭, B, D, F, uses the same diminished scale starting
A♭, B♭, B, C♯, D, E, F, G, A♭

- B dim7 chord, B, D, F, A♭, uses the same diminished scale starting
B, C♯, D, E, F, G, A♭, B♭, B.

NO NATURAL POSITION: THE DIMINISHED SCALE

Like the chromatic scale, the diminished scale has no "natural" position in any major or minor key, and although it can be played anywhere in a key, there will be no suggestion of a tonality.

Even though the symmetric diminished scale has no natural position in any major or minor key, a natural diminished scale or mode does appear as the seventh mode of the harmonic minor key which includes a diminished chord in the same natural position. The diatonic key of C harmonic minor contains a diminished seventh chord built on the seventh degree of the scale. The tone B is the seventh degree of the C harmonic minor scale. The vii dim7 chord in the key of C harmonic minor, built on the seventh degree is diatonically a B diminished seventh chord spelled B, D, F, A♭, and of course the natural scale which corresponds to this B dim7 chord is a diatonic mode from B to B, the seventh degree of the C harmonic minor scale:

B, C, D, E♭, F, G, A♭, B.

A diatonic diminished seventh chord and its corresponding natural diminished scale can be found beginning with the seventh degree of all twelve harmonic minor scales.

The diminished seventh chord contains a double tritone. In the B diminished chord the tritones are B to F and D to A♭. All the intervals of the diminished seventh chord are of the same size: a succession of three minor thirds. The diminished seventh is a highly tensioned chord because of the tritones contained, causing an urgency to resolve outwardly or inwardly. Because of the minor third construction, any one tone of a diminished seventh chord can act as the root of the chord. If any tones of the diminished seventh chord are lowered by a half step, the new chord created becomes a dominant seventh chord. Four dominant seventh chords can evolve from one diminished seventh chord.

CHANGING DIMINISHED SEVENTH CHORDS TO DOMINANT SEVENTH CHORDS

Example:

A diminished seventh chord built on C is spelled C, E♭, F♯, A. If the root C is lowered a half step to B, the notes are now B, D♯, F♯, A which spells a dominant seventh chord B7.

If this same diminished seventh chord is built on E♭ and the E♭ is lowered a half step to D, the notes are now D, F♯, A, C which spells a dominant seventh chord D7.

When this same diminished seventh chord is built on F♯ and the F♯ is lowered a half step to F the notes are now F, A, C, E♭, which spells a dominant seventh chord F7.

When this diminished seventh chord is built on A and the A is lowered a half step to A♭, the notes are now A♭, C, E♭, G♭, which spells a dominant seventh chord A♭7.

The above process can also occur when taking the other two diminished seventh chords and changing them to dominant seventh chords.

A C♯ dim7 chord, spelled C♯, E, G, B♭ produces four dominant seventh chords: C7, E♭7, G7, A7.

A D dim7 chord, spelled D, F, A♭, B produces four dominant seventh chords: D♭7, E7, G7, B♭7.

VARIOUS USES OF DIMINISHED SCALES OVER DOMINANT SEVENTH CHORDS

C diminished scale used as the root of a C7 chord.

C diminished scale used as the third of the A♭7 chord.

C diminished scale used as the fifth of the F7 chord.

C diminished scale used as the seventh of the D7 chord.

C diminished scale used as the flatted ninth of a B7 chord.

C diminished scale used as the flatted third of an A7 chord.

C diminished scale used as the flatted fifth of an F♯7 chord.

C diminished scale used as the thirteenth of an E♭7 chord.

C diminished scale used as the augmented fifth of an E7 chord.

C diminished scale used as the ninth of a B♭7 chord.

C diminished scale used as the eleventh of a G7 chord.

C diminished scale used as the major seventh of a D♭7 chord.

The further down the above list the diminished scale appears, in relation to the root of the chord, the more dissonant the scale will sound.

Following is a list of standard, popular, and jazz tunes that contain the diminished scale completely or in part. Although it is important to learn the diminished scale in all keys or dialects; it is imperative for today's novice composer or improvisor to become familiar with the jazz literature that makes use of the diminished scale. If the student learns, analyses, and memorizes these melodies, improvising on tunes which contain the diminished scale will become easier.

Standard, Popular Jazz Tunes that use Diminished Scales and Chords

All Blues," Miles Davis

"Barbara," Horace Silver

"Black Bottom Stomp," Jelly Roll Morton

"Blue in Green," Bill Evans/Miles Davis

"Desafinado," Antonio Carlos Jobim

"Dippermouth Blues," Joe Oliver

"Donna Lee," Charlie Parker

"E.S.P.," Wayne Shorter/Miles Davis

"Easy Living," Robin/Grainger

"I Remember Clifford," Benny Golson

"Mysterious Traveler," Wayne Shorter

"Night and Day," Cole Porter

"Once I Loved," Antonio Carlos Jobim

"Peace," Horace Silver

"Quiet Nights of Quiet Stars," Antonio Carlos Jobim

"Riverboat Shuffle," Carmichael/Mill/Parish

"Solitude," Duke Ellington

"Thank You," Jerry Dodgion

"The Song is You," Jerome Kern/Oscar Hammerstein

"War Gewesen," David Baker

"Wave," Antonio Carlos Jobim

"What Am I Here For," Duke Ellington

As can be seen by the length of the above partial list of jazz literature which contain the diminished scale in many melodic shapes, a jazz player acquires an abundance of jazz language and style while learning melodies. These tunes, as melodic information stored in the mind's ear, then become part of the total melodic recall to be played in bits or at length when improvising. All great jazz players have hundreds and maybe thousands of jazz tunes at their fingertips that can be used to put together as a puzzle in thousands of different ways over endless chord changes. This process occurs automatically as the improvisor reacts to many new tunes and many new sets of chord changes. The novice player should begin to memorize as many different jazz tunes as possible to expand improvisational fluency and acquire jazz vocabulary and language which should be a continuing process. After memorizing some of the jazz literature listed above, the student should then practice the tunes in as many different keys as possible to expand the student's jazz language even further.

The Pook 7/9 Diminished Scale exercise included in this article is written in both treble and bass clef versions. The study moves through the cycle of fifths progression. Playing this exercise will increase the ability to hear and play the sound of the diminished scale anywhere on your instrument.

The information in this article was taken from *The Diminished Scale* by Emile De Cosmo which has been endorsed by leading educators and instrumentalists including Jamey Abersold, Paquito D'Rivera, Denis De Blasio, Harold Lieberman, Pat La Barbera, Bucky Pizzarelli, Clark Terry, Snooky Young, Arnie Lawrence, Bill Watrous, Clem DeRosa, John Faddis, Slide Hampton, Vincent Bell, Trade Martin, Jack Grassel, Eddie Bert, Joe Cinderella, Friday the 13th film composer Harry Manfredini, Seattle Symphony orchestra conductor Gerard Schwarz, Dizzy Gillespie, Ray Copeland, and Leon Russianoff.

POOK 7/9 DIMINISHED SCALE: TREBLE CLEF

POOK 7/9 DIMINISHED SCALE: BASS CLEF

CHAPTER 28

THE CHROMATIC SCALE

The fundamental music scale used in all Western civilization consists of twelve semitones or half steps called the chromatic scale. The story of chromaticism can be traced to oriental music, which in turn influenced the use of the chromatic scale by the Greeks.

THE CHROMATIC SCALE AND THE TWELVE LUS

The Western world's chromatic scale can be traced back to the twelve lus that evolved out of the Chinese empire. Chinese music influenced the use of the chromatic scale by the Greeks and is probably the oldest musical system in existence. The Chinese chromatic scale is composed of 12 Lus which correspond to the notes in the "circle of fifths" used by the "yellow" Emperor Huang-ti in 2697 B.C. Each note used signified a particular month and hour of day.

The aulos, similar to the oboe having four to sixteen holes, was originally an ancient oriental wind instrument where one could make slight modification of pitch by half covering the holes. According to history the aulos was introduced to the Greeks about 900 B.C. by Olympos, the so-called "inventor of music." The aulos became the most important instrument of the ancient Greeks and influenced the use of chromatics. The word chromatic is a derivative of the Greek "chromos." The Greeks had three types of scales: diatonic, chromatic, and enharmonic.

Pythagorus, who invented the tetrachord, considered the 4th, 5th, and the octave as perfect intervals. The outer notes of intervals were fixed, but the inner notes were moveable and were used as embellishments. In the 14th century references to the chromatic scale were made by theorist Marchettus de Padua. True chromaticism was introduced by Adrian Willaert (1480-1562) and his student Cypriano de Rore (1516- 1565) who used a partial chromatic scale with the notes (B-C-C♯-D-D♯-E-F♯-G) to start the madrigal Calami sonum ferentes in (1561).

During the Baroque period chromatics were used when writing fugues and counter fugal music. In *Art of the Fugue* Bach introduces chromaticism to indicate sadness and mourning. As composers discovered and learned more about the effect that chromatic alteration created its use became evermore present in the music and style of sixteenth and seventeenth composers such as: Monteverdi, Orlando di Lasso. Johann Sebastian Bach made possible an increasing use of chromaticism with his acceptance of the tempered scale where by the octave was divided equal semitones. His *Chromatic Fantasy and Fugue* and *The Well Tempered Clavichord* are great examples of chromaticism.

During the Romantic Era composers such as Chopin, Schumann, and Liszt expressed more emotion in their musical compositions. Wagner followed these composers with his opera Tristan and Isolde. Cesar Frank was a composer who had an individual chromatic, harmonic modulatory style. The use of chromaticism became more frequent in the music of the late 19th and early 20th century composers. The compositions of impressionists Debussy, Ravel, and Griffes, by their style and use of twelve tones, grew into atonality and polytonality.

THE OVERTONE SERIES: THE SOURCE OF THE CIRCLE OF FIFTHS AND THE CHROMATIC SCALE

By analyzing the overtone series one can learn the source of all the musical theory which it produces: intervals of minor seconds, major seconds, minor thirds, major thirds, fourths, augmented fourths, fifths, augmented fifths, flatted fifths, sixths, minor sevenths, major sevenths, octaves, ninths, tenths, augmented elevenths, and thirteenths.

Importance of the overtone series cannot be underestimated. The history and growth of music through the centuries can be traced directly through the overtone series.

Each fundamental produces four chromatic tones at the upper most partials of the overtones:

- The last four tones of the upper partials of the fundamental tone C produces A (the thirteenth) A♯ (B♭) (the flatted seventh), B (the major seventh), and final note C.

- The last four tones of the upper partials of the fundamental tone E produces C♯ (the thirteenth), D (the flatted seventh), D♯ (the major seventh), and final note E.

- The last four tones of the upper partials of the fundamental tone A♭ produces F (the thirteenth), F♯ (G♭) (the flatted seventh), G (the major seventh), and final note A♭.

- The last four tones of the fundamental tone A♭ produces F, F♯, G, A♭. When the last four upper partials of these three fundamental tones (C, E, A♭) are combined they produce the tones of the descending and ascending C chromatic scale.

C descending chromatic scale:

C, B, B♭, A, A♭, G, G♭, F, E, E♭, D, D♭, C

C ascending chromatic scale:

C, C♯, D, D♯, E, F, F♯, G, G♯, A, A♯, B, C

The overtone series serve as the magnetic vehicle of all cadential movement. The fundamental bass moves in descending fifths (C, F, B♭, E♭, A♭, D♭, G♭ (F♯), B, E, D, G).

The cycle of fifths can also be shown ascending (C, G, D, A, E, B, F♯ (G♭), D♭, A♭, E♭, B♭, F). Because of the overtonal influence discussed earlier, the overtone series is in reality a cycle of altered dominant sevenths moving in an endless harmonic spiral of descending fifths. The fundamental and its overtones establish the force of gravity of the musical universe, the strongest and most natural harmonic progression in music.

The gravitational force produced by the fundamental and its overtones causes the forward motion of chord progressions in all styles of composed and improvised music, but the backward direction is used at the discretion of the improviser composer.

CHROMATIC SCALE THEORY

12, 11, 10, 9, 8, 7, 6, 5, 4, 3, 2, 1 = 12 tones

C, B, B♭, A, A♭, G, G♭, F, E, E♭, D, D♭, C =
descending chromatic scale

C, F, B♭, E♭, A♭, D♭, G♭, B, E, A, D, G, C =
descending cycle of fifths

1, 2, 3, 4, 5, 6, 7, 8, 9, 10, 11, 12 = 12 tones

C, C♯, D, D♯, E, F, F♯, G, G♯, A, A♯, B =
ascending chromatic scale

C, G, D, A, E, B, F♯, C♯, G♯, D♯, A♯, F =
ascending cycle of fifths

In summation, the chromatic scale is constructed entirely of half steps. This scale tends to:

(a) lack a usual tonic. (Any tone can be used as a tonic.)

(b) contain the same quality chords on each step of its scale.

(c) have certain special harmonies.

(d) have the same gravitational pull as the cycle of fifths.

(e) contain melodies that are unstable.

(f) create a feeling of tension.

(g) create a forward motion.

(h) have a very moving sound.

(i) empower each tone to be a leading tone.

(j) have a feeling of restlessness.

(k) lack any rules of harmonic progression.

CLOSE RELATIONSHIP OF THE TWO WHOLE-TONE SCALES AND THE CHROMATIC SCALE

The two existing whole-tone scales came out of the chromatic scale; therefore they are closely related. Each whole-tone scale is an arpeggio of each other. For example the C whole-tone scale is an arpeggio of the C♯ whole-tone scale and vice-versa. When the C whole-tone and C♯ whole-tone scales are combined the result is the chromatic scale.

Composers such as Claude Debussy experimented with the whole-tone scales in their compositions. Other composers that used the chromatic and whole-tone scales were Modest Moussorgsky, Ferruccio Busoni, Alexander Scriabin, Ernst Toch, Bela Bartok, Alban Berg, Paul Hindemith, JaCques Ibert, Charles Ives, Maurice Ravel, and Igor Stravinsky. The American composer Wallingford Riegger experimented with both whole-tone scales using them as two halves of a twelve tone row.

In addition to the great composers that made use of the whole-tone and chromatic scales, jazz composers, lead by the high priest of bebop, Thelonious Monk (born October 10, 1920 died February 17, 1982) began a renewal of the use and overuse of the chromatic and the whole-tone scales. Monk also known as "Mad Monk" was one of many pianist composers who made a distinctive contribution to the music of the bebop era. He wrote very angular melodies using sudden chord progressions and chromatic and cycle of fifths changes that were difficult to improvise over. Monk would play and insert whole-tone motives and chromatic colors anywhere and whenever he felt the urge to do so. An excellent example of this is in the song by Monk called Skippy. Because of the relationship of the cycle of fifths chromatic scale and the whole-tone scale Monk uses progressions of chromatic dominant seventh chords moving down or up. He also makes use of cycle of fifths progressions or augmented chords while composing the melody using the two whole-tone scales. The song Skippy was recorded by Steve Lacy on his Reflections album. To quote from the Downbeat magazine article written by Steve Griggs who also transcribed Lacy's solo wherein he states, "Lacy has made a career of studying, performing, and recording Monk tunes. To learn (Monk tunes) I listened to Monk's records hundreds of times and learned a lot more, in the process of listening and practicing than merely the tunes themselves. The harmony, melody, and rhythm are all interesting in Monk tunes. I like their shapes and the way they interlock-the harmony gives the shapes colors."

Another idiosyncrasy of Monk's playing was told to me by Al Lukas, a famous bass player friend of mine who once played with Monk. He said that at times during improvisations Monk would stay on a few measures or sections of the song and improvise over and over until he had exhausted his ideas and then continue with the piece. The late great trumpeter Ray Copeland told me that when he played with Thelonious Monk the same things would take place, especially on intros and bridges.

An example of this type of playing composing is in the melody of *Straight No Chaser*. The melody consists of a repetitive chromatic theme in a different part of each measure, and the reason this works is the song is a blues. The progression holds the song together. Another reason that this type of playing works is because the use of a repeating melody works as well as the use of a bass pedal under a stagnant melody.

Besides abruptly inserting or using either the chromatic scale or whole-tone scale whenever he felt the urge, Monk also wrote vertical melodies with a few notes, using chords but no resolution and playing two part intervals or chord clusters.

In Dave Gelly's book titled, *The Giants of Jazz*, published by Schirmer Books 1986 Gelly writes about Thelonious Monk, "His parents can't have known it at the time, but they gave Thelonious Sphere Monk a name which was to match his music to perfection; the sound of the one instantly calls the other to mind. In the course of his life his public reputation went through three distinct phases from harmless lunatic to fashionable eccentric artist to revered elder statesman. It is entirely probable that Monk himself noticed none of this except for the fact that he was working more regularly during the last two periods and that the pianos were in tune. He arrived on the scene with the bebop movement of the forties, in a sense, he was the most through going bebopper of them all."

It seems that Monk had discovered for himself the close connection that the cycle of fifths and the chromatic scale had to each other. Monk used both chromatic and cycle chords together interchanging with appropriate melodies. Maybe this is the reason Reese Markewich called the chromatic scale the "disguised cycle of fifths" in his book *Inside Outside*.

Leonard Feather a noted jazz historian, critic, author, and composer since the early thirties; best known for his volumes of *Encyclopedia of Jazz* reference books, has written a blues entitled *12 Tone Blues* (c.1960 by Model Music Co.) using the two whole-tone scales that make up a chromatic scale.

In the beginning of the jazz era most of the tunes played or used as vehicles of improvisation were composed with the use of simple chord changes. Usually these tunes included cycle of fifths chord changes that were progressions typically used at the beginnings of jazz. Chromatic progressions appeared later in the history of jazz music and are an outgrowth and are considered the flatted fifth substitute of the cycle of fifths. Therefore they should be learned after one has immersed oneself in the cycle of fifths and the diatonic cycle of fifths and all its dialects (keys).

In the past and present jazz educators instruct students to reproduce everything they play chromatically on their instruments. This is usually ignored because of its difficulty. Practicing this way was suggested because most of the educators were either pianists, instrumentalists who possessed piano skills, composers or theorists.

As the piano is a visual instrument, practicing chromatically is accomplished more easily. Most other instruments that are played are not as visual. The cycle of fifths was understood thoroughly by those who were able to play the piano because most early musical literature made use of the cycle of fifths in part or completely and chromaticism began to appear later.

When harmonic or chord progressions appear in melodic situations they are constructed with the use of five types of movement:

1. Cycle of Fifths: natural harmonic progression of music.

2. Diatonic Cycle of Fifths: natural progression within any key.

3. Minor Seconds ascending or descending: chromatic scale.

4. Whole Steps ascending or descending: whole tone scales.

5. Minor Thirds ascending or descending: diminished thirds

RELATIONSHIP OF THE CYCLE OF FIFTHS TO THE CHROMATIC SCALE

Because of the V to I relationship, which exists between each chord in the chain of dominants the term "cycle of fifths," is employed and established; each note is the fifth of the note it precedes. When you substitute a flatted fifth for every other note in the cycle you arrive at the chromatic scale.

Descending cycle of fifths:
Example: C, F, B♭, E♭, A♭, G♭, B, E, A, D, G, C

Substituting a flatted fifth for every other note creates
Descending chromatic scale:
Example: C, B, B♭, A, A♭, G, G♭, F, E, E♭, D, D♭, C

Ascending cycle of fifths:
Example: C, G, D, A, E, B, G♭, D♭, A♭, E♭, B♭, F, C

Substituting a flatted fifth for every other note creates
Ascending chromatic scale:
Example: C, D♭, D, E♭, E, F, G♭, G, A♭, A, B♭, B, C

This chart shows that the chromatic scale is the "disguised cycle of fifths," (a term coined by Reese Markewich) a flatted fifth substitute of the cycle of fifths either in descending or ascending form which can be used whenever cycle changes are being used.

UPPER PARTIALS OF DOMINANT CHORDS USED IN JAZZ

While famous jazz alto saxophonist Charlie Parker (b. 1920, d. 1955) was playing at a jam session, he became bored with the standard chord changes being used. The song being played was Ray Noble's standard *Cherokee*. While he was improvising, in his mind's ear he could hear other sounds based on the upper partials of dominant chords.

Instead of playing on the roots, thirds, fifths and sevenths he decided to play melodies using the upper partials of the overtones that were heard in his minds ear. He began playing more chromatically and explored, composed and improvised new melodies using the very chromatic upper partials of the overtone series.

In this way he began playing on top of the chord changes instead of inside the changes. This style of playing was new to jazz and became the beginning of bebop. Charlie Parker was inspired to experiment with the upper partials after listening to many great modern composers such as Paul Hindemith, Maurice Ravel, Claude Debussy, Arnold Schoenberg, Bela Bartok, Edgard Varese, Alban Berg, and Igor Stravinsky.

After bebop gave way to hard bop and then to funk, many musicians used the sound of the upper partials melodically while playing their improvisations. One such musician/composer was Horace Silver who wrote many songs among them *Barbara*, *Summer In Central Park*, *Ecaroh*, *Strollin*, *Nica's Dream* and *Mayreh*. John Coltrane was another famous jazz musician who used the sound of upper partials extensively in his improvisations over hundreds of standard tunes in the 1960s. One of today's contemporary jazz musicians, Michael Brecker continues to use Coltrane's progressive sound in his music.

FLATTED FIFTHS IN JAZZ

The progressive jazz players of the late 1940s and 1950s such as Charlie Parker, Dizzie Gillespie, and the bebop "school" of players altered the chord changes of many of the tunes played. Along with the altered chords, they used many of these altered sounds in their melodic lines. The most common altered sound from the bebop school of music was the flatted fifth (or enharmonically the augmented fourth).

Examples: C to G♭ = Flatted Fifth

C to F♯ = Augmented Fourth

Many jazz pieces of that era ended on the flatted fifth. In fact, there was a bebop greeting that gave the flatted fifth sign: a raised open hand with the other hand placed horizontally at the wrist.

In Reese Markewich's book *Inside Outside* he notes, "Ever since the birth of modern jazz the term flatted fifth has been bandied about. Musicians used to make the sign of the flatted fifth when greeting each other in humorous ritual." Reese Markewich also created the term "disguised cycle of fifths" known as the chromatic scale. In the tune *Cool*, written by Howard McGhee the progression Dmin7, D♭min7, Cmin7, F7, appears in measures eight, nine and the first half of the tenth measure.

In the composition *Contours* by Shorty Rodgers the eleventh measure finds this harmonic progression Cmin7, F7, B♭min7, E♭7, a set of ii7, V7 progressions that has perfect chords which can be changed to a minor chromatic progression, namely Cmin7, Bmin7, B♭min7, A7. As a matter of fact whenever any set of ii7, V7 chord changes appear in a song a tritone substitution may be inserted for the ii7 chord.

Charlie Parker used this progression of chords in the composition *Barbados*: Amin7, D7, Gmin7, C7. Flatted fifth or tritone substitutions can be used to change the qualities of some chords to arrive at this:

Cycle chords: Amin7, D7, Gmin7, C7.

Tritone substitutions: Amin7 A♭min7 Gmin7 F♯7.

Anytime you have a iii7, vi7, ii7, V7 diatonic cycle progression that is changed by tritone substitution the roots of the chords that were in cycle will now move down chromatically.

- Chord Progressions in Roman Numerals: iii7 vi7 ii7 V7
- Original chords in the key of C: Emin7 Amin7 Dmin7 G7.
- Tritone substitutions of vi7 and V7: Emin7 E♭min7 Dmin7 D♭7.

Reese Markewich sums it up beautifully in his book *Inside Outside* by stating, "This half step chromatic progression of the roots, or of the II-7s or the V7s, for the matter, is really the cycle of fifths in disguise, a substitution for the original root progression. Thus the chromatic scale, which contains all intervals and chords, is really the cycle of fifths in disguise."

Example: C, E, G, B♭, D, F♯, A, C which is a C13+11 chord.

THE FLATTED FIFTH CONCEPT AND ITS TRADITIONAL HARMONIC ROOTS

Any chord of any species or quality can have for its harmonic substitute a similar type chord built a flatted fifth away from its root called the flatted fifth or tritone substitution. In other words any two similar type chords whose roots are located a tritone apart can substitute for each other. This concept can be traced to its roots in traditional harmony, where augmented sixth chords were used as a type of chromatic harmony and named: Neapolitan, French and German sixths.

CHORD SUBSTITUTIONS MAKING USE OF THE FLATTED FIFTH CONCEPT

Any standard, pop, rock or jazz tune can be embellished by using flatted fifth substitutions of standard chord changes.

QUALITIES OR TYPES OF CHORDS AND THEIR FLATTED FIFTH SUBSTITUTES

C Maj7

would have a G♭Maj7 as its substitution.

C7

would have a G♭7 as its substitution.

C min7

would have a G♭min7 as its substitution.

C min7♭5

would have a G♭min7♭5 as its substitution.

C dim7

would have a G♭dim7 as its substitution.

C Maj7♯5

would have a G♭Maj7♯5 as its substitution.

C Maj7♭5

would have a G♭Maj7♭5 as its substitution.

C 7♭5

would have a G♭7♭5 as its substitution.

C 7♯5

would have a G♭7♯5 as its substitution.

C min(maj7)

would have a G♭min(maj7 as its substitution.

C7 min7♭5

would have a G♭min7b5 as its substitution.

C dim7

would have a G♭dim7 as its substitution.

As can be seen by this list, any type chord can be substituted by the same type chord a flatted fifth away for any harmonic progression. The basic diatonic cycle of fifths can supply the harmonic flow during any progression. Flatted fifth chord substitutions are frequently inserted in this diatonic flow by composers or improvisers.

List of Standard, Popular, and Jazz Tunes that use Chromatic Harmony for It's Chord Changes

Because of the close relationship that exists with the chromatic and whole tone scales we have incorporated tunes in this list that contain both scales. This list of jazz tunes contains whole-tone scales, augmented chords, partials of whole-tone scales, chromatic ascending and descending seventh chords, chromatic ascending and descending two five chords and chromatic bass lines against stagnant or angular melodies that should be played and memorized.

"Air Mail Special," Charlie Christian

"Anthropology," C. Parker/D. Gillespie.

"Armageddon," Wayne Shorter

"Ask Me Now," Thelonious Monk

"Boplicity," Cleo Henry

"Born To Be Blue," Mel Torme

"Brilliant Corners," Thelonious Monk

"Bye Ya," Thelonious Monk

"Cappucino," Chick Corea

"Chippy," Ornette Coleman

"Como En Vietnam," Steve Swallow

"Con Alma," Dizzy Gillespie

"Conception," George Shearing

"Coral," Keith Jarrett

"Criss Cross," Thelonious Monk

"Delores," Wayne Shorter

"Dizzy Atmosphere," Dizzy Gillespie

"Early Autumn," Ralph Burns

"Epistrophy," Thelonious Monk

"Esp," Wayne Shorter

"Evidence," Thelonious Monk

"Fee - Fi - Fo - Fum," Wayne Shorter

"52nd Street Theme," Thelonious Monk

"Good Bait," Dizzy Gillespie

"Gregory Is Here," Horace Silver

"Half Nelson," Miles Davis

"I Got It Bad And That Ain't Good," Duke Ellington

"In Walked Bud," Thelonious Monk

"Introspection," Thelonious Monk

"I Remember Clifford," Benny Golson

"Jessica's Day," Quincy Jones

"Jitterbug Waltz," Fats Waller

"Jody Grind," Horace Silver

"Ju - Ju," Wayne Shorter

"Killer Joe," Benny Golsen

"Le Roi," David Baker

"Let's Cool One," Thelonious Monk

"Little Rootie Tootie," T. Monk

"Meditation," Antonio Carlos Jobim

"Misterioso," Thelonious Monk

"Moments Notice," John Coltrane

"Monkish," Thelonious Monk

"Monks Mood," Thelonious Monk

"Nefertiti," Miles Davis

"Off Minor," Thelonious Monk

"One Note Samba," Antonio Carlos Jobim

"One Up," One Down," John Coltrane

"Our Man Higgins," Lee Morgan

"Played Twice," Thelonious Monk

"Queer Notions," Coleman Hawkins

"'Round Midnight," Thelonious Monk

"Ruby My Dear," Thelonious Monk

"Rythm-A-Ning," Thelonious Monk

"Sister Sadie," Horace Silver

"Skippy," Thelonious Monk

"Spanning," Charles Tolliver

"Stella by Starlight," Victor Young

"Straight No Chaser," Thelonious Monk

"Take the A Train," Billy Strayhorn

"The Duke," Dave Brubeck

"Thelonious," Thelonious Monk

"Well You Needn't," Thelonious Monk

The previous partial list of jazz literature makes use of the chromatic scale, cycle of fifths, for it's harmonic flow. These tunes, have melodic information to be stored in the mind's ear, which then becomes part of the total melodic recall to be played in bits or at length when improvising. All great jazz players have hundreds and perhaps thousands of jazz tunes at their finger tips which can be used to put together as a puzzle in thousands of different ways over endless chord changes. This process occurs automatically as the improvisor reacts to many new tunes and many new sets of chord changes. The student should then learn and play the tunes into as many different keys as possible to expand the student's jazz vocabulary even further.

After getting familiar with and memorizing as many tunes as possible the novice improviser or composer should try to apply some flatted fifth chromatic substitutions to the tunes when encountering cycle changes. The chromatic musical examples in this article are written for C treble clef, B♭, E♭ and bass clef instruments. The exercises are written in every key and move through the cycle of fifths. The exercises should be played with some changes made in octaves to accommodate the range of any particular instrument.

THE CHROMATIC SCALE: TREBLE CLEF / C INST.

THE CHROMATIC SCALE: TREBLE CLEF / B♭ INST.

THE CHROMATIC SCALE: TREBLE CLEF / E♭ INST.

THE CHROMATIC SCALE: BASS CLEF

CHAPTER 29

THE ALTERED SCALE

The altered scale is used by today's leading jazz players to create some of the progressive "outside" sounds of contemporary jazz music.

SOURCE OF THE ALTERED SCALE

The altered scale can be traced back to 1907 in *Sketch of a New Esthetics of Music* by Ferruccio Busoni (B. 1866, d. 1924), according to David Ewens, author of *The Complete Book of 20th Century Music* (published in 1952 by Prentice Hall, Inc., New York, NY), who states,

"To composing, Busoni brought the same trenchant and restless intellect which made him so fine a classical scholar, philosopher, poet, painter, essayist— and one of the aristocratic interpreters of piano music of his generation. His musical thinking was profound (sometimes even abstruse), as perhaps only those who listened to his discussions on esthetics can best appreciate…He invented new scales, and new harmonic schemes growing out of these scales; he tried to evolve a new system of musical notation; he experimented with quarter tones."

The book *Chasin' the Trane* by J.C. Thomas tells about a day in 1958 when Thomas visited the great tenor saxophonist John Coltrane at his home. During the visit, Coltrane was practicing out of a book written by Sigurd Rasher, a German classical saxophone player, that contained 158 exercises dealing with learning the high notes

or harmonics above the normal range of the tenor saxophone. Because the position and tightness of the lips (embouchure) caused considerable pain with Coltrane's teeth, Coltrane stopped working on high notes in that book and started playing a different book. This new book was published in 1947 by Coleman Ross Company, Inc., and was written by the internationally known musicologist Nicolas Slonimsky. It was entitled *Thesaurus of Scales and Melodic Patterns*. In the introduction of this book, there is a quote from Ferruccio Busoni regarding the discovery of what is now called the altered scale. Busoni states, "There is a significant difference between the sound of the scale C, Db, Eb, Fb, Gb, Ab, Bb, C when C is taken as tonic, and the scale of Db minor. By giving it the customary C major triad as a fundamental harmony, a novel harmonic sensation is obtained." Barry Harris is a jazz teacher and pianist who introduced Coltrane to the Slonimsky book and also some of the theory concepts taught by him. Coltrane played the book for endless hours, and if one plays the book, it becomes clear from where Coltrane got his musical ideas.

Many fine jazz players practiced the Slonimsky book after being introduced to it by Coltrane. Miles Davis composed "Vierd Blues" using notes from exercise #831 of the Slonimsky book for the melody. Others who were exposed to Coltrane's playing and Slonimsky's *Thesaurus of Scales and Melodic Patterns* were Oliver

Nelson, Charlie Parker, Woody Shaw, Thelonious Monk, and Yusef Lateef. Many movie film composers and popular recording artists make use of Slonimsky's Thesaurus as a resource for new musical ideas.

After playing and searching through the Thesaurus, I found many partials of sounds that Coltrane and many other jazz players used in their compositions. Some of the sounds Coltrane used were exercises #459b, #193, #448, #286, #646, and #193. This last exercise was the one that was used for the last few measures of Coltrane's famous composition, "Giant Steps," whose chord changes were identical to the bridge or B-section of the Rogers and Hart tune, "Have You Met Miss Jones."

THE ALTERED SCALE OR FLATTED FIFTH SUBSTITUTE OF THE AUGMENTED ELEVENTH SCALE

Just as a C Mixolydian mode (C, D, E, F, G, A, B♭, C) creates a linear sound for the C7 chord (C, E, G, B♭), we find that a melodic minor ascending scale (G, A, B♭, C, D, E, F♯, G) starting from the fifth (G of the C7 chord) named the augmented eleventh scale. This scale provides a linear sound for the upper partials of the C7 chord derived from the overtone series of the fundamental tone C. To arrive at the sound of the altered scale, one must use the harmony of the flatted fifth substitute of the dominant seventh. For example, the (G♭7) F♯7 (flatted fifth of the C7) harmony is used against the sound of the ascending melodic minor scale to create the altered scale sound.

The etudes for this study are written for C, B♭, E♭, treble, and C bass clef instruments. As in previous articles, this study is written combining the altered scale with the harmony of a dominant seventh ♯9th chord as a single sound. Practicing this sound will help begin to form a place for it in the mind's ear for recall during a solo. This etude also moves in the cycle of fifths progression and continues the shape of the POOK 7/9 pattern of altered scale notes. This POOK 7/9 exercise begins with the C altered scale, using the C7 ♯9th chord and proceeds

through the remaining eleven altered scales and their corresponding dominant seventh ♯9th chords.

VARIOUS NAMES USED FOR THE FLATTED FIFTH SUBSTITUTE OF THE ALTERED SCALE

The following scales are used over the flatted fifth substitute of the dominant seventh V7 chord. Each scale starts from the seventh degree of the melodic minor scale, using the harmony produced by a dominant ninth chord: the altered scale, the super-Locrian mode, the Pomeroy scale, the diminished whole-tone scale.

The ascending and descending scale degrees for all altered scales and their respective chords and Roman numerals:

1 2 3 4 5 6 7 1

I II III IV V VI VII I

Altered scale used for B7 chord:
B C D E♭ F G A B

Altered scale used for E7 chord:
E F G A♭ B♭ C D E

Altered scale used for A7 chord:
A B♭ C D♭ E♭ F G A

Altered scale used for D7 chord:
D E♭ F G♭ A♭ B♭ C D

Altered scale used for G7 chord:
G A♭ B♭ C♭ D♭ E♭ F G

Altered scale used for C7 chord:
C D♭ E♭ F♭ G♭ A♭ B♭ C

Altered scale used for E♯7 chord:
E♯ F♯ G♯ A B C♯ D♯ E♯

Altered scale used for A♯7 chord:
A♯ B C♯ D E F♯ G♯ A♯

Altered scale used for D♯7 chord:
D♯ E F♯ G A B C♯ D♯

Altered scale used for G#7 chord:

G# A B C D E F# G#

Altered scale used for C#7 chord:

C# D E F G A B C#

Altered scale used for F#7 chord:

F# G A B♭ C D E F#

In 1941, a hit song called "Autumn Nocturne" was composed by lyricist Kim Gannon, with music by Josef Mirow. Within a single measure, Mirow used the sound of both the altered scale and the augmented eleventh scale. This measure is repeated three times during the length of one chorus; twice in the beginning A section, and once in the last A section.

In 1945, singer Frankie Laine wrote lyrics for a song called "We'll Be Together Again"; music composed by Carl Fischer. The song contains many flatted fifth and augmented eleventh sounds.

Jazz composer Tadd Dameron wrote a piece called "Hot House" (made famous by Charlie Parker and Dizzy Gillespie) based on the chord changes of "What Is This Thing Called Love," which contains numerous examples of the augmented eleventh and altered scales.

A popular title song from the 1965 Broadway musical, "On A Clear Day You Can See Forever," by lyricist Alan Jay Lerner and composer Burton Lane contains an excellent example of the use of the augmented eleventh sound in the second chord change.

An interesting side note is that a famous jazz lick named after the song that it comes from: "Cry Me A River" by Arthur Hamilton, c. 1955, is the retrograde melodic fragment for the opening notes in the composition, "A Night In Tunisia" by Frank Paparelli and Dizzy Gillespie, c. 1944.

Following is a list of standard, popular, and jazz tunes that contain sharp and flatted ninth, eleventh, sharp eleventh, and thirteenth chords, and augmented eleventh scale sounds completely or in part. Although it is important to learn the altered scale in all keys, it is imperative

for today's novice composer or improvisor to become familiar with the jazz literature. If the student learns, analyzes, and memorizes these melodies, improvising on tunes using the altered scale will become more familiar.

Standard Jazz Tunes to Be Learned that Use the Sound of the Altered Scale and Augmented Eleventh Scale Melodically or Harmonically

"A Night In Tunisia - Dizzy Gillespie/Frank Paparelli

"Algo Bueno - Dizzy Gillespie

"Autumn Nocturne" - Kim Gannon/Josef Mirow

"Au Privave" - Charlie Parker

"Barbara" - Horace Silver

"Bloomdido" - Dizzy Gillespie/Charlie Parker

"Blue Seven" - Sonny Rollins

"Boomerang" - Clark Terry

"Boplicity" - Cleo Henry

"Chelsea Bridge" - Billy Strayhorn

"Cry Me a River" - Arthur Hamilton

"Dizzy Atmosphere" - Dizzy Gillespie

"Donna Lee" - Miles Davis

"Donna" - Jackie McLean

"Early Autumn" - Ralph Burns

"Eb-Pob" - Fats Navarro/Leo Parker

"Ecaroh" - Horace Silver

"Emanon" - Gillespie/Shaw

"Gary's Waltz" - Gary McFarland

"Girl from Ipanema" - Antonio Carlos Jobim

"Gregory Is Here" - Horace Silver

"Groovin' High" - Dizzy Gillespie

"Hamburger Helper" - Scott Reeves

"Heaven" - Duke Ellington

"Hot House" - Tadd Dameron

"Iris" - Wayne Shorter

"Jody Grind" - Horace Silver

"Kampala" - Ralph Towner

"Katrina Ballerina" - Woody Shaw

"Killer Joe" - Benny Golsen

"Limehouse Blues" - Braham

"Little Willie Leaps" - Miles Davis

"Lucifer's Fall" - Ralph Towner

"Mayreh" - Horace Silver

"M.D." - Dave Liebman

"Midnight Sun" - Sunny Burke/Lionel Hampton/
    Johnny Mercer

"Morning Song" - Scott Reeves

"Motion" - Jimmy Raney

"Move" - Denzil Best

"Nica's Dream" - Horace Silver

"O Go Mo" - Kai Winding

"October 10th" - Richard Beirach

"On a Clear Day You Can See Forever" - Lerner/Lane

"One Note Samba" - Antonio Carlos Jobim

"Paper Butterflies" - Ruben Rada

"Pee Wee" - Tony Williams

"Pensativa" - Claire Fischer

"Pirana" - Hugo Fattoruso

"Prince of Darkness" - Wayne Shorter

"Scrapple from the Apple" - Charlie Parker

"Serenity" - Scott Reeves

"Signal" - Jimmy Raney

"Soul Eyes" - Mal Waldron

"Stella by Starlight" - Victor Young

"Strollin'" - Horace Silver

"Summer in Central Park" - Horace Silver

"Take the A-Train" - Duke Ellington

"That's What I'm Talking About" - Shorty Rogers

"The Fruit"" - Bud Powell

"Thriving on a Riff" - Charlie Parker

"Travisimo" - Al Cohen

"Trumpet Blues" - Roy Eldridge/Dizzy Gillespie

"We'll Be Together Again" - Carl Fischer/Frankie Laine

As can be seen by the length of the above partial list of jazz literature, which contains the altered scale in many melodic shapes, a jazz player acquires an abundance of jazz language and style while learning melodies. These tunes, as melodic information stored in the mind's ear, then become part of the total melodic recall to be played in bits or at length when improvising. All great jazz players have hundreds, and may thousands, of jazz tunes at their fingertips that can be used to put together, as a puzzle, in thousands of different ways over endless chord changes. This process occurs automatically as the improvisor reacts to many new tunes and many new sets of chord changes. The novice player should begin to memorize as many different jazz tunes as possible to expand improvisational fluency and acquire jazz vocabulary and language. This should be a continuing process. After memorizing some of the jazz literature listed above, the student should then practice the tunes in as many different keys as possible to expand the student's jazz language even further.

Guitarists should play each exercise in every position on the fingerboard from the first through sixth position, and especially in the fifth position, which is the position that most easily accommodates their studies. Thence, the exercises should be practiced above the sixth position, at least up to the ninth. All other instrumentalists should play the altered scale in the complete range of their respective instruments.

The altered scale can be used as a guide for theory, ear training, and harmony, and covers the proper minor modes to be used over the correct dominant seventh chords through the cycle of fifths in all keys.

The altered scale is used by leading educators/ instrumentalists including Arnie Lawrence, Clark Terry, Bill Watrous, Clem and Richard DeRosa, John Faddis and Slide Hampton, Vincent Bell, Michael Becker, Joe Lovano, Jack Grassel, Eddie Bert, Joe Cinderella, and Harry Manfredini.

BOOK 7/9 ALTERED SCALE – TREBLE CLEF INSTRUMENTS

treble clef C instruments

Emile De Cosmo

Music Graphics By Louis De Cosmo
WEBSITE: http://homepages.go.com/~woodshedding/

POOK 7/9 ALTERED SCALE — BASS CLEF INSTRUMENTS

bass clef instruments

Emile De Cosmo

Music Graphics By Louis De Cosmo

CHAPTER 30

THE BEBOP SCALE

In three previous articles from Jazz Player magazine we discussed the overtone series, the cycle of fifths and its flatted fifth substitute: the chromatic scale. Another scale (or mode) that is closely related to the cycle of fifths is the mixolydian mode that gives the linear notes or scale tones for the dominant seventh chord. It is the fifth mode of any major or minor key and is sometimes called the dominant seventh scale. In 1945 Charlie Parker and Dizzy Gillespie met while playing with Jay McShann's band at the Savoy ballroom. Because of their close association Parker and Gillespie were to become known as partners and co-founders of the new jazz movement known as bebop. At this time the frequent use of chromatic notes became important. During the Blues and Swing eras the flatted third and flatted seventh were used, but when the Bebop period began the use of the flatted fifth, flatted and raised ninths, flatted fifth substitutions of dominant seventh chords, and the chromatic scale flourished.

When this happened chromaticism came into prominence. The term bebop scale was named by the great jazz educator/composer David Baker who discovered it through his analysis of the jazz literature of the bebop school of jazz. Even though the use of the term bebop scale started with modern jazz, its roots began with the Greek theorist Pythagoras who developed early Greek modes. The modes were created with tetra-chords whose names were derived from a four stringed instrument called the kithara.

Guido d'Arezzo, a religious musician (995-1050), made an important change to the medieval tonal system. D'Arezzo introduced musical terminology. The Guidonian System presented a six-tone diatonic scale with tone syllables. In ascending order they are: ut (do) re mi fa sol la. (C, D, E, F, G, A) Guido then added the notes B♭, B, C, D, & E. The B♭ was taken from the Greek synemmenon tetrachord. This led to the development of the F major scale but more importantly, with the added B♮, this scale became the beginning of today's bebop scale.

The bebop scale appeared in jazz during the bebop era from many different sources. The chromatic tones of the bebop scale first appeared in music as the last four partials of the overtone series. The overtone series is created from any fundamental tone. If C is used as the fundamental tone, the last four harmonic partials of the overtone series are: (ascending) A, A♯, B, C (descending) C, B, B♭, A.

- If F is used as the fundamental tone, the last four harmonic partials of the overtone series are: (ascending) D, D♯, E, F (descending) F, E, E♭, D.

- If B♭ is used as the fundamental tone, the last four harmonic partials of the overtone series are: (ascending) G, G♯, A, B♭ (descending) B♭, A, A♭, G.

- If B is used as the fundamental tone, the last four harmonic partials of the overtone series are: (ascending) C, C♯, D, E♭ (descending) B, D, D♭, C.

- If A♭ is used as the fundamental tone, the last four harmonic partials of the overtone series are: (ascending) F, F♯, G, A♭ (descending) A♭, G, G♭, F.

- If D♭ is used as the fundamental tone, the last four harmonic partials of the overtone series are: (ascending) B♭, B, C, D♭ (descending) D♭, C, B, B♭.

- If F♯ is used as the fundamental tone, the last four harmonic partials of the overtone series are: (ascending) D♯, E, F, F♯ (descending) F♯, F, E, D♯.

- If B is used as the fundamental tone, the last four harmonic partials of the overtone series are: (ascending) G♯, A, A♯, B (descending) B, A♯, A, G♯.

- If E is used as the fundamental tone, the last four harmonic partials of the overtone series are: (ascending) C♯, D, D♯, E (descending) E, D♯, D, C♯.

- If A is used as the fundamental tone, the last four harmonic partials of the overtone series are: (ascending) F♯, G, G♯, A (descending) A, G♯, G, F♯.

- If D is used as the fundamental tone, the last four harmonic partials of the overtone series are: (ascending) B, C, C♯, D (descending) D, C♯, C, B.

- If G is used as the fundamental tone, the last four harmonic partials of the overtone series are: (ascending) E, F, F♯, G (descending) G, F♯, F, E.

MUSICAL EXAMPLES OF MELODIES THAT LED TO WHAT IS NOW KNOWN AS THE BEBOP SCALE

1. This example is written by the famous American bandmaster and composer. A son of a Portuguese father and a Bavarian mother who studied harmony and played violin from 1864 to 1867, John Philip Sousa was born November 6, 1854 in Washington D.C. and by the late eighteen hundreds had composed numerous marches. In the first four measures of the introduction to the march *The Thunder* Sousa uses two scales from the fifth note of the F scale in contrary motion. Starting on the note C the melody ascends from C to C an octave higher C D E F G A B♭ B C and in the bass he writes a descending line starting with the note C B B♭ A G F E D C. Both scales are derived from the mixolydian mode of the key of F with an added B♮.

2. Friedrich Kuhlau (b. Uelzen, Hanover, Sept.11, 1786 - d. Copenhagen, March 12, 1832). Kuhlau was well versed in piano, flute, harmony, and composition. He wrote many sonatinas that were very chromatic. In *Opus #1* in the last measure of the first section he uses a descending dominant type bebop scale from the note G. In the thirteenth measure of *Opus 20 #2* Kuhlau writes a descending dominant type bebop scale from the note D. In many of his sonatina compositions he uses many bebop type descending and ascending lines too numerous to mention.

3. In 1940 Jimmy Van Heusen and lyricist Johnny Burke wrote a song called "Polka Dots and Moonbeams." It is written in the key of F major and in the A section of the melody they make use of a partial of the F bebop scale: (descending) F E E♭ D. The B section modulates to the key of A major. In the B section, starting from the fourth beat of the first measure, he uses a descending bebop scale against the dominant E7 chord: E E♭ D C♯ B A G♯ E.

4. The song "Tico-Tico," a popular BMI tune from Australia (written in 1943 by Zequinha Abreu, English lyric by Ervin Drake, Portuguese lyric by Aloysio Oliveira) contains a bebop type scale in the four-measure introduction starting in the second half of the second measure. Written in the key of C a descending line starts on the note G, the fifth of the scale, and continues G F♯ F E D C B A G F E D ending on C.

5. In 1945 Benny Goodman used the bebop scale in his solo on "Slipped Disc." The song is in A B A form and is written in the key of A♭. He plays an ascending bebop scale over an F dominant seventh chord starting on the fifth (C). C, D, E♭, E, F, F♯, G, A, B♭. Goodman uses the same line two more times on his last chorus in the thirty-first measure and in the next to the last measure of the four measure tag.

6. "The Jeopardy Theme" (by Merv Griffin, published by Vine music Broadcast Music Inc., copyright 1984) melody notes are C F C F A G F E D D♭ C in the key of F. This is a descending F scale starting on the third, A and descending to the fifth, C using the flatted sixth, D♭. This scale appears throughout the piece at various times.

THE MUSICAL EXERCISED PROVIDED USE FIVE ALTERATIONS OF THE BEBOP SCALE

The following five examples use the C bebop scale.

1. C, D, E, F, G, A, B♭, B, C (ascending) C, B, B♭, A, G, F, E, D, C (descending). The half step occurs between the 7th and the tonic.

2. C, C♯, D, E, F, G, A, B♭, C (ascending) C, B♭, A, G, F, E, D, D♭, C (descending). The half step occurs between the first and second degrees of the scale.

3. C, D, D♯, E, F, G, A, Bb, C (ascending) C, B♭, A, G, F, E, E♭, D, C (descending). The half step occurs between the second and third degrees of the scale.

4. C, D, E, F, G, G♯, A, B♭, C (ascending) C, B♭, A, A♭, G, F, E, D, C (descending). The half step occurs between the fifth and sixth degrees of the scale.

5. C, D, E, F, F♯, G, A, B♭, C (ascending) C, B♭, A, G, G♭, F, E, D, C (descending). The half step occurs between the fourth and fifth degrees of the scale.

A jazz improvisor can become more familiar with the bebop scale by practicing and memorizing the musical examples provided. Applying various rhythms to the exercises will improve technical fluency and creativity when using the bebop scale in an improvisation. All the great jazz improvisers use the bebop scale and its variations in their improvisations.

THE BEBOP SCALE: TREBLE CLEF

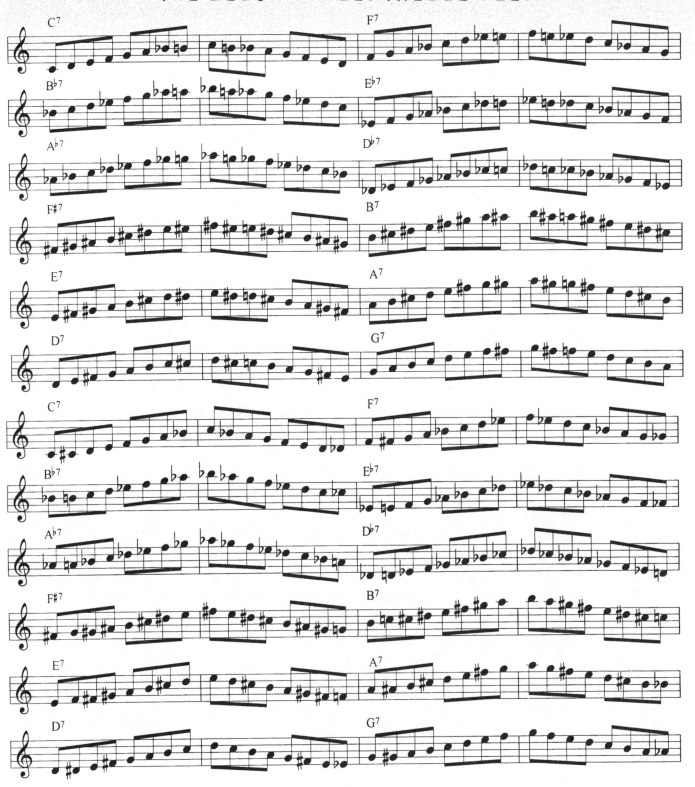

THE BEBOP SCALE (CONT): TREBLE CLEF

THE BEBOP SCALE (CONT): TREBLE CLEF

THE BEBOP SCALE: BASS CLEF

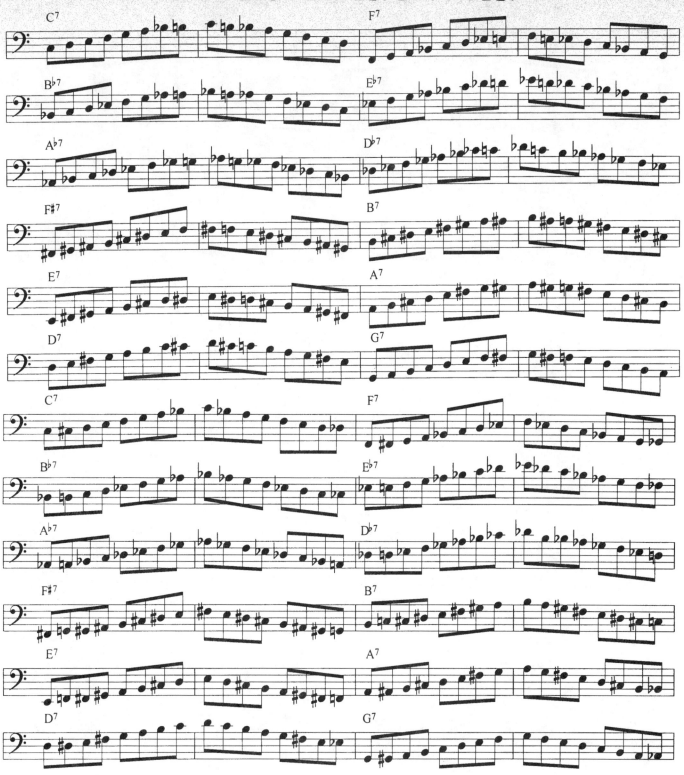

THE BEBOP SCALE (CONT): BASS CLEF

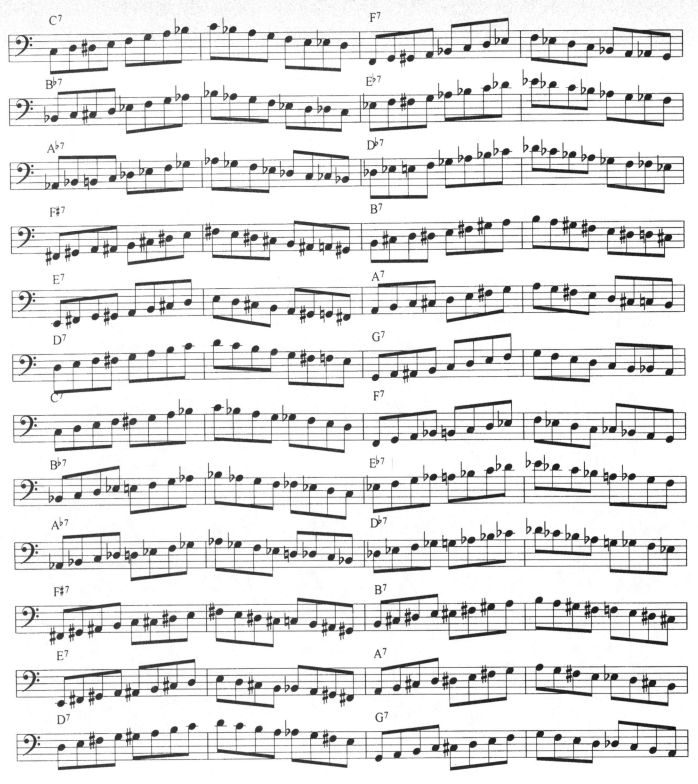

THE BEBOP SCALE (CONT): BASS CLEF

Presenting the Hal Leonard JAZZ PLAY-ALONG SERIES

1. **DUKE ELLINGTON**
   00841644 ....$16.95

2. **MILES DAVIS**
   00841645 ....$16.95

3. **THE BLUES**
   00841646 ....$16.99

4. **JAZZ BALLADS**
   00841691 ....$16.99

5. **BEST OF BEBOP** Vol. 5
   00841689 ....$16.99

6. **JAZZ CLASSICS WITH EASY CHANGES**
   00841690 ....$16.99

7. **ESSENTIAL JAZZ STANDARDS**
   00843000 ....$16.99

8. **ANTONIO CARLOS JOBIM AND THE ART OF THE BOSSA NOVA**
   00843001 ....$16.95

9. **DIZZY GILLESPIE**
   00843002 ....$16.99

10. **DISNEY CLASSICS**
    00843003 ....$16.99

11. **RODGERS AND HART FAVORITES**
    00843004 ....$16.99

12. **ESSENTIAL JAZZ CLASSICS**
    00843005 ....$16.99

13. **JOHN COLTRANE**
    00843006 ....$16.95

14. **IRVING BERLIN**
    00843007 ....$15.99

15. **RODGERS & HAMMERSTEIN**
    00843008 ....$15.99

16. **COLE PORTER**
    00843009 ....$15.95

17. **COUNT BASIE**
    00843010 ....$16.95

18. **HAROLD ARLEN** Vol. 18
    00843011 ....$16.95

19. **COOL JAZZ**
    00843012 ....$15.95

20. **CHRISTMAS CAROLS**
    00843080 ....$14.95

21. **RODGERS AND HART CLASSICS**
    00843014 ....$14.95

22. **WAYNE SHORTER**
    00843015 ....$16.95

23. **LATIN JAZZ**
    00843016 ....$16.95

24. **EARLY JAZZ STANDARDS**
    00843017 ....$14.95

25. **CHRISTMAS JAZZ**
    00843018 ....$16.95

26. **CHARLIE PARKER**
    00843019 ....$16.95

27. **GREAT JAZZ STANDARDS**
    00843020 ....$15.99

28. **BIG BAND ERA**
    00843021 ....$15.99

29. **LENNON AND MCCARTNEY**
    00843022 ....$16.95

30. **BLUES' BEST**
    00843023 ....$15.99

31. **JAZZ IN THREE**
    00843024 ....$15.99

32. **BEST OF SWING**
    00843025 ....$15.99

33. **SONNY ROLLINS**
    00843029 ....$15.95

34. **ALL TIME STANDARDS**
    00843030 ....$15.99

35. **BLUESY JAZZ**
    00843031 ....$15.99

36. **HORACE SILVER**
    00843032 ....$16.99

37. **BILL EVANS**
    00843033 ....$16.95

38. **YULETIDE JAZZ**
    00843034 ....$16.95

39. **"ALL THE THINGS YOU ARE" & MORE JEROME KERN SONGS**
    00843035 ....$15.99

40. **BOSSA NOVA**
    00843036 ....$15.99

41. **CLASSIC DUKE ELLINGTON**
    00843037 ....$16.99

42. **GERRY MULLIGAN FAVORITES**
    00843038 ....$16.99

43. **GERRY MULLIGAN CLASSICS**
    00843039 ....$16.95

44. **OLIVER NELSON**
    00843040 ....$16.95

45. **JAZZ AT THE MOVIES**
    00843041 ....$15.99

46. **BROADWAY JAZZ STANDARDS**
    00843042 ....$15.99

47. **CLASSIC JAZZ BALLADS**
    00843043 ....$15.99

48. **BEBOP CLASSICS**
    00843044 ....$16.99

49. **MILES DAVIS STANDARDS**
    00843045 ....$16.95

50. **GREAT JAZZ CLASSICS**
    00843046 ....$15.99

51. **UP-TEMPO JAZZ**
    00843047 ....$15.99

52. **STEVIE WONDER**
    00843048 ....$15.95

53. **RHYTHM CHANGES**
    00843049 ....$15.99

The Hal Leonard JAZZ PLAY-ALONG SERIES is the ultimate learning tool for all jazz musicians. With musician-friendly lead sheets, melody cues and other split track choices on the included CD, this first-of-its-kind package makes learning to play jazz easier and more fun than ever before. Parts are included for all C, B♭, E♭ and Bass Clef instruments.

Prices, contents, and availability subject to change without notice.

FOR MORE INFORMATION, SEE YOUR LOCAL MUSIC DEALER, OR WRITE TO:

HAL•LEONARD®
CORPORATION
7777 W. BLUEMOUND RD. P.O. BOX 13819
MILWAUKEE, WISCONSIN 53213

For complete songlists and more, visit Hal Leonard online at

www.halleonard.com

0109